S0-BKB-855

Assembling Unity

Women and Indigenous Studies Series

The series publishes works establishing a new understanding of Indigenous women's perspectives and experiences, by researchers in a range of fields. By bringing women's issues to the forefront, this series invites and encourages innovative scholarship that offers new insights on Indigenous questions past, present, and future. Books in this series will appeal to readers seeking stimulating explorations and in-depth analysis of the roles, relationships, and representations of Indigenous women in history, politics, culture, ways of knowing, health, and community well-being.

Other books in the series:

Written as I Remember It: Teachings (ʔəms taʔaw) from the Life of a Sliammon Elder, by Elsie Paul, in collaboration with Paige Raibmon and Harmony Johnson

Indigenous Encounters with Neoliberalism: Place, Women, and the Environment in Canada and Mexico, by Isabel Altamirano-Jiménez

Standing Up with Ga'axsta'las: Jane Constance Cook and the Politics of Memory, Church, and Custom, by Leslie A. Robertson with the Kwagu'ł Gixsam Clan

Being Again of One Mind: Oneida Women and the Struggle for Decolonization, by Lina Sunseri

Indigenous Women and Feminism: Politics, Activism, Culture, edited by Cheryl Suzack, Shari M. Huhndorf, Jeanne Perreault, and Jean Barman

Taking Medicine: Women's Healing Work and Colonial Contact in Southern Alberta, 1880–1930, by Kristin Burnett

Sarah A. Nickel

Assembling Unity

Indigenous Politics, Gender, and the Union of BC Indian Chiefs

UBCPress · Vancouver · Toronto

© UBC Press 2019

All rights reserved. No part of this publication may be reproduced, stored in a retrieval system, or transmitted, in any form or by any means, without prior written permission of the publisher, or, in Canada, in the case of photocopying or other reprographic copying, a licence from Access Copyright, www.accesscopyright.ca.

27 26 25 24 23 22 21 20 19   5 4 3 2 1

Printed in Canada on FSC-certified ancient-forest-free paper (100% post-consumer recycled) that is processed chlorine- and acid-free.

Library and Archives Canada Cataloguing in Publication

Nickel, Sarah A., author
    Assembling unity : Indigenous politics, gender, and the Union of BC Indian Chiefs / Sarah A. Nickel.

(Women & indigenous studies)
Includes bibliographical references and index.
Issued in print and electronic formats.
ISBN 978-0-7748-3798-9 (hardcover). – ISBN 978-0-7748-3799-6 (pbk.). –
ISBN 978-0-7748-3800-9 (PDF). – ISBN 978-0-7748-3801-6 (EPUB). –
ISBN 978-0-7748-3802-3 (Kindle)

    1. Union of British Columbia Indian Chiefs. 2. Native peoples – British Columbia – Politics and government. 3. Native women – British Columbia – Politics and government. 4. Indigenous peoples – British Columbia – Politics and government. 5. Indigenous women – British Columbia – Politics and government. I. Title. II. Series: Women and indigenous studies series

E78.B9N52 2019   323.11970711   C2018-902649-9
                                                                     C2018-902650-2

Canada

UBC Press gratefully acknowledges the financial support for our publishing program of the Government of Canada (through the Canada Book Fund), the Canada Council for the Arts, and the British Columbia Arts Council.

This book has been published with the help of a grant from the Canadian Federation for the Humanities and Social Sciences, through the Awards to Scholarly Publications Program, using funds provided by the Social Sciences and Humanities Research Council of Canada.

Printed and bound in Canada by Friesens
Set in Garamond by Artegraphica Design Co. Ltd.
Copy editor: Barbara Tessman
Proofreader: Helen Godolphin
Indexer: Judy Dunlop
Cover designer: George Kirkpatrick
Cover images: Delegates of the first Indian Chiefs of British Columbia conference, November 1969, photo courtesy of UBCIC

UBC Press
The University of British Columbia
2029 West Mall
Vancouver, BC V6T 1Z2
www.ubcpress.ca

Contents

Acknowledgments

I THOUGHT I HAD already experienced all the writer's block possible for this project, but sitting down to write these acknowledgements I quickly realized I was wrong. The task of genuinely and fully acknowledging all the generous, brilliant, and supportive people who helped bring this work to fruition was overwhelming, so I decided to keep things simple. Because, at its heart, this is a community-engaged study of Indigenous politics, I want to specifically highlight and name the individuals who lent their voices and experiences to this project. I also want to acknowledge that this project began on the unceded lands of the Sḵwx̱wú7mesh, Xʷməθkʷəy̓əm, Tsleil-Waututh, Katzie, and kʷikʷəƛ̓əm Nations, took me across numerous communities in the unceded Indigenous lands now known as British Columbia, and ended in Treaty 6 territory and the Homeland of the Métis at the University of Saskatchewan. In this way, this work has taken me many places, just as I have taken it with me as I moved.

It is no exaggeration to say that this book would not exist today without the generosity of those individuals who shared their experiences of the UBCIC with me. Janice Antoine, Wayne Christian, Adam Eneas (and Sandy Detjen), Delbert Guerin, Percy Joe, Clarence Jules, Marge Kelly, Louise Mandell, Arthur Manuel, Don Moses, Naxaxalhts'i (Albert "Sonny" McHalsie), Clarence (Kat) Pennier, George Saddleman, Sioliya (June Quipp), Saul Terry, Reuben Ware, and (Wahmeesh) Ken Watts offered considerable time in contributing their thoughts about the past and present iterations of Indigenous politics. Through each of these conversations, it was clear that these individuals (and others) have dedicated a lifetime of work to the Indigenous political cause, and it weighed heavily on me to "get this history right." I hope I have done justice to your words and experiences.

During the long gestation of this work, several individuals passed on, leaving me with a greater sense of urgency to get their stories out into the world. The passing of Delbert Guerin, Clarence Jules, Arthur Manuel, and Don Moses left a sizable hole in the collective political-historical consciousness of Indigenous peoples in BC – and I know they will not be forgotten.

Friends and colleagues at Simon Fraser University and the University of Saskatchewan have helped shaped this work through many conversations (perhaps more than any one of them wanted to have), and I am grateful for the insights these brilliant individuals have provided me. My family, too, deserves special mention for the unwavering support they have given to me over these many (many, many) years.

The team at UBC Press worked swiftly and diligently to bring this work to its current form and I'd like to thank Darcy Cullen, Ann Macklem, and the rest of the production staff for their contributions. Thanks also to *BC Studies* and *American Indian Quarterly* for allowing me to republish parts of two articles that previously appeared in their publications. Aspects of Chapter 6 specifically appeared in an article co-authored with Madeline Knickerbocker for *BC Studies*.

Finally, I would also like to acknowledge the financial support received from the Social Sciences and Humanities Research Council of Canada, Simon Fraser University, and the University of Saskatchewan.

Abbreviations

AFN	Assembly of First Nations
AIM	American Indian Movement
BCTC	BC Treaty Commission
BCANSI	British Columbia Association of Non-Status Indians
BCIHA	British Columbia Indian Homemakers' Association
BCNWS	British Columbia Native Women's Society
BCR	band council resolution
CCNM	Cache Creek Native Movement
CEDAW	United Nations Convention on the Elimination of All Forms of Discrimination against Women
CNIBC	Confederation of Native Indians of British Columbia
DSS	Department of the Secretary of State
DIA	Department of Indian Affairs
FABC	Fisheries Association of British Columbia
FLQ	Front de Libération du Québec
HBC	Hudson's Bay Company
HCS	Homemakers' Clubs of Saskatchewan
IHC	Indian Homemakers of Canada
LAC	Library and Archives Canada
LIP	Local Initiatives Program

NAIB	North American Indian Brotherhood
NARP	Native Alliance for Red Power
NBBC	Native Brotherhood of British Columbia
NCAI	National Council of American Indians
NIB	National Indian Brotherhood
NIYC	National Indian Youth Council
NSBC	Native Sisterhood of British Columbia
SRRMC	Stó:lō Research and Resource Management Centre
SUPA	Student Union for Peace Action
SVITF	Southern Vancouver Island Tribal Federation
UBCIC	Union of British Columbia Indian Chiefs
UN	United Nations
UNN	United Native Nations
URC	Union of British Columbia Indian Chiefs Resource Centre

Assembling Unity

Figure 1   Delegates of the first Indian Chiefs
of British Columbia conference, Kamloops, BC,
17–22 November 1969. | Photo courtesy of UBCIC

BEGINNINGS

On a late November afternoon in 1969, approximately 150 delegates of the first Indian Chiefs of British Columbia conference gathered for a commemorative photo to mark the creation of a new pan-Indigenous political organization, the Union of British Columbia Indian Chiefs (UBCIC) (Figure 1). This was a moment that demanded to be captured, as it was the first time so many leaders and representatives from the almost two hundred First Nation bands in what is now called British Columbia had united for a common cause.[1] Of course, there had been earlier attempts at unity, including a number of pan-Indigenous organizations operating throughout the nineteenth and twentieth centuries, but settler colonial interference, as well as geographic, linguistic, and cultural diversity, prevented province-wide collaboration. This conference, hosted by the Tk'emlúps te Secwépemc at the Kamloops Indian residential school, ushered in a new era of cooperation under the UBCIC, which quickly became a leading voice for Indigenous rights in twentieth-century British Columbia.

The above photograph embodies the rich history of this event. The conference's motto, "United we stand, divided we perish," which is visible on the banner in front of the delegates, was not only a poetic statement but also a clear illustration of Indigenous realities in the late 1960s.[2] Attacks on Indigenous social, political, and economic autonomy were staple features in the Canadian settler state, and these took on intense new forms in the 1960s. Visible in the image is Tk'emlúps te Secwépemc Chief Clarence Jules, the conference's official host, who, addressing delegates, said how proud he was that the chiefs had chosen Kamloops for this meeting. He insisted that this important gathering was "the first step in gaining recognition for our wishes, our aims, and our demands."[3] Kamloops is known in Secwepemctsín as Tk'emlúps, which means "where the rivers meet," and the people, the Tk'emlúpsemc, are known as the "people of the confluence." That this conference took place in Kamloops, a traditional meeting place and trade route, and that the meetings were held at the Kamloops Indian residential school – a colonial institution co-opted by an Indigenous rights organization – was highly symbolic, and this meaning was not lost on the delegates.[4]

This photograph also embodies the narratives community members tell about the UBCIC. Between 2012 and 2015, I travelled around the province interviewing dozens of current and former members of the organization – some included in this picture. Almost everyone I spoke to referenced this first meeting and this image, drawing on their own memories or the stories they had heard. Some people told me how cold it was on that November day when delegates gathered for the picture.[5] They talked about where they were standing; some shivered in front of the camera, and others, like Nlaka'pamux Lower Nicola Chief Don Moses, who helped organize the conference, stood behind the lens helping to squeeze everyone into the frame.[6] Children such as Jeanette and Clarence "Manny" Jules, who attended the conference with their father, Chief Clarence Jules Sr., recalled chasing each other around as delegates organized themselves for the camera.[7] Most people referenced the buzz of excitement that took over the gathering as delegates came to terms with the importance of achieving widespread political unity.[8]

The photographic image also symbolizes the political and logistical challenges of unity, as well as participants' unwavering dedication to it. British Columbia has a long history of Indigenous politics and resistance, but with almost two hundred distinct First Nations representing more than thirty language groups (each with different histories and political goals), gathering for a province-wide meeting to develop shared political goals was no small feat. Ongoing state oppression and a long history of attempts to achieve political unity prompted each of the delegates to make the often-difficult trek to Kamloops in 1969. I heard stories from the coast of how community members piled into old cars with brown-bag lunches and sleeping bags, unsure of where they might stay or if they would have enough gas money to get to Kamloops.[9] I also heard about one Gitxsan chief from the northern town of Hazelton who was so intent on attending the conference that, with no other option, he hired a cab for the thousand-kilometre journey. The trip left him with a $700 bill in an era before chiefs could expect their travel costs to be covered.[10] To help offset this personal burden, delegates at the conference passed around the hat for a "little silver collection," much like they did for others with a financial shortfall.[11] Delegates, then, had strong moral and material investments in the UBCIC's success and the overall idea of pan-Indigenous unity. This photograph ultimately represents a wide swathe of experiences: some are visible in the image and others are not, but all are important in capturing the history of the UBCIC.

When these delegates formed the UBCIC in 1969, it was not the first example of pan-Indigenous cooperation or the first pan-Indigenous association to emerge. Indigenous communities had lengthy histories of cooperation through treaties. For instance, the Fish Lake Accord between the Tk'emlúps te Secwépemc and the Syilx people of Sp'áxmen (Douglas Lake) settled a boundary dispute and long history of warfare between the communities and continues to be observed and reaffirmed today.[12] The principles within such agreements were central to the creation of pan-Indigenous political organizations in the twentieth century. The Allied Tribes of British Columbia, the Native Brotherhood of British Columbia, the British Columbia Indian Homemakers' Association, the British Columbia Native Women's Society, and the Indian Rights Association were just a few of the organizations that predated the UBCIC. But these regional, women's, and nation-based bodies were limited in scope, longevity, and/or membership, largely because of continuing intra-community divisions and state resistance. A truly province-wide united front remained elusive, yet highly desired.

In mid-1969, pan-Indigenous unity had been given a boost when Pierre Trudeau's Liberal government introduced its *Statement of the Government of Canada on Indian Policy,* better known as the White Paper. Under the banner of equality, the White Paper proposed to transfer the responsibilities for Indigenous peoples from the federal government to the provinces. To accomplish this, it would abolish the Indian Act, which governed the lives of First Nation peoples; terminate all treaties, which were sacred nation-to-nation agreements meant to continue in perpetuity; and eliminate the special status and recognition of Canada's First Nation population. In British Columbia, where treaty making had been limited and Indigenous rights went unrecognized by the settler state, the White Paper meant that the federal government would permanently ignore the historical reality of colonial dispossession.[13] This was unacceptable to Indigenous peoples in British Columbia (and indeed across the country), and they united in opposition.

Recognizing their structural limitations and inability to fully represent the broad provincial population, leaders from three existing associations operating in British Columbia – the North American Indian Brotherhood (NAIB), the British Columbia Indian Homemakers' Association (BCIHA), and the Southern Vancouver Island Tribal Federation (SVITF) – arranged for a chiefs' meeting to discuss province-wide unity.[14] The 1969 Indian Chiefs of British Columbia conference drew leadership from at least 140 of the province's 192 First Nation bands.[15] With 85 percent of the status Indian population represented, this meeting signified a level of pan-Indigenous cooperation Indigenous peoples had long been seeking.[16] Organizers agreed that the UBCIC would not interfere with community autonomy or supersede existing organizations. Instead, it would act as a coordinating organization where chiefs could develop strong opposition to the White Paper as well as a unified stance on the unresolved British Columbia Indian land question and claims based on Indigenous title.

Considering the long historical push for pan-Indigenous unity and the unique conditions of mid-twentieth-century British Columbia, this book examines why Indigenous peoples sought unity to combat settler colonialism in the late twentieth century and, specifically, how the evolving and multi-faceted concept of unity shaped the modern Indigenous political movement through the sometimes limited, hierarchical, and gender-biased political spaces offered by a provincial chiefs' organization. An old adage claims there is "strength in unity," and this has been the premise of many social movements and political organizations. But how true is this claim, really? How well does unity as a political concept and practice work for the political organization of marginalized groups? And in what ways might "unity" mask underlying inequities (such as those related to gender and status) that are then pushed aside under the emblem of the "greater good"? Who does "unity" really represent and benefit? Does the claim of universality actually serve only to reproduce deeply entrenched structures of inequality? Using the UBCIC as a case study, *Assembling Unity* wrestles with these questions and suggests that, even though unity (as envisioned and practised) by the elite and male-dominated UBCIC could be exclusionary, the reality was far more complex, particularly as a wide variety of interest groups worked towards reshaping how unity was defined and performed within the wider movement. It would be easy to dismiss the UBCIC as a privileged male organization out of touch with its community, but that would ignore the nuances of power operating in Indigenous communities as well as their widespread belief in unity. Surprisingly, this chiefs' organization enabled more egalitarian political action than one might expect. This was entirely because individuals within the organization, as well as those outside it (including grassroots people and members of women's organizations), continually used "unity" as a tool to resist unequal elements of UBCIC directives.

Despite its focus on the UBCIC, this book is more than just a study of an organization. It explores the relationship between BC pan-Indigenous politics and global political channels and ideologies, placing the UBCIC within a local, regional, and international context. It firmly situates UBCIC negotiations of unity within the broader framework of Indigenous politics and resistance at a time when other organizations, as well as the burgeoning transnational Red Power movement, embraced Indigenous unity as a response to settler colonial oppression.

Two principal arguments complicate and contribute to existing narratives of BC Indigenous politics. First, unity was a long-standing and central goal for BC Indigenous peoples, one that not only preceded and extended beyond the UBCIC but was heavily negotiated between UBCIC members, grassroots constituents, and Indigenous women's organizations. Each had unique visions of what unity should look like and strategically used the concept to have their political goals realized within the context of the UBCIC. This process reveals much about pan-Indigenous politics in this era of liberal multiculturalism, Indigenous sovereignty, and global social movements.

Second, to maintain unity and resist settler political formations, the UBCIC and its critics and allies deployed political resistance, recognition, and refusal in highly strategic ways. Building on the works of Glen Coulthard and Audra Simpson, I use the term *recognition* to denote implicit and explicit acceptance of political authority, ideologies, and agendas within and outside of the UBCIC.[17] I use the concept of *refusal* to highlight political resistance where individuals can register their opposition through political non-compliance and by enacting their own strategies. Examining the ways in which the UBCIC facilitated internal and external discussions about political authority, representation, and strategy, this study reveals that recognition and refusal were negotiated not only between BC Indigenous peoples and settler-state actors but also within Indigenous communities and organizations. And these discussions often had a strong gendered dynamic, with Indigenous women consistently lobbying for representation. Exposing and embracing the complexities of how pan-Indigenous politics was negotiated adds important insights into how Indigenous politics works on the ground.

This work makes several core interventions into Canadian and Indigenous histories. By privileging Indigenous political theories and voices, it disrupts established assumptions that Indigenous peoples are not political but, rather, engage only in "activism" or reactive responses to settler colonial political forms, and, further, that the legitimacy and visibility of this "activism" continues to rely on recognition by the settler state. The foremost examples of this trend can be seen in existing discussions of the 1969 White Paper and the constitution debates of the early 1980s, which are falsely credited with, respectively, producing the modern Indigenous political movement and initiating calls for Indigenous sovereignty. According to Indigenous peoples, complex political systems and conceptions of sovereignty existed long before these developments. These myopic moments, then, collapse Indigenous politics – which has long drawn on historical sociopolitical bodies and generations of engagement with settler politics – into flashes of awareness and reaction that seem ungrounded and decontextualized, and therefore invalid. *Assembling Unity* corrects this practice.

This book also redefines the boundaries and expectations of what constitutes politics by unsettling dominant Western and patriarchal ideals. It presents a strong gendered disruption of Indigenous politics by firmly locating Indigenous women in the BC political movement. The UBCIC is, therefore, an ideal case study for understanding the evolution of political movements, concepts of unity and politics, and gendered political expressions.

Scholarly Interventions

Exploring connections between Canadian Indian policy, settler colonialism, global social movements, and Indigenous politics, this study draws on elements of two dominant historiographical trends – narrow community studies and broad political surveys – to demonstrate the strong intersections between local, regional, national, and transnational political expressions. We know about the unique political activities and strategies of specific communities such as the St'át'imc, Nisga'a, and Syilx thanks to work by historians Joanne Drake-Terry, Daniel Raunet, and Peter Carstens.[18] Their studies provide deep historical analyses of long-standing political engagements with neighbouring nations and settlers. Yet, within these works, links to larger political trends, including inter- and intra-tribal coalition and conflict, are somewhat lost. By contrast, broad political and pan-Indigenous surveys explore Indigenous interaction and the impact of Indigenous politics on Canadian political and economic structures. But these studies lack detailed ties to community dynamics and Indigenous identities.[19] Instead, they provide wider lenses through which to understand Indigenous activism, highlighting far-reaching and long-standing political roots, and seeking to insert Indigenous politics into the dominant historical narrative.[20] For example, Paul Tennant's seminal work on Indigenous politics in British Columbia and Laurie Meijer Drees's study of the Indian Association of Alberta analyze provincial trends rather than individual community contexts or culturally specific political ideas.[21] While focused on a provincial organization, *Assembling Unity* explores both broad and narrow political trends, using the concept of political unity as a guiding principle.

This work also firmly situates Indigenous politics within broader transnational networks, including sixties social movements and Red Power, showing how, for instance, Indigenous people in Canada were inspired by the fish-ins in Puget Sound, Washington State, which saw American Indians enacting their treaty-guaranteed right to fish; the 1969 occupation of Alcatraz by the pan-Indigenous "Indians of All Tribes"; and the American Indian Movement (AIM), which set up Canadian chapters in Penticton and Vancouver.[22] Canadian and American activists moved across the border, taking their political ideologies with them and creating strong political partnerships. Indeed, young Canadian Indigenous activists such as Anna Mae Aquash travelled south to participate in AIM activities, including the 1973 Wounded Knee standoff on the Oglala Lakota reservation of Pine Ridge, South Dakota.[23] Meanwhile, American activists came north to lend support to events such as the 1974 Kenora takeover, which saw Kenora's Anicinabe Park occupied by the Ojibway Warrior Society; the 1974 Cache Creek blockade; and the 1975 occupation of the regional Department of Indian Affairs office in Vancouver, which involved local and international AIM members.[24] UBCIC members also worked together with the American

Indian Movement, the National Indian Brotherhood, and the Indian Association of Alberta (among others), and were influenced by the political theorizing and activism of individuals such as Martin Luther King Jr., Mohandas Gandhi, and Harold Cardinal.[25] These ideological and embodied cross-fertilizations shaped the political movement in British Columbia along global political contours and are fundamental elements of this narrative.

Theoretical Influences

Assembling Unity brings together critical Indigenous theory and Indigenous feminisms and uses archival and oral history methodologies to reveal the personal and community contexts informing both political engagements and expansive regional, national, and international political trends. To effectively privilege Indigenous understandings and practices of politics, this work begins with the premise that, while settler colonialism is designed to eliminate Indigenous peoples, cultures, and politics (as Patrick Wolfe convincingly argues), its success is not inevitable.[26] Alissa Macoun and Elizabeth Strakosch are correct in arguing that the settler colonial project remains unfinished, in large part due to Indigenous resistance and the refusal to accept settler sovereignty and political modalities.[27] This book likewise destabilizes assumptions of settler colonial theory and, using critical Indigenous theory, makes room within settler colonial analysis for resurgent Indigenous politics and decolonization. Focusing on a robust history of Indigenous politics and complex practices of resistance, refusal, and recognition, and centring Indigenous voices and histories, we can refocus our gaze away from what the settler project is trying to do, to see how it is failing in many respects and can continue to be disrupted.

Disruption takes many forms, including interrupting dominant Western knowledge systems with Indigenous theorizing, which includes acting politically, thinking, writing, singing, and dancing – all of which are visible in the UBCIC's history. Māori scholar Linda Tuhiwai Smith famously called for Indigenous peoples to implement their own systems of knowledge in order to destabilize oppressive Western research practices, and this work takes up this call.[28] Rejecting the tendency of Indigenous academics to equate theory and research with Western epistemologies and colonizing scholarship, and demonstrating the centrality and importance of theory for Indigenous peoples, I rely on Indigenous peoples' robust theoretical work to understand historical Indigenous politics. Indeed, UBCIC chiefs and community members framed the Indigenous rights movement with Indigenous knowledge and political ideologies, and I not only situate Indigenous actors at the centre of my analysis, allowing them to tell their own histories on their own terms, but also privilege their theoretical frameworks about Indigenous politics, sovereignty, community, and decolonization.

This book also explores Indigenous women's political contributions, particularly within the male-dominated UBCIC environment. Despite a strong body of literature on Indigenous women's politics, we still know very little about how Indigenous women formed their political identities, developed political communities, and strategically leveraged their disadvantaged gender and racial positions to achieve political change. In recent years, scholars in the United States and Canada have re-examined Indigenous women's activities and discovered the deeply political nature of women's work in society, but women's politics remains historically decontextualized and either divorced from or folded into the broader Indigenous rights movement. Some important exceptions to this trend include Patricia Barkaskas's excellent master's thesis on the British Columbia Indian Homemakers' Association and its newspaper, *Indian Voice*.[29] Likewise, Jo-Anne Fiske's work reveals the political roles of Dakelh women in British Columbia, explaining how their participation in community work and voluntary associations relied on their roles and responsibilities as mothers.[30] Outside British Columbia, several important works highlight Indigenous women's political work, including Aroha Harris and Mary Jane Logan McCallum's analysis of eastern Canadian Indian Homemakers' Clubs and the Māori Women's Welfare League. These authors challenge assumptions about the conservative nature of early twentieth-century Indigenous women's organizations and find that, through their clubs, Indigenous women pursued their political and social objectives in ways that were consistent with their lived realities.[31] Likewise, Kathryn Magee's article on Alberta Native Homemakers' Clubs, which suggests that these state-derived clubs served as vehicles of politicization for Indigenous women, also offers important insights.[32] These analyses provide an important foundation in complicating histories of women's activism and Indigenous movements, but more work needs to be done.

Effectively integrating BC Indigenous women's experiences into this narrative demands understanding their unique struggles with colonialism and patriarchy. New Indigenous feminisms provide a robust framework for analyzing overlapping systems of racism and sexism to understand Indigenous women's socio-political realities.[33] Using an Indigenous feminist lens that views women's Indigeneity as a multi-vocal site of strategic political power, *Assembling Unity* explores the political roles of Indigenous mother-hood and homemakers' organizations and uses gender analysis to understand the highly masculine (and heteronormative) nature of Indigenous politics at this time. Unlike earlier expressions of Indigenous feminism that focused primarily on the fraught relationship between some articulations of main-stream feminism and Indigenous women, I use the term "new Indigenous feminisms" to refer to actions and perspectives that use strong feminist and gender analyses, and that critique patriarchy, white supremacy, and colonialism.[34]

Methodological Frames

This research reflects a total of seven years of oral history work with indi-viduals and communities around the province. It draws on interviews with dozens of current and former UBCIC members, as well as female Indigenous activists and activists' family members. Using semi-structured and open-ended interview techniques, I conducted interviews attuned to the ways in which political narratives and the interview space are negotiated across a variety of considerations (including social positions, memory, and political values).[35] My strategy for seeking interviews was to identify current and former UBCIC members and seek them out through my existing net-works, recommendations from others, and the UBCIC. Personal references and limitations on my ability to travel widely meant that the majority of narrators came from central British Columbia and the Southwest Coast. For this reason, just as I recognize the challenges of representation inherent in oral interview work, I also acknowledge that this research is restricted in its ability to speak for activists in communities beyond the Southwest Coast and the Interior. Archival materials, however, provided insights into these and other gaps.

This book draws heavily on UBCIC archival records, including meeting minutes and conference materials, which expose the day-to-day operations of the organization and long-term trends. I used archival sources from the UBCIC's Resource Centre and Indigenous community archives, in addition to government records from the Department of Indian Affairs and the Department of the Secretary of State housed in provincial and national repositories. I also used a wide range of Indigenous newspapers operated by communities and organizations such as the UBCIC, the BC Indian

Homemakers' Association, the Native Brotherhood of British Columbia, and others. These records provide insight into the UBCIC from Indigenous perspectives as well as from settler colonial points of view. Because the UBCIC operated during a time when Indigenous politics became highly bureaucratized, I had access to a broad range of archival sources.

What Follows

This book does not represent a definitive history of the UBCIC or the individuals involved in it. In fact, the types of historical narratives produced through this book are decidedly complex and fragmented. As such, they seem to challenge the very possibility of constructing an intelligible and straightforward narrative. The UBCIC has operated since 1969 and has involved thousands of individuals across the province. Given the organization's longevity, the individual and nation-based membership of the UBCIC shifted, and elected chiefs and councillors changed over time, making identifying consistent protagonists difficult. This study embraces the complexities and contradictions inherent in the UBCIC and follows the general curvatures of the organization's history. Ultimately, this book will show how political unity was negotiated across a wide range of considerations.

Chapter 1 explores how Indigenous peoples sought unity and situates the creation of the UBCIC and new expressions of pan-Indigenous politics within the long history of politics in British Columbia. It counters the dominance of the White Paper – prevalent in most accounts of the modern Indigenous movement – which has tended to obscure important and established political networks, and it places the role of changing Indian policy in conversation with existing Indigenous political patterns. In this chapter, I argue that the UBCIC's formation reflected long-standing attempts at political unity – notably, concerted attempts to create a pan-Indigenous organization throughout the 1950s and 1960s. I also suggest that pan-Indigenous unity was ultimately conceptualized within a framework of band governance, which caused friction later on. Maintaining pan-Indigenous unity between 1969 and 1975 demanded that the UBCIC construct and emphasize its own political authority, and Chapter 2 examines this process. While the UBCIC's dominant concept of unity fostered inequalities between the union, its grassroots membership, and Indigenous women's organizations, I argue that groups who disagreed with the union's position used political interruptions and internal refusals to reconceptualize unity. From marginalized political positions, these groups demanded the increased democratization of unity and more gender inclusivity, which in turn reshaped UBCIC mandates and practices.

By the early 1970s, the UBCIC's engagement with the Canadian state occurred primarily through government funding and increasing bureaucratization. Chapter 3 explains how the organization adapted its political strategies to incorporate a series of recognitions and refusals in order to propel its political agenda and preserve unity while working within state structures. This diplomatic strategy was not ultimately sustainable, however, and by 1975 the UBCIC and its constituents had reached a breaking point. Chapter 4 focuses on the UBCIC's decision in 1975 to reject government funding, which has long been viewed as a turning point for the organization. I suggest that the refusal of funding constituted a significant political interruption to the neoliberal state, yet this move also produced competing internal refusals among UBCIC constituents, many of whom disagreed with the organization's decision and its evolving conception of unity. Indigenous women's organizations were especially vocal against the UBCIC decision and framed their opposition in terms of gender inequality and the preservation of Indigenous communities. This rejection of funding was also accompanied by other radical manifestations of unity during the summer of 1975, notably direct action. Chapter 5 explores this increased radicalism, which resulted from the political decline of the UBCIC and of the Department of Indian Affairs' bureaucracy, new grassroots political channels, and political influences of global social movements. This radicalism demonstrated the power and flexibility of pan-Indigenous unity. Indeed, UBCIC constituents and community members adopted new political roles and ideologies and incorporated them within existing political frameworks. Although direct expressions of radicalism in the mid-1970s were ultimately short-lived, they caused the UBCIC and Indigenous activism in British Columbia to undergo a significant ideological shift. By the 1980s, conversations about Indigenous sovereignty dominated Indigenous organizations and communities. Chapter 6 places the aftermath of the funding decision and the continuing – albeit changing – discourse of unity in this context. It reveals how, at times, the UBCIC used the discourse of unity to define and pursue its own limited concept of male-dominated sovereignty within Canadian state political structures, but also how grassroots activists and Indigenous women continued to resist these limitations.

Assembling Unity traces the history of a movement built on a widely applicable, yet highly fraught and elusive concept, of political unity. Its stories are both unique and common. It examines the similar trajectories of the Indigenous rights movement across Canada and in the United States, and mirrors ideological conversations happening in the New Left, social movements, and other organizations combatting gender and racial inequalities. It offers insight into how movements grow and change over time; how cooperation and unity are negotiated; how hierarchy and power work, and how people shape those processes; and how resistance manifests both internally and externally. This study is the first to tell the history of pan-Indigenous unity in British Columbia as a story of political negotiation, gender differentials, and power. It traces this difficult and fraught work but eschews the temptation to evaluate political success in limited terms of "achieving" unity (a practical impossibility). Instead, it captures the political hope epitomized in Syilx Penticton Hereditary Chief Adam Eneas's 1975 call to action: "My friends, this is unity and this is the way we should be doing it. Our old people are here with us. Let's not talk anymore about the constitution and the white man's laws and how we can fit into them. Let's talk about what we are going to do now."[36]

PART I

Pan-Indigenous Unity

ADDRESSING DELEGATES OF the Indian Chiefs of British Columbia conference in Kamloops on 17 November 1969, Tk'emlúps te Secwépemc Chief and conference host Clarence Jules began by declaring, "I wish to say how proud I am that you have chosen the Kamloops area for this most important occasion." He continued, "I say 'most important' because, as you know, this is the first time in the history of our Province that an All-Chiefs' Conference has been held. May I say that this too, makes me very proud."[1] Convinced that Indigenous peoples needed to unite politically to have their rights and title addressed by the provincial and federal governments, Jules was optimistic about this latest attempt at unity. Yet he was aware of the challenges associated with pan-Indigenous cooperation, including a history in British Columbia of inter- and intra-tribal disagreement and government opposition that had undermined early twentieth-century organizations, and so his enthusiasm for a new organization was tempered with caution. Acknowledging the potential for conflict, Jules insisted that disputes were useful, as "an All-Chiefs' Conference would be of little value unless every Chief expresses his feelings on all subjects to be discussed here." He conceded, "Naturally, there will be many points of view taken. However, this is what we want; this is our democratic right; this is the only way in which we can take a position that reflects the wishes of all Indian people in British Columbia."[2] Also in attendance was Tsartlip leader and president of the Southern Vancouver Island Tribal Federation Philip Paul, who likewise saw unity as the only hope for the future of Indigenous politics and communities. He gravely suggested to delegates that "the history of disunity in this Province gave birth to this Conference you are now attending and depending on the outcome of this Conference is the future of your children and mine."[3] This moment, Paul suggested, was an important one for Indigenous leaders in British Columbia. At this critical juncture, this nod to the past and the future spoke of a need for change, particularly so future generations could avoid the trials of their ancestors. Although political unity would be a challenging endeavour – particularly for a diverse provincial Indigenous population – it was one worth pursuing to achieve Indigenous rights recognition.

THE CHAPTERS THAT FOLLOW explore the political foundations of the Union of British Columbia Indian Chiefs, the first steps towards Indigenous political unity across British Columbia, and the subsequent challenges in maintaining this cohesion. They highlight both the unique historical context of British Columbia in terms of settler-Indigenous relationships as well as multiple attempts at pan-Indigenous unity, which are often divorced from discussions of the modern Indigenous political movement. I situate broad patterns of political work within the framework of the UBCIC and, using Indigenous perspectives on these political histories, demonstrate a degree of continuity that has been underexplored.

1

UNITY

"United we stand, divided we perish"

THE DRIVE FOR PAN-INDIGENOUS unity was not new; it has roots in historical Indigenous cooperation and was active throughout the nineteenth and twentieth centuries, with an explosion of pan-Indigenous organizations in the 1950s and 1960s. There were strong political continuities across this timeframe in terms of political discourses and goals, and the Union of British Columbia Indian Chiefs would build on these. Thus, the UBCIC's creation was simply one expression of political unity within a lengthy history of similar actions. Still, the existing literature flattens these historical complexities and often specifically attributes the UBCIC's creation (and the beginning of the modern Indigenous movement) to the 1969 White Paper of the government of Pierre Trudeau.[1] This direct causality implies that Indigenous politics exists, and is relevant and conceivable, only in relation to the settler state. Such a position not only disregards generations of Indigenous political interactions but also erases the flurry of political activity occurring in the decades before the White Paper. This settler-centric interpretation also ignores Indigenous peoples' understandings of their own political past, and it privileges beliefs about the inherent eliminatory nature of settler colonialism at the expense of explanations grounded in Indigenous thought and experience.

Attending to the processes and products of Indigenous politics, I suggest that Indigenous actors achieved political unity in 1969 through a combination of factors. In addition to Indigenous peoples' united response to the White Paper, these included established Indigenous political practices rooted in historical socio-political bodies, increasingly effective Indigenous leadership, support from Indigenous women's organizations, and emerging liberal discussions of multiculturalism. Together, these factors created space for Indigenous rights discourses and practices to thrive, and this particular historical moment enabled new possibilities for Indigenous politics.

Creating the UBCIC

In 1969, Cowichan leader Dennis Alphonse, Philip Paul, president of the Southern Vancouver Island Tribal Federation (SVITF), Don Moses, president of the North American Indian Brotherhood (NAIB), and Rose Charlie, president of the British Columbia Indian Homemakers' Association (BCIHA) organized the Indian Chiefs of British Columbia conference, where chiefs and delegates discussed their vision for united political action and defined their political goals. Premised on the belief that "it is in the best interest of our people if we speak with one voice on the question of Indian status, land claims, and claims based on Aboriginal title, [and] the administration of Reserve lands," the first resolution of the conference recommended forming a "united body dealing with problems common to all our peoples in British Columbia."[2] With this, the pan-Indigenous Union of BC Indian Chiefs was born. There was widespread support for unity across the culturally and geographically diverse territory (see Figure 2 for a map of the Indigenous peoples of British Columbia), although some communities wanted to build on pre-established traditions of inter- and intra-tribal cooperation, others wanted to initiate political action, and still others wanted to incorporate pan-Indigenous strategies into already developed political frameworks. Indigenous communities in British Columbia and the surrounding areas had long mobilized negotiation, pan-Indigenous cooperation, and treaties to address competition for land and resources. These practices were prevalent before and after the arrival of Europeans in what is now British Columbia. Although the notions of "pre-contact" and "post-contact" are problematic, falsely dichotomous, and difficult to track and prove, it is useful to highlight the multiple ways in which Indigenous communities responded to internal and external political challenges without tethering historical and political change to colonial processes and apparatuses.

For instance, in the interior of the province in 1895, during a time of scarcity, chiefs from the Secwépemc and Ktunaxa Nations agreed to share their hunting territories east of the Rocky Mountains with each other and

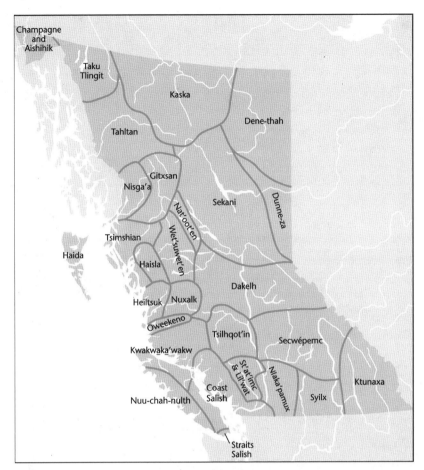

Figure 2 Indigenous peoples of British Columbia. | Cartography by Eric Leinberger

the Stony Nation.[3] This agreement recognized the hardships of bordering nations and used diplomacy rather than military action to seek a solution. Unity was also practised among autonomous communities in response to an external threat. This was the case along the South Coast during the mid-1800s, when "politically distinct" Coast Salish communities united against Laich-Kwil-Tach Kwakwaka'wakw raiders, building fortresses along what is now the Fraser River to defend against attacks and participating in a coordinated attack against one of these Kwakwaka'wakw raiding groups.[4] In the Interior, the Fish Lake Accord negotiated in the 1760s or 1770s between the Tk'emlúps te Secwépemc and the Sp'áxmen (Douglas Lake) Syilx also provides insight into intra-community agreements. This political agreement permitted the Upper Nicola to permanently inhabit the Nicola watershed located in traditional Secwépemc territory known as Secwepem-culw.[5] This was an unprecedented agreement at the time and remains so today; the Upper Nicola is the only Syilx community residing within Secwépemc boundaries. According to former Upper Nicola Chief George Saddleman, this agreement made in the "q'əsapi? times" or "long ago times" not only solidified pan-Indigenous relationships in the past but also served as a strong socio-political foundation long after.[6] Today, the agreement continues to be reaffirmed through ceremony and celebration in both ter-ritories. Thus, the UBCIC provided a forum to renew past relationships and continue pre-UBCIC interactions in a provincial organizational set-ting, and the newly formed organization also drew strength from these existing partnerships. The UBCIC, then, was simply one expression in a long line of political negotiation.

Other communities that lacked strong pan-Indigenous political founda-tions and continuity saw the UBCIC as an opportunity to develop new avenues of political mobilization.[7] This was the case in the Williams Lake District, where existing political organizations such as the Allied Tribes, Native Brotherhood of British Columbia, and Interior Tribes of British Columbia were present but had failed to take hold in any meaningful way due to a lack of representation from the district. The UBCIC, on the other hand, was – according to David Zirnhelt – "undoubtedly the most import-ant organization affecting the political evolution in the Williams Lake district [as] it provided a body of expertise and a source of political strength."[8] In part, this was because the UBCIC sought equal representation from each of the fifteen regional districts of the province (see Figure 3; following amalgamations in 1979, the number of districts was reduced to thirteen) and facilitated strong communication across the districts through fieldwork-ers and annual general assemblies, which were held at different locations each year. The UBCIC was also attractive to the Nisga'a nation, which had highly developed and localized political strategies but was seeking new methods to advance its claims. Before the UBCIC, Nisga'a pursued their land claim through local political bodies including the Nisga'a Land Committee, which later became the Nisga'a Tribal Council.[9] This highly localized approach successfully articulated specific Nisga'a needs but lacked the provincial reach and widespread applicability needed to motivate settler governments into action. While provincial bands and leaders had different reasons for attending the first all-chiefs' meeting, most could agree

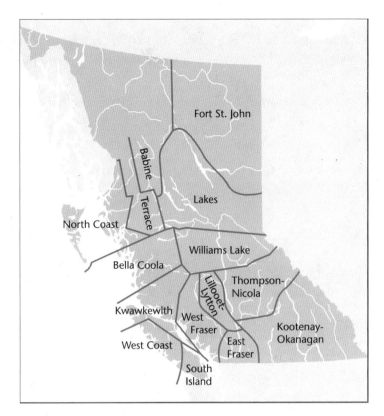

Figure 3 Union of BC Indian Chiefs districts in 1971. | Cartography
by Eric Leinberger, adapted from a 1971 UBCIC map

that government intransigence regarding Indigenous rights and title, current Indian policy that politically isolated communities from each other, and new legislation proposing to end First Nations' status all meant that Indigenous peoples needed to pursue a united front to realize their long-standing political goals. The alternative, which consisted of isolated community- or tribal-based organization and limited pan-Indigenous cooperation, while important and ongoing, needed refining.

Indigenous Women and Political Organization

The widespread support for unity also owed much to Indigenous women, specifically members of one of the two existing provincial women's organizations, the British Columbia Indian Homemakers' Association (BCIHA). It spearheaded fundraising efforts to hold the all-chiefs' conference in 1969, was involved in the original call for participants, and supported the UBCIC's mandate for unity through its auxiliary (and marginalized) political position.[10] This level of political involvement was surprising, given Indigenous women's long history of political exclusion by colonial agents and the organization's inauspicious beginning as a Department of Indian Affairs' project aimed at promoting Euro-Canadian standards of domesticity.

Indigenous women in 1960s British Columbia grappled with deep-seated histories of marginalization. Fur traders, missionaries, and government agents had long promoted European gender norms and heteropatriarchy, which meant that they failed to acknowledge the role of Indigenous women as economic and political leaders, thus disrupting existing dynamics and systems.[11] Even so, before Confederation, Indigenous men and women were legislatively equal. This changed in 1869, with the introduction of the Act for the Gradual Enfranchisement of Indians, the Better Management of Indian Affairs, and to Extend the Provisions of the Act (the Gradual Enfranchisement Act), which specified that the state would consider Indigenous women only in relation to their fathers or husbands.[12] The act also introduced patrilineality and patriarchy as the benchmark for allocating Indian status, with section 6 determining that Indigenous women would keep their status of birth until they married. If a woman chose to marry a non-Indigenous man, she and her current and subsequent children would lose their status.[13] The act "provided always that any Indian woman marrying any other than an Indian, shall cease to be an Indian within the meaning of this Act, nor shall the children issue of such marriage be considered as Indians within the meaning of this Act."[14] Post-Confederation Indian policy, then, expanded and formalized informal practices regularizing heteropatriarchy and gender inequality.

Through later amendments to Indian policy, this sexist provision became increasingly oppressive. In the 1951 revisions to the 1876 Act to Amend and Consolidate the Laws Respecting Indians (the Indian Act), section 6 of the Gradual Enfranchisement Act was reimagined as section 12(1)(b), which summarily retracted many of the remaining allowances offered under the previous act, including women's continued access to annuities, band lands, and resources.[15] Thus, Indigenous women who "married out" immediately lost their status as registered Indians, membership in their band, any reserve lands or right to inherit such lands, annuities or percentages of band revenue, educational and housing support, and the right to be buried on reserve land.[16] This policy had obvious material effects in terms of access to resources, but, by removing women from their kinship networks and ancestral homes, it also had severe social implications.[17] In many instances, women who lost their status relocated to urban areas, where they faced new economic and social pressures. These pressures drove some into intense poverty, homelessness, alcoholism, sex work, and other struggles, while simultaneously promoting the formation of new urban communities and identities.[18] Section 12(1)(b) also amounted to an attack on Indigenous women's reproductive autonomy and freedom to choose sexual and marriage partners, and to an assault on Indigenous family units by imposing hetero-patriarchy on families.

Likewise, the policy intensified women's political dispossession by ex-cluding them from voting in band elections and holding political office. This positioned Indigenous men as self-sufficient leaders and placed women in roles of socio-economic and political dependency, with long-standing repercussions into the twentieth and twenty-first centuries.[19] Historically, male chiefs have greatly outnumbered female leaders, and continue to do so; moreover, male political activity was more highly legitimized and valued by settler agencies (as evidenced through greater funding allocations to male organizations and more men in leadership positions), while female politics was, and continues to be, devalued.[20] Referencing Harry B. Hawthorn's concept of "citizens plus" – which suggested that Indigenous peoples held the rights of Canadian citizenship and also those associated with Indian status – Canadian legal historian Kathleen Jamieson argued that the Indian Act constructed Indigenous women as "citizens minus" by entrenching gender discrimination into a widespread regulatory policy.[21]

This context is crucial for understanding how Indigenous women care-fully negotiated and resisted their political exclusion to support unity and organizations like the UBCIC. They saw the UBCIC's strong potential for achieving the goals of Indigenous communities as a whole as well as Indigenous women's political needs. The women therefore asserted their political agendas, which centred on community well-being, through auxiliary roles in the UBCIC and their own organizations such as the BCIHA.[22]

The British Columbia Indian Homemakers' Association

The creation of the BCIHA in 1968 was in itself an act of political resistance. The association amalgamated local Indian Homemakers' Clubs, which had been created as a part of a Canada-wide Department of Indian Affairs (DIA) initiative earlier in the century. Saskatchewan boasted the earliest Indian Homemakers' Clubs in Canada, which were introduced in the late 1930s. These were modelled after the non-Indigenous Association of Homemakers' Clubs of Saskatchewan (HCS), formed in 1911.[23] Thomas Robertson, the inspector of Indian agencies for the DIA, introduced the notion of extending the HCS to surrounding First Nation communities. In 1937, members of the HCS at the University of Saskatchewan established the first Indian Homemakers' Club, on the Red Pheasant Reserve; the club was administered through the Agricultural Extension Division of the university.[24] Indigenous women who were involved in the club adopted the HCS mandate and took courses on sewing, childcare, gardening, and non-Indigenous food-preservation techniques.[25] By 1940, Indian Homemakers' Clubs were active in fourteen reserve communities across Saskatchewan and quickly spread to other provinces. The Department of Indian Affairs took over responsibility, forming the national Indian Homemakers of Canada (IHC) network.[26] By the mid-1950s, the IHC network was a staple feature in Indigenous communities, with over two hundred clubs operating in the provinces and territories by 1956, nineteen of which were located in British Columbia.[27]

According to the 1951 IHC constitution, Indian Homemakers' Clubs were funded and directed by Indian Affairs as a way to "assist Indian women to acquire sound and approved practices for greater home efficiency; to help the aged and less fortunate, and improve living conditions on the Reserve; to discover, stimulate, and train leadership; to sponsor and actively assist in all worth-while projects for the betterment of the community; to develop better, happier, and more useful citizens."[28] The DIA's original vision for the clubs assumed that Indigenous domesticity and family life needed improvement. Often, these attitudes were grounded in the belief that Indigenous standards of living were too low and that the solutions to these deficiencies lay in redirecting Indigenous motherhood to achieve settler colonial standards of domesticity. Even where standards of living were high – such as in many prosperous Northwest Coast fishing communities – the department was determined to intervene in the homes and lives of Indigenous families. This interference implied that colonial policies, which placed Indigenous peoples on inadequate lands with poorly built houses and little access to sanitary services, education, and health and welfare programs, were not to blame for impoverishment or service gaps. Instead, Indigenous peoples suffered simply because Indigenous women remained unwilling or unable to be effective homemakers. The settler state viewed Indigenous women as the problem and the solution to these challenges.

And yet, despite the obvious colonial, patriarchal, and heteronormative intentions behind the management of Indigenous motherhood, women also believed that they had a distinct responsibility to improve circumstances for their families and reserve communities. This motivated their participation and agency within these and other reserve-based women's clubs.[29] The Homemakers' and other women's clubs held information sessions on nutrition, disease management and prevention, and maintaining healthy pregnancies. They also provided sewing and handicraft lessons, organized community clean-ups, and arranged for shared childcare.[30] The clubs quickly became established community resources; Soowahlie Stó:lō club member Marge Kelly explained: "A lot of them [were] complaining ... because here [the Homemakers' Club women] know what's needed at home. That was our main project – like health, housing, renovations, all that." Noting the challenges of providing community services as individuals with limited resources, Kelly concluded, "but we sure fought hard to get a lot of things."[31] Kelly's insistence that people came to the Homemakers' Club because they knew what was needed at home points to the important roles women played as community mothers, experts, and spokespeople.

The women used their clubs in highly political ways to generate material, knowledge-based, and personal resource networks on and between reserves, and they also provided a local outlet for community members to vocalize their needs. Nevertheless, Indigenous women in British Columbia initially did not see themselves or their clubs as political.[32] They accepted patriarchal definitions of politics, believing they were simply doing the work of good wives and mothers and refusing a wider definition of politics that would encompass their clubs. "In those early years, we were not political," Dakelh Stoney Creek homemaker Mary John explained. "We called ourselves the Busy Beavers and we were just what the name of our club said – we were busy homemakers, looking for ways to make life better for our families and our village. All of us were having babies and raising small children," she continued, "and we believed that we didn't have time for politics."[33] Even Kelly, who insisted the homemakers "fought hard to get a lot of things," did not consider this as political work because she did not view the club as an official political organization.[34] For these women, official politics was limited to (often male-dominated) band governance and state agencies, whereas community or social work was tied to home life and motherhood.

This understanding of women's work as social rather than political was common within the Indigenous rights movement, women's movement, and other global social movements. Anne Terry Strauss and Debra Valentino suggest Indigenous women involved in Chicago's Native American community organizations in the 1960s occupied positions of "invisible leadership," whereby their formal political contributions went largely unrecognized, and Grant Arndt argues this invisibility did not change until the movement shifted towards a "social welfare" focus, although even that focus continued to perpetuate sexism.[35] This gendered exclusion was also common among black women engaged in Black Power movements, where women grappled with racism and sexism in tandem – prompting some to practice what Kimberly Springer terms "interstitial politics" or "politics 'in the cracks'" – as well as among white female activists in the New Left.[36]

For Indigenous women in British Columbia, their political reticence began to change as they acknowledged how underlying structures of poverty and racism (but not yet gender discrimination) thwarted their continued efforts to improve Indigenous lives. They resisted by exposing the inadequacy of the resources that the DIA boasted about in the Indian Homemakers' Club bulletins (written largely by non-Indigenous "experts," including social workers and nurses) and the pages of its publication *Indian News.* Government publications from the late 1940s to the mid-1950s implied that Indigenous women had broad access to the resources they needed to improve their families and communities, including sewing machines and lessons and educational movies on childrearing.[37] Within *Indian News,* the department consistently extolled the introduction of programs "such as sewing, gardening, 4-H Clubs and other activities for young people, community entertaining and welfare work."[38] Gradually, Indigenous women criticized the superficiality of these resources and programs, arguing that a lack of infrastructure on reserves, including adequate housing, sewer systems, and educational facilities, spoke to a much deeper problem that sewing machines and movies could not fix.

Preserving their roles and responsibilities as mothers and accepting their limited gendered spaces, the women critiqued the structural challenges to what Molly Ladd-Taylor has termed "mother-work," which requires meeting children's basic needs for nurturing and protection. In order to provide these necessities, and to be effective mothers, women needed access to material security, bodily integrity, moral autonomy, and political efficacy.[39] Patricia Hill Collins has highlighted the intersectional nature of mother-work whereby "motherhood occurs in specific historical situations framed by interlocking structures of race, class, and gender, where the sons and daughters of white mothers have 'every opportunity and protection,' and the 'colored' daughters and sons of racial ethnic mothers 'know not their fate.'"[40] Indigenous mother-work, then, resides in a unique space where settler colonial attitudes and policies devalued Indigenous mothering practices and denied women access to the necessary resources for successful mother-work. Reflecting this reality, the Indian Homemakers' Clubs lobbied Canadian government agencies for widespread changes to policy and greater material support for Indigenous families, and, through this advocacy, many club members began to recognize their work as political, if not openly feminist.

The Department of Indian Affairs disapproved of the Homemakers' Clubs lobbying efforts and quickly retreated, withdrawing its financial and moral support from the clubs, claiming the women were becoming "too much of a pressure group."[41] The women, in turn, frustrated by their lack of recognized political capital and the narrow and imposed club mandates, sought their independence by creating two new organizations in 1968: the British Columbia Indian Homemakers' Association (BCIHA – an amalgamation of local Homemakers' Clubs across the province), and the British Columbia Native Women's Society (BCNWS – a coordinating organization made up of women's clubs and interested individuals).[42] Stó:lō Chehalis Homemakers' Club leader Rose Charlie spearheaded the BCIHA, while Tk'emlúps te Secwépemc member Mildred Gottfriedson, president of the Paul Creek Women's Club, facilitated the creation of the BCNWS. Together, these forums operated throughout the province, with the BCNWS ultimately more heavily involved in the Interior and the BCIHA on the coast.[43] Both organizations registered under the British Columbia Society's Act, enabling them to seek financial support through other government agencies such as the Secretary of State and to operate without the funding and oversight of Indian Affairs.

Though not without challenges, the BCIHA was able to pursue a more openly political mandate. With a broader representative base, the BCIHA became the first provincial Indigenous women's organization and operated as a reserve-based women's organization representing the concerns of status and non-status First Nation women.[44] With membership open to all

Indigenous people over sixteen years of age, the BCIHA consisted of ninety-two local Indian Homemakers' Clubs and had a leadership structure that included a president, a first vice-president, thirty-two district vice-presidents, and a secretary. The coordinating structure of the association meant that local clubs still had a great deal of autonomy. Yearly general assemblies and the BCIHA's official newspaper, *Indian Voice,* communicated the organization's broader aims. The BCNWS, for its part, emerged as a provincial Indigenous women's council, uniting different women's organizations and serving as a voice for status and non-status women, as well as Métis, urban, and out-of-province women who were not represented by existing organizations. Formed by eight Indigenous women from Kamloops and Vancouver, each with varied experiences in community services and organizing, the BCNWS sought to address the unique concerns of Indigenous women and children around section 12(1)(b) of the Indian Act and to protect Indigenous children's rights. The organization consisted of individual members united under a six-person executive and nine-member board (elected by members).[45] Ultimately, the process of creating independent lobbying groups and expanding the BCIHA's and BCNWS's activities facilitated important consciousness-raising efforts within the Indigenous women's movement, and, by 1969, this movement was firmly established within the province.

In the transition from local, state-led Homemakers' Clubs and women's groups to independent province-wide associations, the BCIHA and BCNWS resisted state attempts to direct Indigenous motherhood. The women proceeded carefully, constructing their politics within the limited spaces available to them. Often, this meant purposefully using their positions as mothers and women, and drawing on acceptable language of community caretaking and "mothering the nation," to promote their political development and strong grassroots agendas. As provincial spokeswomen and lobbyists, members of the BCIHA and the BCNWS called for clarity in the policies affecting Indigenous populations and decried the service inequality between Indigenous peoples and non-Indigenous British Columbians. The women made demands in their capacity as mothers concerned for their families and communities; this strategy both affirmed and challenged the DIA's stated expectations of Indigenous women's roles.[46] At its 1969 convention, for instance, the BCIHA forwarded thirty-eight resolutions to DIA Regional Director J.V. Boys, outlining weaknesses in Indigenous health and welfare, education, adoption policies, housing, Indian arts and crafts programs, and

Canadian law. Among the resolutions were calls for a new school in the Stó:lō community of Sts'ailes, the completion of department-contracted reserve housing, and cross-cultural training for non-Indigenous teachers in the public school system.[47] The BCNWS made similar demands, calling for equal funding for Indigenous children in foster care and for increased education resources (particularly for students living in boarding homes in Vancouver).[48] Department officials had hoped Indigenous women would use their gendered positions to improve reserve conditions, and they commended them for raising "the status of the women themselves on the reserves," but they did not anticipate that women would employ these roles to critique the wider settler socio-political systems, and this development was deeply troubling for the department.[49]

The department likewise did not suspect that Indigenous women (specifically the BCIHA) would play a key role in the creation of the UBCIC, but, as an active provincial organization with strong community contacts, the BCIHA was well positioned to promote the UBCIC. As mentioned earlier, in the lead-up to the first Indian Chiefs of British Columbia conference, the BCIHA was not only involved in the initial call for a chiefs' organization but also helped fundraise to support the costs of the conference by hosting two "moccasin walks" between the Fraser Valley and Vancouver.[50] Like the male leadership, the BCIHA saw the value in pan-Indigenous unity and a chiefs' organization, despite its exclusion from official membership positions. This financial, moral, and political support was central to the UBCIC's formation.

UBCIC Structure

Thanks in part to women's involvement, on 20 November 1969, 90 percent of delegates at the First BC Chiefs' conference voted in favour of a "United Front" resolution, which formally created the UBCIC. By 22 November, the last day of the conference, a newly appointed committee drafted the structure of the organization to ensure band autonomy and non-interference with other Indigenous organizations.[51] Organizers designed the UBCIC as a coordinating association that would facilitate collective responses to common issues facing Indigenous communities in British Columbia. It would not supersede existing band, tribal, or pan-Indigenous associations. Representatives also designed the UBCIC's organizational structure to promote unity.

Comprised of three levels of membership – band chiefs and band councillors, representatives from other political organizations, and hereditary chiefs – the UBCIC solicited representation from communities across the province. Elected band chiefs and elected councillors, known as full and active members, respectively, made up the fifteen-member chiefs' council, which functioned as a board of directors for the UBCIC and was responsible for implementing policies. Each member of the chiefs' council represented one of the fifteen UBCIC districts, which followed Department of Indian Affairs district boundaries. Though some activists were critical of basing political activity on DIA-prescribed structures, this system ensured equal representation from all areas of the province.[52] Outlining the role of the chiefs' council, the UBCIC's newspaper *Unity* reported: "Members of the Council are responsible to report periodically the work of the Union and their participation in this work to the Chiefs of Bands in their respective districts. As individuals they are responsible to promote the work of the Union at Band level and to formulate general policy based upon close contact with the Bands."[53]

Although the arrangement of the organization changed over time, initially the chiefs' council also appointed a three-member executive committee to direct the chiefs' council and oversee general UBCIC operations.[54] The union considered all elected band chiefs full members, and these individuals paid a membership fee based on the band's population. They could hold office in the UBCIC vote at its general assemblies. At the second level of leadership, elected councillors and representatives from other organizations were called active members and could vote at general assemblies and hold office, but only through UBCIC approval.[55] For example, the Native Brotherhood of BC received a voting membership position through this process early on in the UBCIC's history, as did the BCIHA and the BCNWS in 1977. Before this, however, women's organizations remained outside the membership, despite their heavy involvement in the UBCIC. Finally, the third level of membership included hereditary chiefs, who were considered honorary members. They could not vote at general assemblies or hold office, but they provided valued insight and direction as community leaders.[56] The arrangement of the UBCIC was mindful of existing political frameworks, but it also acknowledged the circumstances of Indigenous-settler relations that brought Indigenous peoples together in this time and place.

Settler Colonial Contexts and Histories of Indigenous Politics

The UBCIC was heavily influenced by the unique settler colonial legacy in British Columbia, where limited treaties and refusal to acknowledge Indigenous rights created the conditions for pan-Indigenous mobilization. Unlike other areas of Canada, where, following the terms of the Royal Proclamation of 1763, the Crown negotiated treaties to determine how settlers and Indigenous peoples would share the land and resources and to determine the scope of future social and economic relationships, colonial agents in British Columbia largely refused to follow this law. They preferred to negotiate Indigenous-settler relations on settler terms, which, at times, blatantly ignored Indigenous autonomy and land rights. This, in turn, meant that Indigenous peoples in British Columbia had to articulate their political goals differently than Indigenous populations elsewhere. Whereas Indigenous peoples included under the Numbered Treaties negotiated between 1871 and 1921 sought political unity to demand the proper implementation of treaty rights, Indigenous peoples in British Columbia spoke in terms of the unresolved land question, Indigenous rights, Indian status, and claims based on Indigenous title.[57]

Until the Oregon Treaty of 1846 set the southern boundary of the mainland and the Vancouver Island area and Britain established a colony controlled by the Hudson's Bay Company (HBC), there had been little need to address Indigenous land rights.[58] Indigenous peoples in British Columbia vastly outnumbered settlers, and there was marginal competition for land and resources, and hence minimal newcomer intrusion into Indigenous ways of life.[59] But, by 1849, the situation in British Columbia was changing. Increasing settlement led to the creation of the colony of Vancouver Island. James Douglas, chief factor of the HBC on Vancouver Island and governor of the new colony, was tasked with balancing the expectations settlers had for secure land title through fee simple land policies on the one hand and Indigenous occupation of and relationship to the land on the other. Correspondence with his superiors at the London Colonial Office reveals that Douglas and the HBC felt they had to recognize the Indigenous tribes as the rightful owners of the land and equitably purchase any uncultivated or uninhabited "waste" lands from them.[60] Between 1850 and 1854, Douglas did just that, arranging fourteen treaties in the area around Fort Victoria, Fort Rupert, the Saanich Peninsula, and Nanaimo. In each instance, he negotiated for the complete surrender of the land, with the exception of village sites and enclosed areas, in exchange for continued hunting and fishing rights, and payment in the form of blankets.[61] Douglas did not negotiate similar arrangements for First Nations beyond the limited areas covered in the fourteen treaties, however.[62] Instead, as settlement increased, he began allocating reserve lands without treaties, and this shift towards a settler-oriented system of land ownership and distribution set the precedent for future reserve allocations.[63]

A significant turning point in land tenure and Indigenous-settler relations came with the discovery of gold on the Fraser River near Yale in 1858. The discovery (which came directly on the heels of the California gold rush a few years earlier) brought upwards of 20,000 miners to the Fraser Canyon region, prompting the creation of the mainland colony of British Columbia that same year. The Interior nations were severely affected by the influx of miners to their territories. Miners encroached on and damaged fishing grounds and villages, and brutalized Indigenous peoples from the Nlaka'pamux and Syilx nations. Serious conflict ensued. The result of the "Fraser Canyon War," as it has been dubbed, was the creation of up to eleven verbal peace treaties between American militia leaders and local Indigenous chiefs, which restored law and order and, most significantly, restored Crown sovereignty over lands that had been abdicated to the Americans.[64] The newly created province, in turn, intensified bureaucratic control over Indigenous peoples and escalated geographic containment with reserve allotments.

Increasing state intervention into Indigenous lives through new legislation motivated Indigenous leaders to unite politically. The nineteenth century, in particular, witnessed unprecedented changes to existing patterns of governance, including the 1869 Gradual Enfranchisement Act, which was designed to replace hereditary governance systems with an elective band council system prescribed by the federal government. Under the act, male band members twenty-one years of age and older elected chiefs, who served three-year terms. But the act also limited the overarching authority of these leaders, enabling the governor of the colony to control the jurisdictions of band chiefs and dismiss any chief who displayed "dishonesty, intemperance, or immorality," while in office.[65] The federal and colonial governments unilaterally altered Indigenous political frameworks and gave themselves the ultimate authority to depose leaders according to their own terms. Despite these disruptions, some bands maintained traditional leadership patterns by electing hereditary chiefs or returned to electing hereditary chiefs after a period during which Department of Indian Affairs or churches had made appointments. However, the impact of colonial Indian policy remained visible nonetheless.[66] The 1876 Indian Act amalgamated existing legislation relating to Indigenous peoples and further disrupted Indigenous systems of governance and society. It became a tool for racial definition, defining who Indians were and creating a registry for those who met Department of Indian Affairs criteria. The act solidified changes to band governance and installed department Indian agents to oversee the activities of the reserves. The increasing bureaucratization of the DIA over the course of the nineteenth and twentieth centuries – which led to oversight in Indigenous governance, identity, education, health care, economic development, and land tenure – initiated unprecedented administrative intrusion into Indigenous ways of life. Indigenous communities, in turn, sought ways to combat these disturbances.

Over the course of the nineteenth and early twentieth centuries, BC Indigenous peoples would consistently resist settler colonial expansion through formal political organization, and the legacy of these efforts are visible in the UBCIC. This historical period of Indigenous politics has been well studied by Paul Tennant, R.M. Galois, Hamar Foster, Brian Titley, Keith Carlson, and others and will not be produced here.[67] Instead, this following brief survey of nineteenth-century action serves to locate the roots of the UBCIC and pan-Indigenous cooperation. In the early nineteenth century, Indigenous opposition to colonialism consisted of tribally based demands for treaty or land that were grounded in oral histories and beliefs about Indigenous responsibility to the land and in opposition to reserve allotment policies.[68] In 1872, Coast Salish chiefs and their supporters travelled to New Westminster, where they gathered at the provincial land registry office to demand revisions to land policies that allowed settlers to expropriate land without treaty.[69] Between 1869 and 1873, chiefs from many of the Coast Salish nations came together to write letters and petitions to colonial officials asking for rights to land and resources and protection from non-Indigenous incursion, and, between 1873 and 1887, Salish, Nisga'a, and Tsimshian leaders also initiated pan-Indigenous political strategies within groups that shared similar languages. In 1874, for instance, fifty-six chiefs from Coast Salish and Interior communities gathered to draw up a petition demanding a federal reserve policy of eighty acres per family.[70] This petition, presented to Indian Commissioner I.W. Powell, highlighted the shared grievances among BC Indigenous communities about inadequate reserve allocations but also demonstrated knowledge of land allocations and reserve policies elsewhere – particularly on the Prairies, where treaties promised 160 acres per family. These detailed requests confirmed sophisticated understandings of how colonial land policies influenced Indigenous communities and how, in lieu of mobility and access to geographically wide-ranging resources, reserve communities needed larger reserves to sustain their populations.[71] Under threats of war by the Interior nations, who stood ready to join Chief Joseph of the Nez Perce to fight for the land rights, a Joint Reserve Commission was struck in 1876, but BC nations withdrew from the commission by 1878 and it dissolved in 1910, having accomplished very little. These initial expressions of unity were limited in scope, but provided a strong basis for early twentieth-century organizing.

Pan-Indigenous Organizations

Paul Tennant suggests that the late 1880s produced a "new level of political awareness and organization" that pursued "a very specific set of Indian political demands for recognition of aboriginal title, for treaties, and for self-government."[72] This era of organization was characterized by heavy reliance on the support of outsiders, including missionaries and lawyers, as traditional Indigenous leaders had no formal education, knowledge of the Canadian legal and political system, or ability to communicate in English.[73] Lawyer Arthur O'Meara acted as legal counsel for the Nisga'a, the Indian Tribes of BC, and later, the Allied Tribes, and simultaneously provided legal advice for the predominantly Anglican settler organization, the Friends of the Indians of British Columbia.[74] Likewise, amateur ethnologist James Teit was particularly active among the Interior tribes, aiding in the translating and transcribing of petitions and assisting the formation of the Indian Rights Association.[75] Through this type of advocacy, Indigenous leadership consistently and clearly asserted their right to the land, sending delegations to Victoria, Ottawa, and England and refusing to allow settlers and colonial officials into their territories for surveys and reserve allotments. In 1881, for instance, the Nisga'a brought a delegation to Victoria under the leadership of Chief Mountain to protest increasing newcomer encroachment on their territories. In 1885, Anglican missionary William Duncan demonstrated his support for Indigenous claims by travelling with a delegation of Tsimshian chiefs to Ottawa to meet with Prime Minister John A. Macdonald.[76]

By the early 1900s, it was clear that an established Indigenous rights discourse and patterns of mobilization had been established. Dissatisfied with the intransigence of Canadian and provincial governments, Indigenous leaders took their grievances to the international stage. In 1904, Tk'emlups Chief Clexléxqen (Petit Louis) and Syilx Chief John Chilaheetza travelled with French Oblate priest Jean-Marie-Raphael Le Jeune (a missionary for the Secwépemc stationed at Kamloops between 1880 and 1927) to Europe. They had hoped to meet with King Edward VII to explain the political frustrations of their people but were unsuccessful in obtaining an audience with the king. The trip was not a total loss, however, as the chiefs were able to meet with Pope Leo XIII in Rome and thus initiated some of the earliest international lobbying efforts, a strategy that would be taken up by later activists. Petitions and local pressures continued until 1906, when three Interior and Coast Salish chiefs, Joe Capilano (Squamish), Charley Isilpaymilt (Cowichan), and Basil David (Basil Dick) (St'uxwtews), travelled to England, with Katzie member Simon Pierre as an interpreter, to present a petition to Edward VII outlining Indigenous grievances.[77] Historian Keith Carlson is correct to interpret these actions as Indigenous leaders asking not for new rights to be recognized but, rather, for existing promises made by the Crown to be honoured.[78] Members of these and other delegations proved discerning in their knowledge of historical promises and engagements with the Crown and were determined in demanding what was owed to them. In 1909, in what Hamar Foster fittingly describes as a "turning point" in the early Indigenous rights movement, the Cowichan petition on behalf of the Cowichan tribes, drafted by Arthur O'Meara, Methodist missionary Charles M. Tate, and Toronto lawyer J.M. Clark, was sent to the Colonial Office in London.[79] That same year, a large delegation of Interior chiefs travelled to Ottawa to meet with Prime Minister Wilfrid Laurier. Upon their return, they began to align themselves beyond regional affiliations to encompass the Nisga'a and members of the Coastal Indian Rights Association. These actions precipitated the creation of the pan-tribal Indian Rights Association, followed closely by the unification of Interior communities under the Interior Tribes of British Columbia.

For many participating communities, these actions and organizations represented the first time they were involved in pan-Indigenous political cooperation. While these organizations remained heavily reliant on settler allies to help navigate the settler state's political terrain, a new generation of leaders was emerging to shift the landscape of Indigenous issues.[80] And political pressure from the federal government was mounting, particularly after protests by the Gitxsan demonstrated that Indigenous communities would not soon forget their grievances. In response, Laurier's government arranged an investigation into Indian title, with a particular focus on British Columbia in 1909.[81] Lawyer Tom MacInnes was tasked with producing the report, and, while he failed to consult Indigenous peoples throughout his work, he did acknowledge their lengthy occupation and clear ownership of their lands as well as their illegal dispossession of these lands at the hands of the federal and provincial governments. As a result, MacInnes supported the appeals Indigenous peoples had made to the king and prime minister for reparations. Not surprisingly, Laurier was not keen to take up MacInnes's recommendations to adjudicate title before the courts, and the lawyer's report was ultimately shelved.[82] Laurier was motivated, however, to tour the province, meeting multiple Indigenous delegations in 1910 to assess the issue for himself, and he became more sympathetic to their cause. In preparation for this visit, Interior chiefs came together at Spences Bridge and, with the assistance of amateur ethnologist and their "secretary" James Teit, wrote "The Declaration of the Indian Chiefs in the Southern Interior of British Columbia." Within that declaration, the chiefs called for treaties "the same as all the Indian tribes in the other provinces of Canada," compensation for lands appropriated and pre-empted or bought by settlers, the enlargement of existing reserves, and for land title.[83] The declaration not only demonstrated clear understandings of Indigenous issues elsewhere in Canada but presented demands that would remain consistent among twentieth-century political organizations.

On 25 August, when Laurier arrived in Kamloops as part of his pre-election campaign tour, a delegation of chiefs including Chief Clexléxqen (Petit Louis) (Secwépemc), Chief John Tetlenitsa (Nlaka'pamux), and Chief John Chilaheetza (Syilx) made an oral presentation asserting unequivocal title and sovereignty over their lands. The oral presentation (which had been dictated to and recorded by Teit, and then translated into English by the French Oblate Father Le Jeune) came to be known as the "Memorial to Sir Wilfrid Laurier." The memorial traces the history of Indigenous–non-Indigenous encounters, viewing early relationships with fur traders (labelled seme7uw'i or "real whites") as peaceful and productive, and the arrival of miners as a turning point whereby newcomers (including increasing numbers of settlers) took control of Indigenous lands and resources.[84] The memorial, like past petitions and declarations, is a statement of Indigenous sovereignty and a call to action for government officials to observe Indigenous rights and title.

Between 1909 and 1911, numerous Indigenous nations across British Columbia including the Cowichan, Nisga'a, Tahltan, and Lillooet forwarded similar petitions and delegations to outline their discontent with government officials and to reiterate their desire to settle the land claim. The Nisga'a were particularly tenacious in their demands, becoming increasingly politically active after 1888 and forming several political organizations between 1907 and the 1980s to pursue their claims. Still, the political spaces opened through these channels were not yet matched by a willingness on the part of governments in Canada to address Indigenous claims; when confronted by a delegation of BC chiefs in 1911, Premier Richard McBride flatly rejected their pleas to settle the land question.

Over the course of the next few years, continued Indigenous pressure and a shift in federal politics with the election of Robert Borden's Conservatives led to the creation of the Royal Commission on Indian Affairs for the Province of British Columbia (commonly known as the McKenna-McBride Commission). Between 1913 and 1916, the commissioners visited reserves to inspect the land base and hold public hearings on reserve land issues. While it was a significant step for the federal government, its agents did not design the commission to address the land question in the manner preferred by Indigenous peoples. Instead, the commission was concerned primarily with the suitability of Indigenous reserve allotments, not with issues of Indigenous rights and title. The commission worked under the expectation that Indigenous peoples would follow state mandates, not vice versa, and placed the onus on Indigenous peoples to conform to settler political modalities. Although Indigenous peoples had demonstrated their ability to adapt, Michael Posluns argues that "the feasibility of social change with a minimum of violence does not depend upon a colonized people learning to express their aspirations in the language of the colonizer as much as it depends on the ability of the colonizers to hear what indigenous people have been saying all along."[85] This inability or unwillingness to hear Indigenous political demands is a dominant thread running through the history of Indigenous-settler relationships and prompted strong resistance.

Even in this era of limited formal organization, BC Indigenous people remained highly political and strategic in their engagements with government agents. Community members concurrently recognized the political legitimacy of the McKenna-McBride Commission (by participating in its hearings) and rejected the commission's underlying goals (by ignoring the commissioner's directions). The newly appointed deputy superintendent general of Indian Affairs, Duncan Campbell Scott, believed the commission would provide finality on the land claims issue by delivering the definitive word on reserve allocation. He assumed this relatively quick survey and limited adjustment of reserve lands would satisfy Indigenous demands for land title, but his conception of Indigenous rights and title and economic needs completely mistook Indigenous peoples' understandings of their own rights and what they were prepared to accept.[86] At the hearings, the five appointed commissioners quickly learned the depth and breadth of discontent among Indigenous peoples in British Columbia and often found it difficult to restrict Indigenous people's testimony to commentary on reserve apportionments.[87] Indigenous political leaders and community members spoke knowledgeably and consistently of Indigenous title and rights, rather than limited reserve lands, insisting that they needed treaties to protect their lands and resources. Elders criticized government hunting and fishing restrictions and the negative impact these were having on their families and communities, and they outlined health problems and difficulties securing access to physicians.[88] Indigenous peoples simply refused to follow the prescribed commission mandates, yet, by participating in the hearings, they leveraged this strategic involvement to speak on issues they found important.

Indigenous peoples' actions during the commission both reflected and facilitated political fluency. The McKenna-McBride hearings had the unintended consequence of providing Indigenous leadership and community members with the opportunity to co-opt and reshape state arrangements in order to express and further develop their own political discourses. Structured according to Canadian legal standards while allowing Indigenous peoples to give testimony in their own languages through the aid of interpreters, the hearings introduced a political middle ground. The commission not only represented continuity with treaty-era engagements (by travelling to Indigenous communities and accommodating the use of Indigenous languages), but also provided Indigenous peoples with practical experience in Canadian political forums. This exposure served to further politicize individuals including Andrew Paull, a Skwxwú7mesh (Squamish) community member who, up until his role as an interpreter for the commission hearings, had been heavily involved in organizing Indigenous hop-pickers and fishermen across the province but was not yet involved in the British

Columbia land question.[89] The McKenna-McBride hearings galvanized Paull and other Indigenous peoples across the province.

In response to the much-anticipated *McKenna-McBride Report,* the various Indigenous organizations operating across the province decided to unite. In 1916, a conference in S̲k̲w̲x̲wú7mesh territory attended by approximately sixteen Indigenous nations resulted in the creation of the Allied Tribes of British Columbia, a new pan-Indigenous organization incorporating the Indian Rights Association, the Interior Tribes, and the Nisg̲a'a Land Committee. This new organization allowed Nisg̲a'a, Interior Salish, and southern nations to pursue the overall land claim of BC nations rather than to continue to pursue "local and divided actions based on piecemeal petitions about individual grievances," as George Manuel would later state.[90] Indigenous peoples had long valued widespread political unity as a strategy against settler policies and were now in a better position to achieve it as a cohesive force.

Still, the federal government remained staunch in its opposition to negotiating the land claim issue, forcing the Allied Tribes to pursue political change through other means. With its principal mandate to negotiate the land claim, the organization focused on combatting the recommendations of the McKenna-McBride Commission, after its report was released in 1919. The report called for the creation of 482 new reserves, encompassing 87,291 acres, and eliminating a total of 47,058 acres from existing reserves (affecting twenty-three band communities).[91] Although the recommendations increased the overall reserve acreage across British Columbia, Indigenous communities insisted the additional land was worth much less than the eliminated lands, and they refused their consent. In spring 1920, representatives from the Allied Tribes spent several months in Ottawa challenging Bill 13 (which would adopt the *McKenna-McBride Report* and final recommendations) and Bill 14 (which would approve compulsory enfranchisement of all status Indians). These bills were proposed in combination because, as Hamar Foster notes, "the Indian Act provided that land could not be removed from a reserve without the consent of the band for whose benefit it was held, [therefore] Bill 13 had to dispense with this requirement."[92] When the Allied Tribes failed to halt the approval of the report, they turned to challenging its implementation. Here, too, they faced an uphill battle. British Columbia executed the report via order-in-council in July 1923 and Ottawa followed suit the next year. To circumvent the federal government, the Allied Tribes decided to pursue the land claim through the courts.[93] The government, however, was equally innovative, and, in 1927, when the Allied Tribes attained a hearing with a Special Joint Committee to discuss the land question, Canadian officials, building off the criticism of some Interior bands not involved in the Allied Tribes, claimed the organization's support was too limited.[94] In its decision, the Special Joint Committee identified similar problems about representation and additionally questioned the role of non-Indigenous individuals such as O'Meara and Teit in the British Columbia land question.[95] With the Allied Tribes weakened by the Special Joint Committee's ruling against them, the federal government was poised to deal its fatal blow. In 1927, agents made a strategic amendment to the Indian Act by introducing section 149A, which prohibited Indigenous peoples from hiring lawyers to pursue land claims.[96] This amendment was a devastating setback to the Allied Tribes, but the organization had also been struggling to maintain a strong financial base and wide representation.[97] In 1927, it formally disbanded, but it remained a strong source of inspiration for pan-Indigenous unity throughout the twentieth century.

The 1927 Indian Act amendment generally limited political activity in this era, but the Native Brotherhood of British Columbia (NBBC), founded at Port Simpson in December 1931, proved that Indigenous politics could persevere in spite of formal policy. In part, this was due to the increasingly subversive nature of political organizations and the NBBC's strategic adherence to Indian Act regulations. The NBBC formed "primarily as a response to the economic despair of the depression," particularly in the Indigenous fishing industry, rather than as a land claims organization, and thus it was off the Department of Indian Affairs' radar.[98] And while it was not initially concerned with Indigenous rights and title issues, delegates still took measures to hide the political leanings of the organization. Xʷməθkʷəy̓əm (Musqueam) Chief Delbert Guerin explained that the NBBC openly structured itself as a Christian organization, whereby delegates would meet in churches, sing hymns to begin their meetings, and hide their political papers in bibles in case the Indian agent happened by.[99] Many leaders at this time were devout Christians and incorporated spiritual beliefs into their political practices, but this outward and calculated emphasis on religion rather than politics demonstrates well-developed political manoeuvres. Of course, this type of socio-political strategizing was not new. The federal government's ban on the potlatch and other Indigenous ceremonies and practices in the 1880s had also produced sophisticated tactics to avoid attracting the settler state's attention.[100] NBBC membership built on these well-established resistance strategies in formal political channels.

Through its work with fishermen predominantly on the northwest coast of British Columbia, the NBBC emerged as a unified, pan-Indigenous organization emphasizing non-land-based Indigenous rights. The political evolution of the brotherhood occurred gradually – not extending beyond the immediate economic concerns of fishermen until well into the 1950s.[101] Unlike the other organizations focused on securing Indigenous title and rights to hunt, fish, and gather, the NBBC concentrated on equal access to commercial fishing and fair prices for goods. By the late 1950s, it explicitly incorporated notions of pan-Indigenous unity into its lexicon and, boasting an expanded membership including the coastal tribes and some Interior tribes in the province, began lobbying for changes to the Indian Act; old age pensions for First Nations; improved medical services, education, and housing; liquor rights; and the provincial and federal vote.[102] As the organization matured, its leadership hoped to establish the NBBC as the representative provincial Indigenous political organization.

At the 1959 NBBC convention, James Sinclair, president of the Fisheries Association of British Columbia (FABC), praised the NBBC's work not only in the fishing industry but also "in forests, farming, traffic and [Indigenous] rights" and suggested that the brotherhood was "a single authority for the BC Indian."[103] He urged the NBBC to act as the official political voice for BC Indigenous peoples, allowing the population to finally "speak with one voice."[104] Yet the NBBC's political priorities (which did not include the land claim) did not align with other Indigenous organizations, which viewed the organization as, at best, irrelevant to the wider BC land question and, at worst, antithetical and damaging to Indigenous rights. The question of First Nation enfranchisement, in particular, elicited significant debate, as some felt "that the extension of the federal vote would weaken their position in retaining their aboriginal rights and possessions."[105] In other words, some feared that enfranchisement would communicate to the Canadian government that Indigenous peoples were satisfied and no longer concerned about residual land title and rights issues. These widespread fears prompted Minister of Citizenship and Immigration Ellen Fairclough to make an official statement in the NBBC's newspaper, *Native Voice,* reassuring First Nation peoples that their special status would continue regardless of their citizenship.[106] Such reassurance did little to help the

NBBC's cause, however. While its focus on Indigenous rights and its limited constituency, principally within Northwest Coast fishing communities, ensured its survival in a draconian era of government Indian policy, as Guerin and former Syilx Upper Nicola Chief George Saddleman noted, too many people saw the NBBC as simply a coastal fishing organization and nothing more.[107]

A Strong Push for Unity

Despite organizational limitations, Indigenous politics in the mid-1960s was dominated by the discourse of unity, and this heightened the drive towards establishing a province-wide association, with activists articulating their politics in ways that the UBCIC would later mirror. In March 1966, members of the Southern Vancouver Island Tribal Federation and the North American Indian Brotherhood gathered at xʷməθkʷəy̓əm (Musqueam) to form the Confederation of Native Indians of British Columbia (CNIBC), which, according to Tennant, "was intended to be a *co-ordinating forum* which would neither replace nor supplant existing organizations, but would serve their common interests."[108] This structure – which was echoed in the framework that the UBCIC would adopt in 1969 – appealed to existing BC Indigenous organizations interested in trying new strategies but not wishing to sacrifice their political autonomy. By the time the CNIBC held its first meeting in November 1966, representatives from the NBBC, the Nuu-chah-nulth Tribal Council, and the Indian Homemakers' Clubs had decided to join as well.

The CNIBC built on existing political genealogies, but it also struggled amid competing Indigenous politics. The organization had not yet identified a workable framework to overcome challenges of representation, especially in areas where formal organization was less developed, such as the Northeast. By 1967, the CNIBC's initial assurances that it would merely coordinate (rather than supplant) existing BC political organizations seemed misleading, as the association began developing into its own organization, complete with an elected executive and a draft constitution. With the bulk of support coming from Salish communities and organizations, the CNIBC emulated the limited constituency of the NBBC, and this prompted some to question whether the confederation was looking to replace existing organizations or duplicate the associations and services already in place.[109]

The Department of Indian Affairs also criticized the CNIBC's limited representation: Minister Arthur Laing refused to consult with the organization until it represented at least 75 percent of the status Indian population in British Columbia.[110] Appalled by this unrealistic condition, Benjamin Paul, leader of the CNIBC, scoffed, "Could Mr. Laing muster 75 per cent of his constituents[?] I would like to remind him that his own elected party has only 51 per cent of the popular vote."[111] The DIA's demand not only highlighted the double standards imposed on Indigenous political representation but also ignored the department's own role in sabotaging past attempts at Indigenous political unity. Only a few years prior, the department had used district divisions to isolate bands and deter political unity, and now it was insisting that Indigenous peoples designate a representative organization before Laing would even entertain the idea of direct consultation. Department amnesia must have also prevented officials from recalling that Indigenous communities in British Columbia were not homogeneous or easily united, as the experience of the Allied Tribes had demonstrated thirty years prior. This new demand was timely and was likely an attempt to delegitimize the relatively popular and growing CNIBC. Once again, settler state officials confirmed their unwillingness to listen to or accept Indigenous expressions of their own political realities. Instead, Indigenous peoples were pushed to conform to the changing will of the state – something they refused to do.

The 1967 edition of the *Native Voice* highlighted the continued attempts by leaders of the main BC Indigenous organizations to unite. At the February 1967 NBBC convention, delegates echoed plans for unity and passed a resolution to create a constitution outlining the terms of such union:

WHEREAS various British Columbia Indian organizations have agreed, in their respective conventions, with the principle of Indian unity;

WHEREAS British Columbia Indian organizations have agreed with the principle of uniting their respective executive bodies on a common ground for a common purpose;

WHEREAS one Indian voice is necessary to provide a united front in the consideration of the unsurrendered Aboriginal title of the Indians of British Columbia;

THEREFORE BE IT RESOLVED that the executive head of each existing British Columbia Indian organization meet forthwith to prepare for signature, a constitutional basis for Indian unity.[112]

The language here is strikingly similar to – and, at times, perfectly matched – that which appeared in James Sinclair's 1959 address at the NBBC convention and what would be seen two years later in the organizational materials of the UBCIC. The continuity in the discourse and ideology that surrounded BC Indigenous political organization from the late 1950s to 1969 suggests that the UBCIC's achievement of unity drew on the ideologies and goals of previous political activity. The well-established trend towards pan-Indigenous unity is noteworthy, especially when placed in conversation with the academic literature that emphasizes 1969 as a watershed moment in pan-Indigenous politics. Considering how Indigenous actors understood these political developments and their own political histories, it is clear that the White Paper played a more marginal role in BC pan-Indigenous political unification than the existing literature suggests.

Instead, the formation of the UBCIC in November 1969 is best understood in the context of established attempts at unity and competing organizations. Political unity was highly desired, not only to appease the Department of Indian Affairs, which wanted a single representative organization through which it could achieve certainty on the land claim issue, but because Indigenous peoples in British Columbia also believed that unity provided the solution to claims for Indigenous rights and title. Yet, if unity was the agreed-upon aim of Indigenous peoples in 1969, the question remains: What prevented an existing organization from becoming the new representative voice of BC Indigenous communities? Why create yet another organization? The CNIBC proved that BC Indigenous peoples were not interested in replacing existing organizations with a provincial institution but, rather, needed a coordinating organization that would not seek independence as the CNIBC had. Existing nation-based organizations such as the SVITF and the Nisga'a Tribal Council – and national organizations such as the NAIB, which maintained ties to separate organizations in specific regions and associated with specific issues – were likewise unsuited to becoming provincial bodies. The CNIBC and the NBBC, while broadly representative by the 1960s, were not structured to work as coordinating organizations; they drew their membership from band members rather than leadership, which made it difficult to enact decisions in communities. Indigenous peoples determined a need for a chiefs' organization, with representatives from each band community who could speak authoritatively and legitimately for the majority without weakening community politics. Thus, the UBCIC was the product of an established inclination towards political cooperation that emerged due to specific local circumstances.

Towards the White Paper

The White Paper was a strong catalyst for unity, and an important political tool for mobilizing support, but it was by no means the only factor at work. Like Indigenous political unity, the White Paper was not a unique occurrence but part of a long-standing political trend. Officially, the White Paper was a policy document designed to correct Indigenous peoples' inequality and oppression, but it rested on the same racist and assimilative tendencies that had characterized Canadian Indian policy since the nineteenth century. Notably, the authors of the White Paper falsely assumed that Indigenous subjugation resulted from First Nation peoples' special legislative status and believed that abolishing the Indian Act and historic treaties and eliminating the special rights and recognition of Canada's Indigenous population could ameliorate these conditions.

This well intentioned, if misguided and paternalistic, interpretation was consistent with the national and global political mood at the time. Many saw the policy – developed by Minister of Indian Affairs Jean Chrétien – as the culmination of changes in public sentiment and government attitudes in the 1960s against the oppressive nature of Indian policy. In 1968, when Pierre Elliott Trudeau's Liberals came to power, global decolonization movements and new social movements, particularly the civil rights, student, and anti-poverty movements in the United States, forced many Canadians to shift their critical gaze from the rest of the world to the injustices on their doorstep.[113] Canadian citizens adopted and reshaped emerging political ideals from global movements and applied them to local and national issues of Indigenous rights, Quebec nationalism, and poverty.[114] These shifting political beliefs manifested in formal politics and in citizen-led movements. In federal politics, Lester B. Pearson's war on poverty, initiated in 1965, proposed to eliminate Indigenous destitution through the Community Development program. Groups such as the Waffle – a militant socialist caucus within the New Democratic Party – formed in 1969 to support New Left politics and to voice opposition to the Vietnam War and colonialism in Quebec and to support the labour and women's movement.[115] In the same vein, the Student Union for Peace Action (SUPA), created in Regina in 1964, provided a framework through which young radicals could "challenge the systematic inequality that was foundational to the nation-state."[116]

SUPA members spent time in Métis and First Nation communities to learn first-hand about the types of conditions created under settler colonialism and to help Indigenous peoples escape this environment through politicization. Peeling away the façade of what many believed was a "humanitarian" and "protectionist" Indian policy, Canadians began to see the poverty, isolation, and dehumanization the Indian Act created, and they demanded change. A series of exposés on First Nation reserve conditions throughout this era also hastened Canadian political awareness and motivated grassroots responses.[117] Organizations like the SUPA, however, had uneven success and attracted varying degrees of criticism. For instance, many SUPA members lacked the critical positionality and understanding of colonialism needed to ensure their work did not become voyeuristic or serve to simply re-entrench white paternalism. Bryan Palmer has argued that, despite the often genuine concern for Indigenous peoples and the desire to help alleviate oppression, SUPA community outreach failed to accomplish anything concrete, and in fact many community members believed the radical students were spies for the Department of Indian Affairs or welfare agencies.[118] This distrust revealed the gap between Indigenous and non-Indigenous lived realities and attested to the challenges inherent in relationships between communities with unequal social, political, and economic status. Yet these groups also exposed an important political shift in public consciousness that settler allies would build on throughout the 1970s. And, of course, just as Canadian citizens were becoming more politically aware, Indigenous peoples were simultaneously drawing strength and direction from developing political movements, particularly those associated with global decolonization and ethnic nationalisms.

In developing and articulating their own political ideologies, UBCIC members George Manuel and Philip Paul were influenced by the ideas of Martin Luther King Jr. and Mohandas Gandhi. As Manuel explained, "The increasing contact of Indian youth with the young people of other disenfranchised groups may ... point to a whole new set of examples from which we can learn and benefit. An unwritten alliance is already emerging between the Indians, black, and Chicano youth across North America."[119] Manuel visited decolonizing countries in Latin America and Africa (particularly Tanzania) to expand his political knowledge, but he remained critical of decolonization processes and sceptical that Third World politics were applicable to Canadian Indigenous peoples. Specifically, Manuel disapproved of the manner in which decolonizing Third World nations practised internal colonization after achieving independence. He suggested that this tendency came from Third World nations' belief that they were underdeveloped and that they needed to bolster their economic and social capital by exploiting weaker nations.[120] Manuel wholly rejected this principle of underdevelopment, as it subscribed to social Darwinian ideas of societal evolution. Instead, he believed in the ability of Indigenous nations within settler states to develop their own social, political, and economic paths, and this belief influenced his approach to Indigenous politics. Similarly, Tsartlip Chief and UBCIC member Philip Paul was influenced by "non-violent civil disobedience, Gandhi, Martin Luther King, and some of the more radical nationalists and leaders."[121]

At the national level in Indigenous politics, the North American Indian Brotherhood and National Indian Brotherhood (NIB) offered forums for broader conversations around issues affecting First Nation peoples, and several key players from British Columbia's political scene, including Andy Paull and George Manuel, were active in these organizations. In 1948, Paull had left the NBBC to create and lead the NAIB, where he focused on more general interest matters including voting rights for First Nations (without giving up Indian status), liquor rights, as well as achieving better pension, welfare, and employment supports.[122] The NIB was created in 1968 – a successor of the National Indian Council, which had been founded in 1961. It further developed as a federation of the provincial and territorial organizations emerging around the White Paper. Representing the status First Nation population and crossing provincial boundaries to bring broader representation of Indigenous issues to Canadian consciousness, the NIB offered a strong, unified voice for Indigenous communities. It worked closely with provincial organizations such as the UBCIC, but its hands were tied in terms of its authority to speak for the specific concerns and goals of local groups.

It was in this context that changes to Indian policy took place. Sensitive to changing public sentiment and building on Pearson's anti-poverty mandates, Pierre Trudeau, Pearson's successor as Liberal leader and prime minister, developed a framework for greater public participation, equality, and more streamlined policymaking. Under his "Just Society" directive, Trudeau rejected the notion that any group could be accorded a position separate from the rest of the population and was convinced that removing the legislated difference between Indigenous and other Canadians could cure Canada's "Indian Problem."[123] Yet, discounting the role of historic injustice in enabling Indigenous oppression, Trudeau misunderstood Indigenous realities and ignored how liberal concepts of individualism, freedom, and equality ran counter to Indigenous peoples' history, collective rights, and self-identification.[124] In 1969, Cree activist Harold Cardinal emphasized this settler ignorance, arguing that Trudeau's Just Society did not apply to First Nation peoples and that his White Paper represented cultural genocide.[125] Cardinal was not alone in his assessment. As UBCIC staff member Reuben Ware explained, "the White Paper was a direct attack on Indians and most positions their leadership stood for. It was seen as forced termination, non-recognition of Indian status aboriginal rights, and administrative and legal assimilation – all this without ending racism and separation."[126]

BC Indigenous peoples used consultations preceding the White Paper and the release of the policy paper itself to continue their drive towards unity. From June 1968 to May 1969, Indigenous leaders and senior policy officials held national consultation meetings where participants discussed changes to the Indian Act. During these meetings, Indigenous leaders in the National Indian Council were vocal and united in their opposition to abolishing the Indian Act and the treaties, insisting they "wanted their special rights honoured and their historical grievances, particularly over lands and treaties, recognized and dealt with in an equitable fashion."[127] They called for "direct and meaningful participation in the making of policies that affected their future," but, in the end, the federal government ignored their wishes – articulated continuously over the eleven-month consultation process – and the resulting White Paper policy reflected this.[128] The policy, released in June 1969, championed a settler-oriented framework of justice and equality through dismantling the Department of Indian Affairs, retracting the Indian Act, and rejecting the special status guaranteed through the Indian Act and the treaties.[129]

The White Paper demonstrated the federal government's ignorance of Indigenous issues and prompted a strong call to arms. At first glance, the policy appeared to be thoughtful and forward thinking in its conception: allowing Indigenous peoples to participate in Canadian institutions and ideologies as individuals, equals, and of their own volition, rather than regulating Indigenous existence through the Department of Indian Affairs and the Indian Act. But the White Paper was severely flawed. First, it ignored

Indigenous peoples' complex feelings towards the Indian Act and their commitment to the continued recognition of their collective special status. Certainly, widespread derision of the Indian Act should have produced support for the White Paper, but Indigenous peoples understood that, while the act was paternalistic and authoritarian, it also recognized the special status of First Nations and allocated reserve lands. It likewise protected the Crown's fiduciary obligations to provide housing, education, and health and welfare services. In fact, reflecting on her initial reaction to the White Paper at the 2009 UBCIC annual general assembly, Rose Charlie, president of the BC Indian Homemakers' Association and member of the UBCIC, supported the ideals of equality for Indigenous populations but remained apprehensive about the retraction of important land, taxation, education, and health care rights, all of which stemmed from the Indian Act.[130] Moreover, Teme-Augama Anishnabai scholar Dale Turner has argued that the White Paper reflected a larger ideology he has labelled "White Paper liberalism," which erroneously saw freedom, equality, and individualism as the de facto remedy for Indigenous difficulties.[131] Such attitudes are clearly visible in the White Paper's interpretation of the treaties as outdated and politically outlandish arrangements, since, according to White Paper liberalism, it was impossible for one part of society to make a treaty with another part.[132] This unilateral rejection of Indigenous nationhood completely misunderstood and dismissed Indigenous understandings of the treaties as nation-to-nation agreements and ignored Crown promises that were to be "carried out as long as the sun shines above and the water flows in the ocean."[133]

The White Paper also denied the historical reality of colonial dispossession by suggesting a policy could erase Indigenous inequality from Canadian history and memory – a move Menno Boldt has categorized as "amnesia" as a cure for injustice.[134] White Paper liberalism ignored the legacy of colonialism, failed to consider the unique nature of Indigenous rights, and assumed the infallible legitimacy of the Canadian state in defining, granting, or retracting Indigenous rights. It also did not acknowledge the need for genuine Indigenous consultation and participation in discussions about Indigenous rights.[135] Finally, the White Paper severely overestimated the extent to which Indigenous peoples, even if they desired to do so, could simply shrug off the Indian Act and seamlessly transition into full Canadian citizenship and equality. It disregarded the degree to which settler colonialism continued to influence the lives of Canada's Indigenous peoples.

The White Paper reflected both continuity and change in Canadian Indian policy. On the one hand, it encompassed the same thinly veiled assimilationist tendencies that had always dominated Canadian Indian policy.[136] Whether cloaked in the language of morality and good intentions for "uncivilized" Indigenous peoples, as was evident in many areas of the pre-1951 versions of the Indian Act, or in the modern context of White Paper citizenship and equality, the underlying assumption of Canadian Indian policy remained the same: "the only good Indian is a non-Indian."[137] On the other hand, the White Paper sought to change how Indigenous peoples in Canada were conceived of and treated by abolishing the factors that many believed kept them marginalized. This policy reflected the first time the Canadian government had attempted to produce a framework for Indigenous justice, and, in the months that followed, it (along with Indigenous political action) provided an opening for Indigenous political discourse.

Established organizations such as the National Indian Brotherhood, the Indian Association of Alberta, and the Manitoba Indian Brotherhood responded by preparing scathing press releases and counter-proposals expressing their outright rejection of the White Paper policy, while other Indigenous peoples organized new associations in order to formulate a response.[138] While most opposed the policy itself, many were also critical of the way in which it had been developed without the genuine input of Indigenous peoples. Sally Weaver argued that, "for its critics, the policy was, at best, a perversion of 'consultative democracy' and, at worst, a case of duplicity."[139] Frustrated early on with the consultation process, leaders began using the regional meetings to formulate their own political goals. Many current and former members of the UBCIC suggest that the organization reached its embryonic stage during these failed consultation meetings, as the gatherings provided Indigenous leaders from across the province a still rare opportunity to engage in face-to-face political discussions with bands outside of their traditional territories.[140] By the time the consultation meetings were wrapping up in May 1969, BC Indigenous leaders had formulated their response, a pan-Indigenous political organization.[141]

White Paper Responses

Shortly after its founding, the UBCIC researched and prepared an official response to the White Paper, intent on speaking for and protecting the interests of First Nation communities in the province. The organization represented a unique Indigenous population who were predominantly without treaties, but the UBCIC was also part of a national trend towards pan-Indigenous unity and mobilization against the policy paper. The Indian Association of Alberta under Cree leader Harold Cardinal famously authored a document entitled *Citizens Plus,* which argued that, rather than eliminating the special status of Indigenous peoples and abrogating the treaties, federal and provincial governments should enact Harry B. Hawthorn's 1966 recommendations that "Indians should be regarded as 'Citizens Plus.'" Hawthorn's report, *A Survey of the Contemporary Indians of Canada: Economic, Political, Educational Needs and Policies,* argued that, "in addition to the rights and duties of citizenship, Indians possess certain additional rights as charter members of the Canadian community."[142] For Cardinal and the Indian Association of Alberta, these "additional rights" centred principally on the treaties signed between Prairie First Nations and the Crown in the 1870s, and the association's report, known colloquially as the "Red Paper," insisted that treaty and other rights needed to be protected in perpetuity.[143]

In contrast, the UBCIC's November 1970 position paper, *A Declaration of Indian Rights: The BC Indian Position Paper,* later known as the "Brown Paper," focused on non-treaty rights, addressing First Nation rights and identity, legal status, reserve lands, legislation affecting First Nations, and relations between First Nations and governments in Canada.[144] The Brown Paper – drafted by UBCIC lawyer E. Davie Fulton, a non-Indigenous man and former minister in John Diefenbaker's Conservative government, and UBCIC member and Kwakwa̲ka'wakw law student Bill Wilson – represented the organization's dedication to pan-Indigenous unity and reflected competing politics in action. The position paper was the organization's first attempt at advancing a political position on behalf of its constituents, and it relied on Wilson and Fulton's legal expertise to advance the UBCIC's position.

Fulton represented the UBCIC, but his presence as a non-Indigenous professional meant that the position paper combined Indigenous and non-Indigenous political forms. The Brown Paper brought together a distinct form of politics that amalgamated the priorities and political understandings of Wilson, Fulton, and the UBCIC executive. For instance, while a clear supporter of the UBCIC's political mandates, Fulton was unwilling to speak in definite terms of Indigenous land title. Instead, the Brown Paper proposed protecting reserve land bases and the authority of First Nations band governments, seeking recognition of Indigenous rights through treaties, and compensation for land and resource expropriation.[145] It made no mention of Indigenous title based on Indigenous sovereignty and inherent Indigenous rights. Explaining Fulton's work on the Brown Paper, UBCIC staff member Reuben Ware insisted that "he wasn't going to put anything down there about 'this is our land,' that's for damn sure."[146] Fulton's reluctance to accept the UBCIC's position stemmed from his belief in the legitimacy of British legal history, which "awarded" land sovereignty to the Canadian state, as well as his experience in government. This position departed from the tactics of other organizations such as the Nisga'a Tribal Council, which relied on concepts of Indigenous sovereignty, governance, and historical occupation to demand rights and title recognition. In the end, the Brown Paper's unique approach had little impact. By the time it was presented to the prime minister, the UBCIC leadership learned the federal government had already begun to re-evaluate the policy paper, officially retracting it on 17 March 1971.

This Indigenous-centred analysis of the province's political history and the broader context of the White Paper challenges dominant narratives that attribute the creation of the UBCIC directly and solely to the White Paper. The White Paper, in part, created the space for a more open discussion about Indigenous rights and title. It was therefore an important component in Indigenous politics, but it was not the only one. Focusing solely on the White Paper and on Indigenous "responses to" settlers ignores the reality that colonialism was simply one phenomenon out of many (including cataclysmic flooding, warfare, and environmental changes that shifted the availability of resources) that Indigenous peoples have always navigated and adjusted to.[147] Historically, Indigenous peoples have looked to a variety of sources to affirm and develop their place in the world, including community-based knowledge and colonial histories, and these primed Indigenous peoples for provincial unity. This chapter is intended to shift our understanding of the advent of the modern Indian movement in British Columbia specifically, and perhaps Canada more broadly. It demonstrates how the concept of unity persisted across space and time, and reminds us that the narratives Indigenous peoples tell about themselves are often quite different than those told about them. Of course, the creation of the UBCIC was not the ultimate solution to Indigenous political concerns. Unity was not a foregone conclusion, and, as a challenging, yet highly desired strategy, it was also not maintained without considerable negotiation.

2

AUTHORITY

"Ordinary Indians" and "the private club"

AS A CHIEFS' ORGANIZATION, the Union of British Columbia Indian Chiefs was built on political structures that were fundamentally hierarchical and exclusionary, but grassroots peoples who were unofficially involved in the organization challenged this order – many envisioned the UBCIC as their organization. At the 1975 UBCIC general assembly, Raymond Jones, frustrated with how bureaucratic procedures excluded the grassroots from official UBCIC business and created different political classes, used sarcasm as resistance. As he stepped up to the microphone without the appropriate credentials or official permission to speak, his presence was, in itself, a significant assertion of political will. When he identified himself to the delegates (as was common when addressing the conference), he referred to himself as an "ordinary Indian" of the "Indian club."[1] Here, Jones offered a critique of the unequal political authority accorded to official conference attendees and, in doing this, created the space for his political voice. This transgression was significant amid a discussion that saw delegates debating the power and accountability of the leadership and the disaffecting nature of the UBCIC's bureaucracy. Sarcasm, then, also enabled non-qualified delegates to interrupt these patterns of authority and bring authority to their own voices.

THE UBCIC WAS, in many ways, a paradox. Its principal goal of achieving pan-Indigenous unity was necessarily tied to political authority and representation, and, because the UBCIC's vision of unity was premised on the representative authority of the chiefs – which reinforced status- and gender-based inequalities among UBCIC constituents – the organization was intrinsically unequal. And yet Indigenous peoples across the province overwhelmingly supported unity as the most effective way to achieve state recognition of Indigenous rights and title and thus consistently worked to redefine the union's parameters. Organizing members designed the UBCIC as a representative democratic association, where the 192 provincial chiefs elected fifteen of their number to represent each district as the chiefs' council, and three of these fifteen were chosen as an executive. This process created a tiered representative democracy, with community members indirectly electing the UBCIC executive (because they had elected their community chiefs).[2] At the bottom of the organization's structure were band chiefs elected by their membership to take local concerns to their UBCIC district representatives and participate in UBCIC committees and discussions. The chiefs who were district representatives then brought their region's issues in the form of individual band or district resolutions to the annual general assembly, where the entire organization could address them. At the top of the UBCIC structure was the chiefs' council and executive council, which also met throughout the year to debate larger questions of land claims and Indigenous rights.[3] As the organization developed its political legs, first responding to the White Paper policy and then addressing the "Indian land question" largely writ, it became clear that the political authority vested in unity was uneven, and this became a strong point of contention.

Community members sought to shape the UBCIC and pan-Indigenous unity to fit their needs and challenged UBCIC leadership with broader and more egalitarian interpretations of unity and democracy. They called for direct rather than representative democracy, and Indigenous women reminded the organization that Indian policy had systematically excluded them from formal political channels and communities.[4] In fact, Indigenous women across British Columbia demanded revisions to the Indian Act to protect against membership loss and argued for political recognition and inclusion. Looking at political recognition among Indigenous peoples and arguing that political reciprocity cannot exist under unequal political, gender, and status considerations, I explore the ways in which the politics of recognition and refusal occur among Indigenous communities – not just between Indigenous peoples and the state – and demonstrate how community members and sympathetic leaders confirmed, critiqued, recognized, and refused political modalities according to their own priorities and political positions.

The UBCIC and Political Authority

Immediately after the UBCIC began operating, community members and some leaders questioned the organization's framework of representation and democratic decision-making. Initially, the configuration of the organization was meant to ensure that the chiefs remained accountable to their people and that the UBCIC executive was responsible to the other chiefs. Nevertheless, the UBCIC's structure attracted criticism as early as 1970, with at least one delegate suggesting changes to the organization's constitution. Addressing representatives at the annual assembly, Ted Watts advocated changing the name of the organization to the "Union of BC Indians," eliminating "Chiefs" from the title.[5] Watts and other constituents such as Skwxwú7mesh Chief Joe Mathias believed that this name change would prompt changes to UBCIC structure, ensuring the organization became a voice of the people rather than a sounding board for the chiefs. Watts reasoned that, while the organization would still include elected representatives, these actors would not come only from a limited pool of elite leadership – the chiefs – but would also come from the grassroots. It is telling that, less than one year into its mandate, members were already concerned with the limitations of UBCIC leadership. Watts's proposal was entertained, but rejected on the basis that another incorporated society had already taken the suggested name – a convenient turn of events for those who wanted to preserve the UBCIC as a chiefs' organization.[6] In the end, the name and structure of the UBCIC solidified it as a chiefs' organization, but the tension between the grassroots and the leadership continued to build, ensuring persistent debate about what kind of organization the union should be, how it should serve its constituents, and who should be in charge.

Just because the UBCIC was created as a chiefs' organization does not mean it exclusively acted like one. The negotiation of politics was also evident within the UBCIC general assemblies, as members with varied positions, backgrounds, and political goals got involved. Kwakwaka'wakw member Bill Wilson quickly joined the charge against the potential unchecked political authority of the UBCIC: "We are setting up hopefully an organization that you can control from the grassroots level of Indian people. It is every Band making decisions, setting priorities so that we can act on them. If you want to turn it into a bureaucracy like the Department of Indian Affairs, fine. We have a lot of Indian candidates who are willing to be bureaucrats."[7] Here, Wilson outlined two common fears among constituents: first, that UBCIC leadership would assume control over the political movement and fail to act in the best interests of the communities, and, second, that Indigenous political practices would be co-opted by outside ideologies and non-Indigenous institutions such as the Department of Indian Affairs (DIA). Many were concerned that the latter phenomenon was serving to fuel the former, with the DIA working to channel decision-making powers into an organized administrative hierarchy, which, according to Wilson, simply changed the colour of bureaucratic power from white to brown and left oppression intact.

Fears of Indian Affairs puppet regimes were well founded, considering the chief and council structure prevalent in most Indigenous communities was an Indian Affairs invention and imposition. Many worried the UBCIC would likewise become a tool of Indian Affairs rather than one of the communities. This fear exposed another layer of contradiction within the organization that would continue to haunt it: the problem of building Indigenous resistance within state structures. Leaders needed to engage with government agencies to have their concerns met. In order to position itself as an organization capable of liaising with government agencies and proposing a strong political claim, the UBCIC needed professional leaders and administrative support, and it looked to government agencies for a strong political model. This created practical and ideological barriers between the union and activists with diverging priorities. The UBCIC executive in many ways was in an unenviable position, working to streamline the association so they could mobilize easily to make decisions and implement policies and programs without alienating their people or "selling out" to Indian Affairs. Thus, they demanded the space and authority to do so.

Grassroots Members and Direct Democracy

Other UBCIC members resisted the executive by positioning themselves as advocates for the grassroots and supporters of direct democracy. In 1973, Haisla Chief Rocky Amos echoed Wilson's and Watts's concerns about chiefs and councillors acting without band members' input: "Too seldom are the opinions and wishes of the communities heard first hand. Too seldom are they made to feel they are actually participating in the destiny being made out for them. Too seldom are they allowed their voice in the plans which govern their daily existence." Instead, like Indian Affairs, leadership acted paternalistically towards band members. Even more frustrating for Amos, however, was the perceived "dictatorial" nature of the UBCIC executive and chiefs' council (the highest level of UBCIC leadership), including one executive who argued that UBCIC member nation chiefs "had no right to question the Union council."[8] This hierarchy undermined regular chiefs' authority and highlighted the image of the "private club" that community members and some chiefs accused the chiefs' council and executive committee of perpetuating.[9] And if this hierarchy silenced the already privileged political voices of all but the highest-ranking chiefs, Amos wondered where this left ordinary community members. On paper, the tiered democracy of the UBCIC promoted grassroots involvement since community members elected their chiefs, but in practice it did not necessarily or automatically protect the interests of those outside the executive or chiefs' council.

The uneven nature of UBCIC democracy led politically involved outsiders to question the validity of the union. In February 1974, Hattie Ferguson of the North West Indian Cultural Society concluded that the attempts by the "men dominated organizations" to achieve unity through the UBCIC had "died an ignoble death."[10] She was not convinced the UBCIC could or would see any success as a unified representative organization, and lost interest in the ideal of unity. Others, like Neskonlith Chief Joe Manuel, were not yet ready to give up. At the 1975 Chilliwack assembly, Manuel stressed the need for communities to influence the political movement by directly electing UBCIC executive leadership and having a voice in the organization. "I would like to remind the assembly that I've visited the reserves and people ask how the Union is structured," Manuel began. "To create involvement," he continued, "we should have the people at the bands voting on who they want. Ever since 1969 I hear people say that they want the grassroots level people to decide, well we should let those grassroots people vote for who they want to make some decisions."[11] To this end, the Neskonlith Band passed a band council resolution in March 1975 calling for positions in the organization to be elected at the band level, and it introduced the same resolution at the UBCIC meeting.[12]

UBCIC leaders were not keen on community members' involvement in elections; nevertheless, Manuel's proposal prompted two suggested changes to UBCIC structure in 1975. The first would alter the organization's configuration so the assembly rather than the chiefs' council would elect the three-person executive committee. The second would allow community members rather than district chiefs to elect their district representatives.

These compromises were designed to dismantle UBCIC hierarchy and elitism. In theory, these would also allow grassroots activism to replace the supposed unimpeded political authority and "brown bureaucracy" Wilson worried was dominating the UBCIC.[13] The first recommendation was widely accepted as a way to facilitate direct democracy within the UBCIC, but, far from being a drastic change, it simply opened voting up to a wider selection of elected leaders and still excluded community members' involvement. This criticism is not meant to undercut the recommendation's significance, as it expanded the number of electors of the executive committee from 15 to 192, the larger number ensuring more local input and genuine debate.

The second motion prompted greater debate, with many chiefs hesitant to relinquish control to the grassroots and feeling alienated by what they perceived to be attacks on their leadership. Chief Forrest Walkem was the most vocal opponent. In denouncing the proposal, he sarcastically introduced himself as "president" of the Cook's Ferry Band, declaring, "I heard people get up to the mike and say that we do not have elected leaders and I guess this is where I must step down as a Chief; I feel like President Nixon." After a brief pause, he continued: "I go along with [the] resolution to let the Chiefs of British Columbia at a general assembly do the voting and electing. If the people at the band level are not satisfied with the person they have elected and they are not satisfied with the decisions that he is making then they should do that at the band level." Concluding, he insisted, "I think they give the Chief a certain responsibility and it doesn't matter *which club* you belong to, they all come to a general assembly like this and carry on their elections."[14]

For Walkem, this proposal amounted to an attack on the chiefs' elected positions and political authority. Political conflict among leaders and the grassroots could run high, and sarcasm often crept in as a defensive, and, at times, confrontational political strategy. He is clearly incredulous at the suggestion that he is not an elected leader, and his somewhat dramatic reference to American president Richard Nixon was both timely, considering the 1972 Watergate scandal (which resulted in Nixon's resignation), and pointed in comparing the disgraced and corrupt Nixon to the chiefs. Maybe he hoped this reference would remind constituents that their chiefs were in no way comparable to American presidents and, further, that community complaints were best registered by voting for someone else in the next election. Of course, Walkem could joke about his political precariousness and call on members to simply elect someone else next time, but, in reality, he was in no imminent danger of losing his position. He resisted calls by Joe Manuel, Rocky Amos, and Bill Wilson for direct democracy, and instead advocated representative democracy, which gave band members control over their band leadership but promoted autonomy for UBCIC leadership. Manuel, Amos, and Wilson, on the other hand, wanted to ensure genuine and sustained political participation from the ground level, and, in their speeches to the UBCIC, they proved that such a system was possible.

As non-voting members, community members occupied liminal spaces within the organization by becoming involved in the assemblies or in the UBCIC itself as staff members. Such membership was not without significant challenges. UBCIC assemblies were strictly regimented, and conference attendees without leadership credentials could attend meetings but could not participate in motions, voting, or debate, unless expressly invited through a formal motion (which was rare). Speaking time, then, was limited to official delegates (chiefs and councillors, and their documented proxies), yet grassroots folks could and did ignore these rules, taking to the microphones on the assembly floor. At the 1975 meeting, several grassroots members used sarcasm to challenge their exclusion from UBCIC political processes. These men, including Kerry Frank, addressed the delegation introducing themselves as members of "the club" and holding up fake cards to indicate that they possessed the appropriate credentials to speak.[15] This was a pointed criticism of the UBCIC's hierarchy and bureaucracy, and, through these deliberate transgressions, individuals such as Frank demanded space within the organization that purported to represent him. The continuity of these speeches delivered over the course of six years exposed a growing division between the grassroots and their allies in leadership, and the opposing chiefs. These statements directed criticism at certain chiefs but also proved that people viewed the UBCIC as an organization they could potentially exert influence on and as one that could protect their interests. Although the union continued to guard the authority of its chiefs, continued resistance reaped small rewards, including this second motion's eventual acceptance.

The often-times difficult dialogues between the grassroots and leadership also remind us that political authority was not unidirectional or stable, but was exhibited through a complex series of shifting and permanent positions. While clear political hierarchies existed within the UBCIC, it was also the case that divisions between "grassroots" and "leadership" were blurred. The power dynamics in the UBCIC were not fixed. They were shaped by frequent elections, which shifted leadership positions. Chiefs who failed to secure re-election in their band lost their political role in the UBCIC and became members of the grassroots. Reuben Ware highlighted this reality and insisted that the chiefs "had to win an election. I mean they weren't chief if they didn't win an election, so, all the politics took place around that."[16] Electoral power could be a powerful bargaining chip for the grassroots, who could use their political support to direct their chief's political agenda. Concern about elections could also have the opposite effect, however, leading chiefs to actively avoid controversial decisions in order to preserve their position.

Chiefs and councillors could also inhabit different spaces within the ranks of leadership. In an organization composed entirely of elected chiefs that became further stratified with the creation of an executive, "leadership" became a complex and shifting category. Non-executive chiefs and councillors could occupy a middle position between the leadership of the organization and the grassroots, allowing them to ally themselves with the communities or the executive at any given time. Indeed, as apparent earlier in the discussions on UBCIC leadership, Chief Joe Manuel aligned himself with the grassroots and used his political power as a chief to censure the actions of the executive committee. Forrest Walkem, on the other hand, used his role to support the executive. Indigenous women also took part in these discussions – believing in the potential for Indigenous political unity – but challenging the UBCIC's definitions of limited gender-based citizenship and political authority.

Indigenous Women and Political Authority

Women's participation in the UBCIC was restricted through the organization's adoption of the Indian Act's definitions of status, band membership, and citizenship, but women consistently challenged these limitations by using the language of unity. While the UBCIC viewed pan-Indigenous unity as a way to achieve rights and title along the band membership lines, Indigenous women increasingly used the discourse of unity to advocate for their inclusion as community members who had a stake in the outcomes and therefore should have a voice in the process. Thus, they intervened in the Indigenous rights movement through a series of networks, including the British Columbia Indian Homemakers' Association (BCIHA), the British Columbia Native Women's Society (BCNWS), and informal community channels. To access political authority within the BC movement, then, Indigenous women had to challenge the structural privileging of male actors as well as established ideologies that coded "male" *political* issues such as sovereignty and land claims as more significant than "female" *social* issues such as housing, education, and health. Increasingly Indigenous women's organizations viewed male leadership as a barrier to women's political effectiveness, insisting that, although women had much to say about the state of their communities, the chiefs were not listening.[17] This position introduced levels of gendered analysis and feminist ideologies previously muted in the women's organizations, and many began to overtly challenge the Indian Act, demanding recognition as political citizens.

Women in the provincial organizations drew on national Indigenous feminist debates, as well as cautious alliances with white feminists, to combat legalized sexism. Gender inequality was well established. Nineteenth-century Canadian Indian policy and state attitudes had undermined Indigenous women's political capital and left them underrepresented in the principal Indigenous political organizations, so women targeted national Indian policy to amend this situation. Like the male-dominated organizations and broad Indigenous rights movement, which built on global social movements, Indigenous women in British Columbia built on the Canadian and global women's movement, participating in the 1967 Royal Commission on the Status of Women as well as an international conference of Indigenous women held in Albuquerque, New Mexico, in 1971.[18] Through these engagements and their own organizations, Indigenous women participated in consciousness-raising activities, which strengthened their political voices and prepared them for the upcoming national debate on Indigenous women's legal status.

When in 1973 Jeannette Corbiere Lavell and Yvonne Bédard mounted a series of legal challenges against the Indian Act on the grounds of sexual discrimination, the BC Indigenous women's organizations kept close tabs on the evolving issue. Lavell, using the Bill of Rights' protections against sexual discrimination, argued that the patrilineal membership provisions in the Indian Act – which had removed her status when she married a non-Indigenous man – violated her human rights. Judge Benjamin Grossberg of the Ontario County Court disagreed, and in his ruling argued that Indigenous women who "married out" of their communities actually had more rights as Canadian women than they would have had as status Indigenous women. Grossberg had clearly missed the point. Not only had he disregarded the material and cultural benefits of status, including (among other things) kinship and community connections, and access to reserve housing, but he had also ignored a primary gendered issue. The Indian Act granted different rights to men who married non-Indigenous women than women who married non-Indigenous men. This blatant oversight ensured that Grossberg would not have the final word, and Lavell quickly took her case to the Federal Court of Appeals.

That court ruled in her favour, finding evidence of legislated gendered bias, but the increasingly controversial case eventually ended up in the Supreme Court of Canada, where Yvonne Bédard, who had been prevented from returning to her reserve after separating from her non-Indigenous husband, joined Lavell. Ultimately, the court ruled against the women, arguing that, while the Bill of Rights guaranteed equality in the law, no inequality was *inherent* in section 12(1)(b) of the Indian Act. Further, the court decided that the Bill of Rights could not supersede section 91(24) of the British North America Act and influence how Parliament administered lands with respect to Indians.[19] Indigenous women across Canada were appalled by this decision, which further fuelled their resistance. Women in British Columbia were already politically active in many capacities before the *Lavell* decision, but the case initiated a new level of awareness of gender discrimination.

Women were not just challenging government; they sometimes came up against Indigenous men as well. Male-dominated organizations (particularly the National Indian Brotherhood) and band councils were deeply troubled by the membership question, with some individuals suggesting that revisions promoting women's equality could potentially strain limited reserve resources as women returned home and that this issue distracted from the Indigenous sovereignty movement.[20] In January 1973, the UBCIC quietly stated its disapproval of the *Lavell* case, emphasizing that communities should be able to determine their own membership, and thus used its authority to sanction women's exclusion. It resented attempts to impose changes to the act through litigation, as in *Lavell,* or through the Department of Indian Affairs. A UBCIC spokesperson explained: "While the Union is concerned with the possibility of reserve lands being over-run by reinstated women members and their non-Indian spouses, not to mention countless children of mixed blood, people within bands are the ones to be inevitably affected so it stands to reason they should decide who will live among them."[21] In promoting internal decision-making processes in Indigenous communities, this representative used racialized language to "other" and exclude women and their "countless children of mixed blood." The gender bias of this individual is also clear: the statement made no mention of reserves being "over-run" by Indigenous men's non-Indian wives and *their* mixed-blood children. Instead, ignoring women's political exclusion, the representative invoked the issue of sovereignty: "Any other method of determining membership and status can only be looked upon as yet another attempt to make Indian people feel that they are incapable of running their own lives."[22] Although many leaders disagreed with the intrusion of the Indian Act in their communities in many other capacities, in this case they were content to maintain the status quo. Adopting a position of Indigenous self-determination and political sovereignty, the UBCIC explained that band members, not civil servants, should determine membership.

On this last point, the UBCIC and the women's organizations agreed, but the women insisted that gender equality in citizenship needed to come first, as current categories of "band membership" already excluded many Indigenous women, leaving them without decision-making powers. Indigenous men, on the other hand, maintained stable membership. BCIHA president Rose Charlie lamented that no one consulted Indigenous women on political decisions and mandates at the band and provincial levels; rather, community men viewed women as political observers or mere extensions of the men.[23] Charlie challenged the limitations of women's supportive roles and the subsequent political damage caused by exclusion from UBCIC conceptions of pan-Indigenous unity. The BCIHA and BCNWS used their conventions, correspondence, and newspapers to promote change, and some of the male leaders were listening. In July 1973, one month after Charlie's criticisms appeared in the UBCIC's paper, *Nesika,* an editorial in the same paper warned the leadership of the loss of politically perceptive and important individuals as women left the union to join women's organizations:

> We are standing by watching our strength being drained off by the formation of women's organizations within our ranks. Why are we not ensuring that our associations give women full representation and an unrestricted voice in all of our activities? A change in the by-laws to provide for a male president and a female vice-president, or vice-versa, would ensure that our women would be given a chance to hold office. A change in the requirements for appointing delegates to the annual assembly, making it mandatory that each local send an equal number of both sexes as delegates,

would give our women equal rights in our organizations. A change in by-laws on the terms of office of a president that would prevent him, or her, from running for a third term, would prevent the formation of a family compact. Such a change would also give the president more incentive to stay home and work for the people, rather than spend his time and taxpayers' money on the campaign trail.[24]

While the identity of the author is unknown, this person was a UBCIC member who not only recognized the lack of female representation in official political channels but also believed gender inequality was undermining the movement as a whole. This editorial represents a particular perspective within the UBCIC that "unity" included all Indigenous peoples, and therefore is a strong transgressive voice against the status quo of UBCIC politics, which undermined women's voices and ignored their specific gendered concerns.

By April 1974, it appeared that the organization would take Indigenous women's concerns and political voices seriously after all. Philip Paul called for their involvement in revising the Indian Act and put forward a motion claiming that, because women were responsible for raising children, maintaining communities, and preserving Indigenous values, they deserved a role in determining their own legislative futures.[25] This statement followed a well-established trope of Indigenous women as community caretakers and "mothers of the nation," using women's supposed natural talents to justify greater political participation. It shows the limitations of the UBCIC's views on gender, though it did ultimately result in a shift acknowledging women's rights. The motion was carried, allowing "Indian women in the Province of BC [to] be *fully involved* in *any and all* revisions to the Indian Act, now and in the future."[26] And yet there is no further evidence to suggest that the women were ever *actually* involved. They continued to be excluded from official political channels and, when the Supreme Court of Canada struck down *Lavell* in 1974, their unequal social and political roles continued.[27] This lack of progress was unfortunate not only because Indigenous women constituted a viable political voice and the UBCIC had promised to include them, but also because they had long supported men's organizations and politics despite not having the favour returned. The BCIHA and BCNWS not only predated the UBCIC, but BCIHA members were directly responsible for supporting the call for a chiefs' organization and raising a significant portion of the funds needed to hold the first chiefs' conference.[28] In return, the chiefs supported the women's work in education, child welfare, and other so-called women's areas but did not effectively address their precarious membership status or their exclusion from debates on Indigenous rights and the land claim. Notwithstanding continued rhetoric of equality, in practice the chiefs continued to narrowly define Indigenous politics and allocate less importance to the work of "women's groups."

The loss in *Lavell* and the continued intransigence of male-dominated organizations led the BCIHA to unite with the BCNWS and the British Columbia Association of Non-Status Women in October 1974 at a workshop designed to address the rights of Indigenous women. The workshop gave women the opportunity to liaise with like-minded and politically active women, and, after two days, the women formed a committee and drafted a series of resolutions that they forwarded to Minister of Indian Affairs Judd Buchanan. The women explained that they continued to be ignored in discussions surrounding the Indian Act, despite the resolution passed by the UBCIC earlier that year guaranteeing them a central role. They criticized the "traditional male dominance [that] denies native women equal rights" and called on "the Minister of Indian Affairs and major organizations [to] recognize this Committee to represent the native women of BC."[29] Shifting their strategies to appeal to government officials rather than their community men, Indigenous women were still forced to operate within a highly masculine political arena that relied on men recognizing their political authority. Ultimately, the state and the UBCIC were not willing to address women's legal status, yet Indigenous women had developed a clear political agenda and demonstrated their ability to place their concerns within the UBCIC's purview. The resolutions highlighted male dominance in Indigenous leadership and the negative effects this had on the rights of Indigenous women, and confirmed women's perception of political unity as both pan-Indigenous and gender inclusive.

Barriers to Political Authority

Even Indigenous women's vision for gender equality was not without its own set of privileges, as organizations were fundamentally premised on normative sexualities and traditional gender roles. They drew on the centrality of motherhood, family, and community, and narrowly defined Indigenous women's identities as heteronormative. Women did not allow room for alternative gender realities or expressions of womanhood outside mothering.

Over time, the associations and some specific women developed strong feminist identities and critiques, but these too remained staunchly heteronormative and continued to be deeply tied to motherhood. I interpret these activities and attitudes through the lens of Indigenous feminism to make room for the feminist homemaker, while also understanding that the women's organizations excluded individuals who were non-conforming on the basis of gender and sexuality.

The heteronormativity and heteropatriarchy of BC Indigenous politics excluded political actors who did not conform to these ideals. The UBCIC was a highly heterosexual, masculinist space where male chiefs and councillors debated concerns about sovereignty, land claims, and Indigenous rights within a high-stakes political environment. UBCIC meetings and post-meeting socialization also consisted of traditionally male activities such as drinking in bars. Tk'emlúps te Secwépemc Chief Clarence Jules explained that the budget for the first Indian Chiefs of British Columbia conference in 1969 allocated $1,500 "just for drinking" at a "Happy Hour," but that the organizers ultimately spent $3,800.[30] Drinking served a variety of purposes, including allowing activists to decompress after intense political meetings, to continue serious political conversations, and even to mend relationships. Penticton Chief Adam Eneas and an anonymous activist also made reference to heavy drinking in hotel bars after UBCIC meetings, and noted that, in one instance, drinking facilitated the unlikely political alliance between Bill Wilson and George Watts, who were intense rivals.[31] Amid these discussions of drinking were also vague and direct references to womanizing and infidelity. These socio-political spaces made no room for women as political colleagues, alternate sexualities or gender identities, or divergent masculinities. Accompanying the political roles of chief, council, and the UBCIC was a specific expectation of one's social and sexual lifestyle. The BC Indigenous political movement was stratified in multiple ways along the axes of gender and sexuality. This reality paired with hierarchies of socio-economic and political status meant that the organizations, despite being considered representative by government agencies, actually reflected the goals and identities of only some of the population.

JUST BECAUSE THE UBCIC was designed as an elite and hierarchical organization does not mean it always operated that way or was immune to resistance and change. The workings of the organization on the ground orient us towards the nuances of power dynamics and community relationships in ways that challenge the notion of unequivocal UBCIC authority. Were UBCIC leaders, chiefs, and band councils allocated significant power and prestige compared to other community members? Certainly. Did this mean that their power went unchallenged or stayed the same over time? Definitely not. To ignore the fact that some chiefs wielded power irresponsibly and in ways that ignored their people would be a mistake, but so too would it be incorrect to assume that all chiefs were disconnected from their people simply because they held formal power in band councils and in the UBCIC. It is clear that others without formal political power were able to use these formal systems to make themselves heard, and to reshape how the UBCIC worked – ensuring that it was not always or solely an organization of chiefs but a people's organization too.

Unity continued to be a flexible concept, consistently challenged and negotiated through complex interactions and gradations of political refusal and recognition within UBCIC politics. While the union envisioned pan-Indigenous unity as a foundation for developing strong political demands, not everyone accepted the underlying assumptions framing the organization's political authority. Community members did not universally approve of the chief and council structure or of some chiefs' interpretations of democracy. Grassroots membership decried inequalities and, drawing on their own understandings of unity, demanded direct participation in the political direction of the organization. Indigenous women also condemned the dual political oppression they faced through the Indian Act and the UBCIC's use of the act's structures to administer political authority.

3

MONEY

"A blessing and a golden noose"

AT THE FIRST UNION of British Columbia Indian Chiefs meeting in
1969, Delbert Guerin, a xʷməθkʷəy̓əm (Musqueam) longshoreman and
burgeoning Indigenous political actor, was introduced to the actual cost of
political participation when he received a thirty-five dollar per day honorarium to attend the UBCIC conference. The honorarium (which covered
meals and accommodations but not travel) was a welcome incentive to
attend the meeting in Kamloops, but, when considered alongside lost wages
from the waterfront and the cost of travel, it was grossly inadequate.[1] For
Guerin, as for other activists who worked full time in addition to their
voluntary political involvement, political participation could directly
threaten economic stability. Not everyone had the workplace flexibility or
economic freedom to engage in conferences and other meetings. Political
involvement, then, was both class-based and deeply gendered. In the 1960s,
Indigenous political actors were caught in the slow transition towards professional politics, and, while many wanted to dedicate themselves to
Indigenous politics full time, they recognized that relying on government
funding to accomplish this was undesirable.

IN THE MONTHS AFTER the UBCIC's formation, conceptions of pan-
Indigenous unity continued to evolve. This work was challenging, considering the complex political and economic circumstances the organization
was operating within. Throughout the early 1970s, influenced in part by
Indigenous militancy in the United States – particularly the occupation of

Wounded Knee – the Canadian government was increasingly willing to discuss Indigenous issues, and it channelled unprecedented amounts of funding into UBCIC coffers.[2] This outward affirmation of support for Indigenous politics, however, was not as promising as it first appeared. The federal government's assimilationist agenda remained intact, and the focus of the Department of Indian Affairs (DIA) on devolving services to local band governments was not accompanied with adequate training for community folks, leaving many to believe this practice was a deliberate attempt to demonstrate Indigenous peoples' ineptitude at managing their own affairs. Against this backdrop, UBCIC member nations strategically countered elements of Indian Affairs' new direction they disagreed with, and often used department policy to do this. For many Indigenous actors at the time, working within this system was controversial. Not surprisingly, government money often came with strings attached. Certainly the advent of government funding aided in the professionalization of UBCIC politics and Indigenous actors, but, also unsurprisingly, these benefits were not realized equally. Just like members of New Left organizations and global social movements (particularly student and feminist groups), grassroots membership and Indigenous women had demanded broader interpretations of democracy within UBCIC politics and envisioned unity as economically equal.[3]

Government Funding and Professional Politics

Significant government funding for political work (Indigenous and non-Indigenous) was a new phenomenon. In its first few years of operation, the UBCIC relied on limited and isolated government grants as well as membership dues to finance its operations.[4] To facilitate political work, chiefs and councillors received small honorariums and, out of these funds, sometimes had their travel expenses covered, depending on the level of fundraising or government support secured for a given conference. At the first UBCIC convention, organizers obtained a grant of $50,000, and this, paired with the fundraising efforts of the British Columbia Indian Homemakers' Association (BCIHA), provided enough money to support limited travel disbursements and accommodations for chiefs and councillors.[5] Similar support was generally not extended to community members, however, and those who decided to travel to Kamloops in 1969 did so on their own dime. The experience of Stó:lō Soowahlie band member Marge Kelly, who carpooled to Kamloops with a group of locals, packing brown-bag lunches for the road, was not uncommon.[6] Experiences such as these demonstrated the dedication to political work, the personal cost borne by these individuals, as well as the inequity among those who attended meetings like the one in Kamloops.

In the late nineteenth and early twentieth centuries, government funding for any sort of political organizing was unheard of: activists relied on their own personal wealth and community fundraisers to support their activities. During the heyday of the Allied Tribes in the early 1920s, Andy Paull depended on "Indian money," raised by "passing the hat," to travel around the province and organize the people.[7] Though precarious, this practice was effective enough until a timely amendment to the Indian Act in 1927 banned fundraising for the purposes of pursuing the land claim, in an attempt to quash the developing political movement. Until the amendment was retracted in 1951, activists such as George Manuel and Paull simply incorporated political work into their existing lifestyles, which for many Indigenous men in the mid-twentieth century included wage labour. Personally funding one's political labour required a high level of dedication and sacrifice and limited the types of organizing individuals could take part in. Balancing paid work with unpaid political activities necessitated having the time and flexibility, as well as the financial resources, for meetings, travel, and correspondence.

Reflecting on the difficulty and thanklessness of this early political activity in voluntary associations and band governance, former UBCIC field worker Janice Antoine (Nlaka'pamux) confirmed that "there was nothing glamorous about it. The chiefs here all worked full time and worked at very physically taxing positions, and then they would meet in the evening. And if they didn't get their business done they would meet almost until it was time to go to work, and then work all day, and the next meeting was similar." She concluded, "They put in a lot of hours with no pay and probably no recognition."[8] Speaking from experience with a politically active family, Antoine recalled the work of her grandfather and her uncles, who all served on the band council and participated in provincial politics while concurrently working in agriculture. As the Indigenous rights movement grew and became more demanding, it was increasingly unsustainable for activists to volunteer their labour and wages to ensure the success of the movement.

Through much of the 1970s the UBCIC received financial support from various government departments, and this tested its philosophical stance on independence and intra-governmental relationships. The UBCIC, like many voluntary organizations, needed financial stability, but members were wary of government support and particularly the oversight that would undoubtedly accompany it. As a result, the UBCIC moved unevenly towards funding. In 1970, it publicly rejected a provincial First Citizen's Fund grant of $53,000 as an act of protest against the ways in which the program was handled. The funding agency promised that Indigenous peoples would administer funds, but, instead, the UBCIC found that a committee of non-Indigenous cabinet ministers oversaw the grants. The handling of the grant money, UBCIC representatives argued, set a precedent for a paternalistic relationship with the province, and, thus, returning the money would refuse this relationship and assert UBCIC independence.[9] This was not to say the UBCIC was wholly against government money (as it drew on such funds throughout the 1970s); rather, it would not accept dependency or political inequality as preconditions for financial support.

In the aftermath of the White Paper, the federal government was keen to convince Indigenous peoples that it encouraged Indigenous self-determination. Yet, federal funding followed an assimilationist agenda that sought to discharge the federal government from its financial and moral obligations to First Nation peoples. The extension of neoliberalism involved "devolving, or returning responsibility for, First Nations and Indigenous peoples' economic grievances (endemic poverty, poor housing, and joblessness) to Indigenous communities to solve, as a matter left eventually to their own self-governing economic development initiatives."[10] For Indigenous peoples in Canada, this policy meant decentralizing program and service administration away from government agencies and into Indigenous communities, which required a strong national organization and fully representative provincial organizations that could effectively administer programs and services to Indigenous communities.[11] Convinced that transferring government-administered programs and services to Indigenous communities would promote productivity, the federal and provincial governments began funding social movements and rights-based organizations like the UBCIC.[12]

The Turn to Government Funding

In the early 1970s, the UBCIC began receiving regular grants from the First Citizens' Fund, the Department of the Secretary of State (DSS), the Canadian Mortgage and Housing Corporation, and the Local Initiatives

Program (LIP).[13] In addition, drawing on the recommendations of the 1971 federal Interdepartmental Committee on Indian and Eskimo Policy, the DSS developed a core-funding program for a limited number of national and provincial Indigenous organizations across Canada.[14] The DSS would fund one status and one non-status organization within each province and stipulated that, in order to qualify for support, these associations had to represent the entire provincial status or non-status Indian population.[15] In 1971, the UBCIC easily positioned itself as the representative status organization in British Columbia, with almost universal membership, and the DSS accordingly transferred unprecedented amounts of money into the association. The department provided yearly grants, generally in excess of $500,000, for five-year terms, under its "core and communications" funding program. This program, according to Tennant, was designed

> for ethnic minorities and classified both status and non-status Indian organizations as eligible recipients. Core funds were intended to cover the basic, or core, aspects of operating an organization, including the payment of full-time salaries to executive officers; communications funds were intended to provide for publication of the newspapers, purchase of audio-visual equipment, and salaries of field workers engaged in community development.[16]

The Department of Indian Affairs also provided capital, operations and maintenance funds, and core funds "to reinforce and support the leadership and representation roles of Band Councils."[17] These funds financed the operation of band offices, including salaries and travel costs for chiefs and councillors.[18] The resulting financial security allowed the UBCIC to generate paid executive and staff positions, to provide chiefs' honorariums and travel expenses, and to operate its offices, the Land Claims Research Centre, the Resource Centre, and its newspaper, *Nesika*.[19] This was a new era of legal and political action and, as George Manuel and Michael Posluns insist, "the B.C. land question that took root at this time [came] to dominate."[20] By 1972, the UBCIC had prepared and presented a brief on Indigenous title to the federal cabinet, and the Nisga'a were likewise pursuing their land claim in the Supreme Court. Federal funding certainly facilitated this action but did not guarantee provincial or federal willingness to solve the BC land question.

This level of funding was not limited to the UBCIC: other regional and national Indigenous organizations, such as the National Indian Brotherhood, received similar support, as did non-Indigenous citizen-participation groups, including the BC Civil Liberties Association and the Company of Young Canadians. By the mid-1980s, the Secretary of State was funding over 3,500 organizations across Canada, and, while the level of funding received followed predictable gendered patterns, the availability of funding also ushered in a new era of Indigenous politics.[21]

Strategic Resistance

There were divergent opinions about the wisdom of accepting government funding, especially after Indian Affairs began transferring housing, social services, and education portfolios to the bands in its devolution agenda.[22] This agenda, while seemingly supportive of Indigenous sovereignty and independence, transferred services to communities ill-prepared to administer them, and it failed to adequately fund these enterprises to ensure success. Chief Delbert Guerin insisted this shift intentionally distracted the organization from the land claim by overburdening it with service provision. Guerin, who served on multiple committees for these new services, explained that the fiscal and organizational challenges of administering services at the band level meant that bands had little time to discuss land claim strategies at the local or provincial level.[23] Likewise, the UBCIC's 1974 Annual Report, written by administrator Lou Demerais, questioned whether the UBCIC, bands, and districts were "embarked on the right course in handling government-funded programs." Labelling the still piecemeal nature of funds as a "'carrot-on-a-stick' designed to lead us away from the ultimate goal: settlement of our land claims question," Demerais chastised UBCIC members for allowing themselves "to be led astray."[24] In addition, the term-based funding model did not provide stability: there were no assurances that money would continue to flow. Philip Paul and Clarence Pennier were likewise wary of accepting money from an agency in order to oppose it – "biting the master's hand," as Pennier put it.[25] UBCIC lawyer Louise Mandell perhaps best captured these complexities when she described government funding as both "a blessing and a golden noose."[26] Funding enabled muchneeded political capacity building but also constrained Indigenous peoples under state agendas and budgetary considerations.

Yet, even as the UBCIC accepted government dollars and tacitly recognized the authority of the Department of Indian Affairs and other government agencies, it consistently employed its own vision for political autonomy. The UBCIC liaised with government departments to facilitate the delivery of health, education, and housing programs, and developed associated committees tasked with understanding the programs and the needs of Indigenous communities and ensuring those needs were met. But many leaders and communities saw such service provision as part of broader self-determination rather than following government devolution agendas.[27] For example, the UBCIC's Brown Paper explicitly called for "improved services and programs" that are "managed and operated by us," and framed this demand in terms of escaping government oversight.[28] Thus, the UBCIC was willing to cooperate with the department's aims to decentralize operations and devolve responsibility for government programs to Indigenous communities, but, ultimately, it wanted to shape its activities according to its own agendas. In fact, in 1974, Delbert Guerin challenged Indian Affairs Minister Jean Chrétien on his department's practice of transferring programs to bands without subsequent reductions in Indian Affairs staff. Guerin reasoned that, if bands were administering services independently, there would no longer be a need for as many department officials.[29] For Guerin, the reduction of Indian Affairs bureaucracy was just one component of recognizing Indigenous rights and independence. For Indian Affairs, however, the ultimate goal was never Indigenous sovereignty; it was Indigenous self-sufficiency and provincial rather than federal responsibility.

Other UBCIC member nations explicitly rejected government intervention into band services, and they strategically used Indian Affairs' own goal of devolution to seek more political autonomy than the department intended. A 1974 band council resolution from Williams Lake that sought to fire the Department of Indian Affairs financial adviser in favour of an adviser from the Williams Lake District used the department's goal to justify their request. The resolution explained: "It is common knowledge that Indian Affairs would like the Indian Bands to take control over more of their own affairs," and therefore the band wanted to hire its own adviser, who would be accountable to the Williams Lake District and paid by the department.[30] Similar letters and resolutions came from the Babine District.[31] Government funding certainly came with a degree of government oversight, yet financial security also promoted an administrative configuration that prepared communities for self-government. Funding, then, could be used strategically as part of the UBCIC's political agenda to realize Indigenous political goals. And, while opinions varied about whether accepting government funding made sound political sense, Indigenous peoples in British Columbia agreed that money was owed them. Funding was not viewed as a "hand up," or even a reflection of changing government attitudes surrounding disadvantaged peoples, but rather as compensation for expropriated land and resources, and long-standing policies of political, cultural, and economic dispossession.

Indigenous Youth Training and UBCIC Streams

Using government funds, between 1973 and 1975, the UBCIC expanded its staff and expertise and solidified a strong position on Indigenous rights and title. It also capitalized on a growing number of educated Indigenous youth: UBCIC leaders Philip Paul, Don Moses, Gordie Antoine, and Bill Mussell invited Bill Wilson, George Saddleman, Clarence "Kat" Pennier, and Saul Terry (who were completing postsecondary education in law, accounting, and fine arts) to work for the organization. Professionalizing and politicizing a new generation of Indigenous people solidified the UBCIC as a respected and representative organization and gave individuals and the union the tools needed for its mandate.

Developing a strong land claim position required research and community consultation, and the UBCIC pursued these through its newly established office at xʷməθkʷəy̓əm (Musqueam) and extensive provincial travel.[32] Saddleman, whose ancestor John Chilaheetza had been part of the 1904 delegation to Rome, was hired as the UBCIC bookkeeper (having completed a program at Cariboo College). He accompanied Pennier, the newly appointed finance person, and the UBCIC executive on consultation tours around the province.[33] The union was committed to taking direction from the people and invested time, money, and staff in these field excursions. Saddleman and Pennier made all the travel and meeting arrangements for these consultations and provided honorariums and travel reimbursements for the chiefs.[34] Both men spoke at length about the value of travel for political purposes in terms of getting to know Indigenous peoples outside their own communities and the politicizing effect these trips had on them. In fact, Pennier – now Grand Chief of the Stó:lō Tribal Council – explained that, before joining the UBCIC, he knew nothing about Indigenous political concerns, and he was not alone.[35] Several other former UBCIC members and staff had similar stories about their politicization.

To accommodate the UBCIC's growing mandate and coordinate the influx of employees, the organization's leadership developed three "streams," or areas of interest: community development, band administration, and land claims. Bill Mussell led the community development and band administration streams, working to educate band members on a host of administrative concerns, such as accounting so that bands could run their own finances.[36] This stream also coordinated appeals to government agencies to address policy inconsistencies, access to resources, poor education, health and welfare, and other concerns.[37] In the summer of 1970, Cowichan Chief and South Island UBCIC representative Dennis Alphonse and UBCIC administrator Bill Wilson wrote separately to Jean Chrétien, minister of Indian Affairs, protesting his Department's education assistance policy. Both letters outlined UBCIC and community outrage at the department's decision to offer assistance only to on-reserve First Nation peoples, arguing that this policy discouraged individuals from seeking opportunities off reserve and punished those who already lived outside their home communities.[38]

In a similar vein, the UBCIC often took a public and unified stance against other government agencies like the Department of Fisheries and Oceans when agents attempted to constrain First Nations' access to resources.[39] The UBCIC offered provincial solidarity to communities that would otherwise face government departments on their own. The organization would "go where they were needed," and at times this included taking on local concerns with non-government agencies.[40] In 1970, the UBCIC challenged Marshall-Wells, a Fraser Valley hardware store that had a policy of automatically rejecting credit applications made by First Nation individuals from a reserve. The UBCIC used its newspaper *Unity* to publicly chastise this business and call for change, demonstrating the extent to which the UBCIC pursued both local mandates and big-picture political concerns.[41]

The three streams worked together to fulfill the organization's major mandate, particularly through the creation in 1973 of the Land Claims Research Centre, which Philip Paul ran in Victoria.[42] Paul sought the talent of community development workers, including Brendan Kennedy, Winona Wheeler, Reuben Ware, and Janice Antoine, who used their experience with political travel to begin researching the land claim. The UBCIC provided local support by funding and organizing district-level meetings and sending community development workers to provide land claim research and front-line support for Indigenous rights and title struggles all over the province.[43] Workers were assigned to one of the fifteen regional districts. Antoine noted, "We were doing a lot of community organizing and roadblocks, and just wanting to bring attention to the issues that were happening during that period. It was a very exciting time."[44]

Through their work in First Nation communities as fieldworkers, in the case of Kennedy, Ware, Wheeler, and Antoine, or bookkeepers, in the case of Saddleman and Pennier, UBCIC staff members facilitated a direct connection between grassroots membership and the UBCIC executive, and, through government funding, became professional political actors. As individuals with a penchant for politics took on full-time jobs within the UBCIC, they could focus on attaining the skills and knowledge necessary for political progress. Other obligations no longer distracted them, and, ideally, the more time they spent in their professional capacity, the more adept they became as activists.[45] Funding, therefore, facilitated the professionalization of activism, and this capacity building has had a lasting legacy across the province particularly as former staff members such as Saddleman and Pennier went on to become leaders.

Professionalization

Despite increases in funding, the transition from volunteer to professional politics was slow, uneven, and gendered. Funding created paid administrative staff positions, but UBICIC member chiefs were expected to incorporate their work for the union into their already underpaid chief and council duties, which many did alongside other paid labour. UBCIC involvement and the professionalization of politics, then, was costly. Guerin's experience with honorariums highlighted at the beginning of the chapter is evidence of this. Even at the peak of government funding in 1974, full-time paid political work was rare, leading Larry Seymour of the South Island District to insist that chiefs and band councils needed full-time pay for full-time political work. As he explained, "I'm wasting my time working for MacMillan Bloedel. I'm wasting my time in working with some company for my wages so that I can live. It is a waste of time for Chiefs and Council to be working outside of the community when we've got so much work" to do for the community. He continued, "We've got to stabilize ourselves.

Stabilize our reserves, bring about stability in our community and this ... is a full time job: it's a full time job for Council, it's a full time job for Chiefs."[46] There was an unspoken expectation that politics was something extra or added and that Indigenous peoples "should" sacrifice to do this work. Seymour resented having to balance wage work and Indigenous politics and hinted that the absence of full-time wages for political work diminished the roles of chief and council. Others agreed with Seymour that Indigenous politics was suffering because leaders had their focus diverted by other things, yet adequate funding for professional leaders was not forthcoming.

Of course, Guerin and Seymour, despite lost wages, were in relatively privileged economic positions compared to others who simply could not afford to miss paid work for unpaid political labour or who did not have the workplace freedom needed to take time off (even if it was unpaid). Their sacrifices were significant and widespread but also demonstrate the multiplicity of working men's experiences in politics. For instance, Guerin had more workplace freedom than some xʷməθkʷəy̓əm members and, despite lost work, he ultimately had the financial stability needed to participate in provincial politics. After he secured a spot on council, other leaders often asked him to attend political meetings when they were unable to leave work. This prompted Guerin to joke that he was the president of the "you-go club."[47] This humorous perspective offers insight into a phenomenon where the "burden" of political work was placed unevenly on those perceived as able to bear it. Maintaining balance between paid labour and unpaid or underpaid political work proved challenging for many activists. In April 1975, Chief George Watts, when introducing members of his West Coast District to the UBCIC assembly, drew attention to the fact that they had "taken five days off work [and] have taken money out of their bank accounts to get here."[48] Engaging in such unpaid work was no small sacrifice for working people, and gender considerations added another dimension to this problem.

Indigenous Women and Professional Politics

Indigenous women lacked the same formal political opportunities as men. Patriarchal gender structures coded Indigenous women as mothers and community caretakers, thus equating women with "the home" through their "natural" inclinations. These internalized gendered hierarchies created significant barriers in terms of political participation, which then undermined women's political professionalization. They were largely excluded from UBCIC politics because they could not access leadership roles in the band governance system; even after 1951 (when the Indian Act no longer barred women from band leadership), few were able to secure these positions. In fact, in the mid-twentieth century, female chiefs and councillors were so rare that they warranted special attention in the Department of Indian Affairs' publication *Indian News*.[49] When women did participate in the UBCIC, they often did so as unpaid support workers and members of auxiliary organizations such as the BCIHA and BCNWS. Within the UBCIC, this unpaid gendered labour included taking meeting minutes, receiving and organizing receipts from chiefs and councillors, and making coffee and refreshments at meetings.[50] Women did secure paid positions as staff members and accessed formal political work in this way, but the UBCIC hierarchy did not value these positions as much as elected leadership roles. Just as other social and political movements at this time built capacity and strength on the backs of women's administrative and caregiving roles, so too did the UBCIC. Women could keep meetings running and play support roles, but they were largely prevented from political decision-making outside their own organizations.

At the same time, women's work in the BCIHA, while self-directed, was viewed by government agents and Indigenous men as social rather than political and, as such, received limited funding and attention. Despite the strong unofficial role they played in the UBCIC, including working to place community concerns about housing, education, and social welfare on the union's agenda, the women's organizations operated without an official voice or vote in the UBCIC until 1977. Not surprisingly, then, BCIHA operating budgets typically constituted one-third of the money received by the UBCIC, while, depending on the budget year, executive salaries ranged between $300 and $1,200 per month in the Homemakers' Association compared to between $600 and $1,500 per month in the UBCIC.[51] This gap can be attributed to two interrelated beliefs: that women's roles were in the home, not in the workplace (and therefore they did not need to be breadwinners), and that women's organizations were not designated as the "representative" provincial organization (and were therefore viewed by the federal government as superfluous).

In addition, work, marriage, motherhood, and gender expectations could prevent women's political involvement. While some male workers from resource industries had flexibility for political involvement, thanks to shift work and seasonal work fluctuations, women, who were already excluded from state-sanctioned governance patterns for ideological reasons, often had constant domestic duties that made it a practical challenge to participate in meetings. Ts'ishaa7ath (Tseshaht) activist Wahmeesh (Ken Watts) recalled that his mother, Matilda, did not get involved in formal politics until after his father, Chief George Watts, died. Explaining that this stemmed partially from "an old school mentality" of separate spheres, Watts suggested that men's activities sometimes compromised women's political potential.[52] Yet he also provided evidence of the flexibility of women's politics, emphasizing the important role Nuu-chah-nulth women played in supporting their husband's political pursuits. In Nuu-chah-nulth culture, he explained, "you don't say 'behind every great man there's a great woman,' it's actually beside." He continued, "If you ever have the opportunity to see, at a feast or some-thing, there's a leader ... and his wife stands right beside and a bit behind him and they'll talk back and forth as he's speaking as a leader, and I think that's what my mom was like; she was such a support for my dad."[53] Of course, this idealized gendered language could mask some women's political oppression under the guise of "tradition" and support, and ignored the difficulties women faced in running the household alone while men practised formal politics.

Still, many Indigenous women carefully incorporated multiple expres-sions of political work into their existing paid and unpaid labour patterns. Examining a picture of a 1969 meeting of the East Fraser District Chiefs and the Indian Homemakers' Association in Chilliwack, Stó:lō Cheam Chief Sioliya (June Quipp) pointed out the strong family connections between the two organizations, including many husband-and-wife teams.[54] Identifying her father, the late Chief Albert Douglas in the picture, Quipp revealed that her mother, Edna Douglas, was also prominent within the Homemakers' Association. Noting her mother's absence in the image, Quipp mused, after some quick mental calculations, that "she was off having a baby."[55] Edna Douglas's political involvement had to be incorporated into her domestic duties, and this meant she had less flexibility than her hus-band. This example suggests how some Indigenous women struggled to politicize while others, like Homemakers' Club members, merged mother-hood and politicization.

Despite these obstacles to women's political power outside of auxiliary roles, settler colonial economic and political systems could compete with each other to produce political opportunities for women – though these did not disrupt deeply entrenched views of women as apolitical. Among the Nuu-chah-nulth of Gold River, men's involvement in wage labour in the 1960s and 1970s opened up political avenues for women that had long been unavailable. As community men went to work in logging camps away from Gold River, they found themselves with little time for band politics. The result was that women stepped in to fill these political roles through temporary local arrangements.[56] Stó:lō Soowahlie band member Marge Kelly had a similar experience in the Fraser Valley when her brother-in-law Thomas Kelly (a chief and dairy farmer) asked her to attend band and UBCIC meetings as his proxy.[57] Notwithstanding these changes in local powers, it was clear that women were viewed, and often viewed themselves, as simply "standing in" for men who were too busy to fulfill all their duties. Community members regarded the female leaders in Gold River as temporary replacements, leaving women's traditional roles as supporters intact. Kelly similarly occupied a provisional and gender-specific role as her chief's proxy, which ensured that she did not have access to any real political power but rather acted simply as an intermediary between the legitimate power of the chief and that of the UBCIC. She also insisted that she was "just helping out" when the political men in her family asked her and was adamant that she did not have any political experience or knowledge. Even when the UBCIC gave her a proxy vote, Kelly deferred her judgment to the male chiefs and would align her vote with theirs because, as she argued, "they were experienced and I wasn't."[58] This outlook extended into Kelly's overall assessment of women's politics, revealing the dominance of masculinist politics. While she conceded that the early Homemakers' Club members played important roles as community experts, she was reluctant to frame women's work as politics, even after the BCIHA was formed.[59] Here Indigenous women's experience was similar to that of many women of colour and white women in the New Left – only in specific circumstances did space "open up" for women, often in the absence of men able to take up political roles.[60]

Funding Gaps and Grassroots Involvement

Political and economic inequalities also existed between Indigenous communities and UBCIC leadership, and these became a source of political refusals against the UBCIC. Communities envisioned political unity and

UBCIC goals as promoting economic equality. As a result, they were critical of leadership and the UBCIC more broadly when they perceived disparities. The economic context in which the UBCIC was operating fuelled these divisions, after the government created paid leadership and staff positions within an organization where previously none had existed. In the mid-1970s, these paid positions included the three-member UBCIC executive, who each received $1,500 per month, and administrators and researchers, who received between $900 and $1,000 per month.[61] Before 1976, members of the chiefs' council also received $250 per month in addition to $50 per day honorariums for meetings.[62] The UBCIC budget also included targeted travel funding for the executive at $200 each per year, and separate funding for conferences, meetings, and workshops, which included honorariums and travel funding for participants.[63]

Community members in the mid-1970s were predominantly concerned with funding, as UBCIC budgets appeared to be substantial, prompting some to imagine their leaders living large off government money rather than filtering funds down to the communities. In some instances, this perception that leadership was benefiting economically in ways that the communities were not was accurate. Chiefs Adam Eneas and Delbert Guerin explained that some leaders refused to attend UBCIC events or meetings unless they received generous honorariums and adequate accommodations. The Marble Arch Hotel near the UBCIC offices on West Hastings Street was a favourite spot for UBCIC leadership, and activists recalled meeting there often.[64] Reflecting back on these days with a mixture of humour and revulsion, Eneas noted that leaders often joked that they were getting "sick of steak and lobster" – a common catch phrase reflecting UBCIC leaders' elite status and expectations.[65] In contrast, band members who were also attending political meetings made sandwiches or stews to feed themselves while their leaders were eating in restaurants, and this state of affairs fuelled frustration and resentment.[66]

On its own, the chief and council system created power differences and hierarchies, and funding within the UBCIC deepened these inequities. The relative political and economic inequalities between the grassroots and leadership – which intensified with the influx of government money – created distrust. UBCIC staff member Janice Antoine explained: "Whether there was or not, there was a belief that the top was skimmed off the money coming into the British Columbia region for the organizations and then it was distributed. So a smaller pot was distributed [to the communities]."[67] Although Antoine admitted that there never was enough money available to the communities and that leadership did many good things for their people, she cautiously questioned some of the privileges available to the chiefs and council and denied to community members. The most visible of these benefits were honorariums and travel funding for leaders to attend political meetings. "I mean, how many people during that period had actually stayed in hotel rooms or even got per diems?," Antoine wondered. "Most people could barely put gas in their car to go to a meeting, and so to know that a bureaucracy was getting it or a few people had access to that ...," Antoine said, trailing off. "It's not that they weren't doing good work with it," she insisted. "It's just that it seemed like a real luxury when there was such a contrast [with] what was happening in our communities."[68] Antoine's balanced and cautious reflection shows the weight of these issues and the role perception plays in people's evaluation of leadership.

This contrast between grassroots experiences and those of chief and council was also visible at UBCIC when Neskonlith Chief Joe Manuel publicly thanked Stó:lō Skwah Chief Bill Mussell for giving band members a place to stay during the annual general assembly. Manuel explained: "On Sunday, some of our band members came down [to Chilliwack]. We all chipped in for gas and paid our own way down. About 30 in all came ... [and] we [didn't] have enough money to buy motels. Bill Mussell has given us a little area in his park across from his house so we could set up camp. We feel great about this."[69] Community members and sympathetic leaders like Manuel consistently raised these experiences at UBCIC gatherings, often as evidence of the heightened political dedication and sacrifice of community members and criticism of Indigenous leaders. At times, publicly raising this issue seemed strategic – a way to motivate UBCIC leaders to act in the best interests of the grassroots who relied on them, such as the case noted above where Watts drew attention to the sacrifices made by delegates from his district. For many, these economic costs demonstrated that even those lacking political and economic capital could make important contributions to the political movement. Again, the notion that proper political work required personal sacrifice was prevalent, and leaders such as Larry Seymour fought determinedly to unseat this expectation as bad political practice. Despite some similarities between the two groups, it was clear that leaders and grassroots were experiencing politics and pan-Indigenous unity differently.

Chiefs' increasing economic privilege in this period exposes underlying assumptions about Indigenous peoples' relationship to wealth, including expectations that Indigenous peoples are inherently impoverished and that any wealth accrued must therefore be suspect. Indigenous leaders have an added expectation that they should not be personally wealthy but should only promote the economic well-being of their communities.[70] Chiefs Adam Eneas and Wayne Christian explained these expectations in terms of traditional holistic leadership, which demanded that leaders see themselves first and foremost as members of their communities, not individual or self-interested workers.[71] Communities also maintained specific ideals about their leadership, and, while they did not expect leaders to remain impoverished and underprivileged, they believed that chiefs, as political representatives and members of communities with shared cultures and historical experiences, had a duty to remain connected to experiences of poverty in their communities and ensure that extra wealth was distributed.

Gender and kinship obligations added another layer to these beliefs, as male leaders were expected to ensure necessary resources were available for their families. Reuben Ware and UBCIC staff member Rosalee Tizya spoke highly of leaders such as Philip Paul and George Manuel who lived according to the standards of their communities, refusing to spend money on frivolous expenses such as fancy clothes and accommodations, preferring to use any extra money to progress the movement. Epistemological differences between those who saw political work as a paid labour and leadership as a traditional practice were at odds here, and navigating these competing systems proved challenging. Still, Indigenous leaders frequently liaised with senior government officials, and expecting chief and council to bring sleeping bags and brown-bag lunches to these important meetings would send a message that Indigenous leaders were not legitimate or serious political actors.[72] Indigenous leaders were, therefore, forced to walk in two contradictory worlds: one where they were accountable to the grassroots and not accessing too many privileges their people did not have available to them, and one where they could move easily in a heavily paternalistic and capitalist state and where it was imperative to demonstrate that leadership could interact with government officials professionally.

In 1969, Indian Association of Alberta president Harold Cardinal outlined the need for the National Indian Brotherhood to be strengthened and the need for the continued creation of strong provincial Indigenous political organizations. He noted the importance of government funding to support these burgeoning organizations, but, like many other organizations in the early 1970s, the UBCIC experienced a crisis of conscience with the turn to government money. The availability of these funds exposed layers of tension along gender- and class-based lines, again raising the question of whether pan-Indigenous unity could ever mean full equality or could thrive within state structures. With these unprecedented levels of funding, the UBCIC reluctantly promoted the federal government's neoliberal and assimilationist agenda, intensifying existing divisions within the organization. And yet it also promoted important degrees of political professionalization that, ironically, would give UBCIC members and allies the skills needed to pursue fiscal and political independence.

PART 2

A Philosophical Revolution and Competing Nationalisms

O N THE MORNING OF 21 April 1975, Stó:lō Yakweakwioose Chief Richard Malloway found himself at a crossroads.[1] Speaking to delegates of the Union of British Columbia Indian Chiefs' seventh annual general assembly, Malloway revealed his conflicted feelings about the BC Indigenous political movement, setting the tone for what would become the most contentious meeting in the history of the pan-Indigenous provincial organization. As a respected leader of the wider Stó:lō host community, and a direct descendant of the four original ancestors of the Ts'elxwéyeqw (Chilliwack),[2] Malloway, who was the current carrier of the tribal hereditary name, Th'eláchíyatel, was well-positioned to reflect on the current and future state of Indigenous political organization.[3] As representatives arriving at the Evergreen Hall in Chilliwack settled in to begin the five-day convention, Malloway spoke poignantly about his forty-year involvement with the Indian land question. Speaking with a mixture of exhaustion and optimism, he noted, "I've been in this work for over forty years and ... nothing has happened in the land question. We've gone to Ottawa and Victoria and we haven't got any answer."[4] Malloway was not alone in his frustration, and his speech captured a disillusioned movement looking for change. A mere six years after BC Indigenous peoples formed the UBCIC, constituents were growing impatient with halting attempts to have Indigenous rights and title formally recognized by provincial and federal governments. Malloway vocalized and legitimized this dissatisfaction, providing fuel for subsequent discussions about the political vision needed to realize the UBCIC's land claim agenda.

The 1975 UBCIC general assembly and the summer of 1975 were pivotal moments for the UBCIC and the Indigenous political movement in British Columbia. By the time the assembly ended in April 1975, the organization had undergone a massive transformation, with several leaders stepping forward to re-envision the UBCIC as financially and politically independent from the Canadian state. Since its inception in 1969, the UBCIC sought to resolve the land question through policy papers and political mediation, but the Department of Indian Affairs (DIA) soon overwhelmed the organization with bureaucratic service delivery. Frustrated with department interference and paternalism, as well as inadequate program funding that left Indigenous communities perpetually underserviced, the UBCIC and its member communities decided to "become radical" and declare political and fiscal independence from government agencies. They resolved to reject all forms of federal and provincial funding and use coordinated occupations, blockades, and strategic law-breaking for one month, beginning 1 May 1975, to achieve their stated aims. This two-pronged strategy – rejecting funding and what would become known as "militant May" – fundamentally shifted the trajectory of the UBCIC. This section details these simultaneous changes, focusing on the rejection of funding, "militant May," and Indigenous sovereignty.

4
REFUSAL
"Empty words and empty promises"

BUILDING ON INCREASING frustrations over slow progress on the land claim in British Columbia, Ts'ishaa7ath Chief George Watts complained, "We have heard a lot of empty words over the last five years as far as Land Claims is concerned. We have heard a lot of empty promises. We have heard a lot of empty resolutions that mean nothing. We wonder when we are really going to get down to the business of committing ourselves to this thing?"[1] Viewing the federal government (particularly government funding and accompanying oversight) as a significant barrier to the goals of the Union of British Columbia Indian Chiefs, the attendees of the 1975 UBCIC annual assembly proposed restructuring the UBCIC as a grassroots organization and rejecting federal and provincial funding and programming as an expression of sovereignty. This proposal included refusing operational funding for bands and organizations like the UBCIC, as well as funds for education, housing, and social welfare (that were normally transferred to the bands to administer). This grand political gesture was not only unachievable but had gendered and class-based consequences that deepened existing conflict within the UBCIC. Yet it also motivated collective political responses that would ultimately reshape the movement.

BETWEEN APRIL AND JULY 1975, the UBCIC attempted to transition from a state-recognized Indigenous bureaucracy to an independent people's movement by rejecting all forms of government funding and programs. Ultimately, the UBCIC's decision ignored the political goals and lived realities of its constituents, who publicly critiqued the funding decision and worked to dismantle UBCIC authority to implement it. Indigenous women's organizations led the resistance, arguing that refusing government funding did little to advance the movement and ultimately harmed and silenced community women and children. Through their distinctly gendered refusals, use of politicized motherhood, and strategic alliances with government departments and like-minded communities, Indigenous women's organizations used their own political strategies to resist UBCIC directives and to advocate for a more inclusive vision of pan-Indigenous unity.

The UBCIC's decision to reject funding was a response to growing concerns about political inaction, bureaucracy, elitism, and government dependence that had been building within the organization since 1969. In many ways, this crisis of conscience mirrored key developments in the Red Power movement in the United States, which, for instance, saw the direct action–oriented National Indian Youth Council break away from the more bureaucratically minded National Congress of American Indians in the early 1960s.[2] Across the United States and Canada, Indigenous political actors were increasingly frustrated with the slow pace of change wrought by conservative and bureaucratic political forms, and they called for more direct challenges to the settler status quo. Within the UBCIC, Chief Richard Malloway's introductory speech at the April 1975 meetings, quoted above, primed delegates for change – as did the first two days of the conference, where tensions ran high during discussions about UBCIC progress. But the principal catalyst for the decision to reject funding was a telex from National Indian Brotherhood (NIB) leader George Manuel. As the national coordinating organization, the NIB looked to unite Indigenous peoples in Canada on issues of mutual concern, and, in 1975, it was concerned with ill-conceived changes to policies and programming. The telex, which was read aloud to delegates, called for the UBCIC, as a member of and in solidarity with the NIB, to reject unfair Indian Affairs programs, particularly the controversial Grants to Bands program (a federal initiative operated by Indian Affairs that allocated funding to bands based on federally determined per capita grant formulas).[3] In 1974, when the program introduced a new formula that effectively cut band funding in half, communities denounced this decline in resources and the unpredictable nature of the program. Chiefs and councillors reasoned that it was impossible to provide funds and services to their membership when their budgets could fluctuate so drastically and with little warning.[4] Further, this and other program decisions were made unilaterally by the Department of Indian Affairs, and Manuel, a well-respected leader and long-standing member of the modern Indian movement, argued that Indigenous peoples needed to reject this level of outside control. This perspective followed familiar trajectories of intensifying political strategies in response to government inaction. The bureaucratic status quo was not working.

The telex brought a broader national discussion about government oversight and intervention to UBCIC concerns and provided a clear political path. In the intense emotional atmosphere of the conference, however, delegates misinterpreted Manuel's suggestion, believing that he was asking the UBCIC to unequivocally reject all funding for bands and organizations. Manuel had never intended to suggest total financial independence; rather, he wanted Indigenous peoples to reject specific programs such as the Grants to Bands in order to register their discontent.[5] But his message perfectly captured the UBCIC assembly's frustration with the federal government and articulated a practical solution to their challenges. With an organization poised for change and an assembly that activists described as having "taken on a life of its own," delegates read Manuel's telex according to their own political desires and local needs, and proposed a motion to refuse all government funding.[6] In this proposal, the BC Indian movement maintained a strong connection to its national context, but was shaped locally.

The original motion, introduced by Tl'azt'en (Stuart-Trembleur) Chief Edward John of the Lakes District, specifically criticized the DIA's programs for band administration, health, education, and housing, arguing that they provided inadequate per capita–based funds while expecting bands and organizations such as the UBCIC to effectively administer these services.[7] In his motion, John called for delegates to reject their dependency on the department by refusing government money.[8] John reasoned that financial freedom would enable the UBCIC to pursue its own mandates and pressure the department to "negotiate on [an] equal basis with respect to our provincial and national leaders."[9] Despite the massive implications of this proposal, which would undermine the sources of UBCIC and community financial stability, the motion attracted relatively little debate among conference delegates.

Of course, political refusals are not simply all or nothing – they can exist on a spectrum and can overlap and compete. For some, the UBCIC original motion did not go far enough in registering disdain for government policies, and, shortly after the motion was presented, Diitiid7aa7tx (Ditidaht) Chief

Charlie Thompson recommended an amendment that would reject all forms of provincial and federal government funding and programs, not simply UBCIC funding and limited band money.[10] This revision meant that Indigenous communities would refuse funding for band administration, housing, education, health and welfare, and cultural development, the Department of the Secretary of State's core and communications funding, as well as services from all federal and provincial sources (see Table 1).[11] Defunding would instantaneously financially incapacitate the UBCIC and Indigenous communities, but the move would also send a strong message to government about the resiliency, pride, and political independence of Indigenous peoples.[12] Chief Thompson's motion represented a robust political ideal that was well intended, but it reflected problematic top-down decision making and was politically short-sighted in anticipating the economic challenges communities would face without stable funding.

The broader rejection of government funding proposed by Chief Thompson was a strong political statement grounded in a sophisticated understanding of how neoliberalism was compromising the land claim and Indigenous rights. It was also a spontaneous and emotionally charged response that was impulsive and ill-conceived. Decisions were made relatively quickly with no opportunity for consultation with community members, outside of those present at the general assembly. This fact was not lost on Seton Lake's Victor Adrian, who warned delegates to keep a level head: "We are all deeply emotional right now and we say these are our leaders, we stand behind them. Well, let's not be emotional."[13] Likening this moment to rash moments of intimacy where someone goes to bed with a person, regrets it the next day, and then kicks that person out of the house, Adrian called on delegates to pause and consider whether they truly wanted to support Thompson's motion and would continue to support their leaders in the light of day. This reference to emotion is deeply gendered and perpetuates a dominant trope that men (particularly political men) should not act out of emotion. Politics, then, is rational, not emotional.[14] Calling on fellow delegates to practise rational rather than emotional politics reminds us that both gender and status played a significant role in the debate.

Thompson's amendment prompted increased discussion, but this was still limited to those present at the assembly. Delegates discussed the amendment with attendees from their respective districts, and non-voting members were able to weigh in on the issue and influence their district's vote. Most of these district breakout sessions were mired in confusion and panic, which

Table 1 Proposed funding refused by original and amended motions at UBCIC meeting, April 1975

Funding agency	Type of funds	
	Original motion	Amended motion
Department of Indian Affairs	Band administration and core funds	Band administration and core funds
	District administration and core funds	District administration and core funds
	Band and district housing projects funds	Band and district housing projects funds
	Band and district education projects funds	Band and district education projects funds
	Band and district social assistance	Band and district social assistance
	Cultural project funds	Cultural project funds
	Economic development funds	Economic development funds (e.g., Indian Fisherman's Assistance Program)
Secretary of State	Organization core funding	Organization core funding
	Organization communication funding (specifically UBCIC core and communications resources)	Organization communication funding (specifically UBCIC core and communications resources)
National Health and Welfare		Health care
Province of British Columbia		First Citizens Fund*
		Human Resources
		Economic Development
		Department of Agriculture
		Department of Education
Central Mortgage and Housing Corporation		Mortgage insurance subsidies
Canada Manpower		Job placement programs

* The First Citizens Fund was created by the BC government in 1969 to support the cultural, educational, and economic development of Indigenous peoples. Ministry of Aboriginal Relations and Reconciliation, http://www.gov.bc.ca; "First Citizens Fund," *Unity: Bulletin of the Union of British Columbia Indian Chiefs* 1, no. 1 (1970): 13–14.

Source: Data adapted from Library and Archives Canada, RG 10, vol. 1994-95/412, box 1, file 987/24-2-12, Union of BC Indian Chiefs, 1972–1981, news release: Bulletin #3, 5 May 1975; UBCIC Resource Centre, Union of British Columbia Indian Chiefs, 1972–1981 and minutes of the Union of BC Indian Chiefs General Assembly Held at Evergreen Hall, Chilliwack, BC, 24 April 1975.

greatly influenced the outcome of the final vote. In the Fraser West District session, for example, interactions between District Chief Earl Commodore (Stó:lō Soowahlie), xʷməθkʷəy̓əm (Musqueam) Chief Delbert Guerin, and Stó:lō Soowahlie councillor Marge Kelly exposed marked differences in how each interpreted the amendment. Guerin and Kelly were concerned primarily that most UBCIC delegates did not understand the full implications of the defunding decision, and Kelly recalled that this confusion was apparent not only in the meeting but also in the communities afterwards.[15] She explained: "That was a hectic meeting. Everybody panicked when they were talking about funding. They were going to take it away. We couldn't understand, eh? Our Chief [Commodore] was trying to [say] they'll take our money out of our bank. But I don't know – I told him, 'You can't take it out now, we can't do that.'"[16]

Guerin also challenged Commodore's interpretation of the funding decision. At the district session, Commodore asked Guerin to explain why he opposed the motion. Surprised that so many delegates were willing to support a proposal with such grave consequences, Guerin disputed Commodore's understanding of the proposition, hoping to change his mind. Guerin narrated the resulting interchange to me. "'Earl,' Guerin said, 'Let me ask you this question. You've got quite a few sisters, right? Your mom and dad are still alive, right?' He said, 'Yeah.' I said, 'Well, do you want your mom and dad to reject their pension cheques? And your sisters and brothers and your families to reject their family allowance for their children?' 'Oh,' Commodore said," realizing the extent of the motion.[17] According to Guerin, Commodore focused on the strong message the motion would send to government but failed to grasp the magnitude of the proposal. Guerin, on the other hand, focused on the practical impact this motion would have on families. Yet Guerin also misunderstood the proposal, falsely believing that community members would lose access to old age pensions, family allowances, veterans' and disability pensions, and unemployment insurance, all payments not included in the proposed funding rejections.[18] This type of confusion was widespread and, after the motion was passed, led to uneven implementation across the province, where some communities – often at the discretion of chief and council – refused payments not included in the decision.

These district sessions created space for delegates and grassroots members to try to make sense of the proposed amendment and direct their district chief's vote, but there was no formal mechanism for grassroots delegates to vote on the funding motion, and many community members were not present to take part in the district discussions. The decision – which would have a direct, immediate, and significant impact on community members' lives – resulted, therefore, from the leadership's, rather than the communities', democratic decision making. Community members had consistently desired to be heard within the formal channels of the organization, but they were not, and this intensified pre-existing criticisms about the inadequacy of representative democracy and about band and UBCIC structures. And yet several leaders were aware of grassroots opinions and brought these voices onto the assembly floor. Doing so added another layer to the complex gradations of political authority and position and lessened community silences. American Indian Movement member and former St'uxwtews (Bonaparte) Chief Ken Basil advocated for community members by denouncing the funding decision as further separating ideological politics from community concerns and lived realities on reserve.[19] Chief Dennis Alphonse agreed, suggesting the leaders in favour of the motion were "playing politics with peoples' lives."[20]

Despite the controversy and misunderstanding surrounding the motion, it passed. With government funding rejected, the UBCIC chose to activate a vision of politics premised on state refusals and financial and political independence. The newly elected UBCIC executive, Tsartlip Chief Philip Paul, Ts'ishaa7ath (Tseshaht) Chief George Watts, and Kwakwaka'wakw Chief Bill Wilson, supported the funding decision but found the exclusion of grassroots opinions unacceptable and vowed to reconcile this neglect amid fiscal independence. It was a well-intentioned and noble ideal, but ultimately could not be realized.

The Post-Chilliwack UBCIC and Community Resistance

The impact of the "Chilliwack decision," as it came to be known, was immediate. The post-Chilliwack UBCIC more closely resembled its 1969 incarnation – before government funding produced a staff of approximately 100 people working out of several offices. In the aftermath of Chilliwack, these administrative positions disappeared almost instantaneously, with the Vancouver UBCIC office and Victoria Land Claims Research Centre closing shortly after the conference. At the UBCIC offices, a skeletal staff remained after what *Vancouver Sun* reporter Ron Rose described as "the happiest mass layoff in BC Indian history."[21] Emphasizing the political capital behind the decision to end government funding, Rose and some members of the UBCIC viewed the layoffs as evidence of Indigenous political independence, and therefore cause for celebration. The UBCIC fired approximately eighty staff members as it packed up its offices and relocated to a smaller, more cost-effective location, but volunteers, including many fired employees, joined the few remaining paid staff to continue operations. Focus immediately shifted away from administrative arrangements for service provision (which required liaisons with the Departments of Health and Welfare and Indian Affairs in order to develop and execute programming) and towards community-based organization focused solely on a land claim. This was both a pragmatic response in the absence of funding – since the UBCIC was no longer accepting government money for these basic services – but it also reflected an ideological desire to embrace a different form of political organization.

Not everyone shared the optimism reported by Rose. UBCIC Land Claims staff member Reuben Ware lamented the changes to the organization and the lost opportunities that accompanied them: "[The UBCIC] just, boom, went straight down. It was such an abrupt ending."[22] These closures, although necessary without a budget, eliminated staff the UBCIC had hired to bridge the gap between the grassroots and members, as well as programs and infrastructure the union had designed to pursue the land claim and Indigenous rights. In effect, the funding decision, in its attempt to promote independence and grassroots activism, erased the progress that had been made in these arenas, sacrificing the most useful elements of the organization. Because of this, as far as Ware was concerned, the UBCIC was "dead after Chilliwack."[23] Of course, Ware was speaking figuratively here: the UBCIC, though very different after Chilliwack, did not cease to exist as a political entity, but in Ware's mind, it had lost the essence of its success. Ware's perspective is not surprising: his role as a fieldworker and one of the formative members of the Land Claims Centre in Victoria enabled him to see the benefits of the organization's hard work.

The Chilliwack decision also had a distinct ripple effect in the communities it supported. Stó:lō Chief Clarence Pennier shared Ware's sentiment: for Stó:lō, the rejection of funding directly compromised their cultural revival work, as they lost critical funding needed to develop the Coqualeetza Cultural Centre.[24] Stó:lō communities were embroiled in a legal battle with the Department of Public Works to have the important cultural heritage site of Coqualeetza returned to them. The funding they received was essential to the struggle. In their discussions about Chilliwack, both Pennier and Ware emphasized a phenomenon that made the funding decision particularly hard to accept: both revealed that the financial and political sacrifices made after Chilliwack were not spread evenly across the organization or the province, or among individuals; rather, communities and local groups were hardest hit, and the "community development [and] community resourcing–type people," who were directly benefiting the grassroots, lost their jobs and their programs. All the while, the UBCIC and its executive levels of leadership were in a position to weather the storm and remained relatively unscathed during the transition.

Overall, community responses to the funding decision varied. Those that fully supported the mandate recognized UBCIC authority and implemented local strategies to adapt their lived realities to the funding rejection. Some communities, including the Upper Nicola, Scw'exmx (Shackan), and Neskonlith, for instance, turned to traditional economic practices to make up for lost band funding. Upper Nicola leader George Saddleman explained that, because the decision happened during the spring, communities were well placed to care for their members by hunting, gathering, and growing food during the summer months. Implementing the relationships and practices of the "q'əsapi? times" or "long ago times," communities shared food and even wages.[25] Scw'exmx Chief Percy Joe's community used similar strategies to survive five months without funding in 1975. He explained that families on social assistance turned to hunting and fishing to make up some of the shortfall. While acknowledging the hardship his membership experienced, Joe insisted, "We were quite proud that we were independent and people were able to survive those times when there was no money."[26]

Neskonlith band members likewise intensified their reliance on traditional economies, but also adapted their politics to include direct action in the form of the Harper Lake Road blockade to support the rejection of funding and promote community survival.[27] On 29 May 1975, band members, wanting to protect important fish stocks from non-Indigenous fishers, blocked non-Indigenous access to Harper Lake, located on the Trans-Canada highway just south of Chase. Highlighting the loss of much-needed provincial welfare payments, a Neskonlith band spokesman defended the blockade "as a matter of survival." In a written statement to the UBCIC, the spokesman argued that, "as the Indian people in BC have elected to reject all welfare programs, we must depend upon our own resources, and the resources of the land. We must hunt and we must fish; we must build our homes out of these resources. We therefore feel it mandatory to protect our traditional fishing and hunting grounds. Harper Lake is one of our traditional grounds."[28] The decision gave added boon to safeguarding Indigenous rights and title, and this blockade was both an expression of unity and support for land claims and Indigenous economic independence and a practical method of safeguarding community welfare. It was also situated within a broader move towards grassroots radicalism across North America. The Puget Sound fish-ins, the occupations at Alcatraz and Wounded Knee, as well as local practices of disregarding fish and game laws were likely on the minds of those involved in the blockade and were in line with the activism occurring across the province, particularly during the month of May.

Other communities took an alternative approach to the funding decision, choosing to adopt only those aspects of the UBCIC mandate that made practical and ideological sense for them. On 26 May 1975, the Owikeno Council of Chiefs sent a telex to Minister of Indian Affairs Judd Buchanan outlining its overall support for the UBCIC decision, with several provisos.[29] The council explained: "We the Owikeno people have voted 98 percent in favour of the Union of BC Indian Chiefs in rejecting the program and funds of the DIA, *except in the area[s] of health, welfare, education, and public services.*"[30] Implementing its own brand of politics, which included a community vote and rejecting elements of the UBCIC's proposal that did not suit its communities, the Owikeno council tailored UBCIC politics to support both local and pan-Indigenous unity. On the one hand, it called for the transfer of band funds held in Ottawa to the council of chiefs for independent administration, and, on the other, it demanded negotiations and liaison with government departments to improve continued services in health, welfare, education, and public services. The Owikeno council, then, supported greater political and economic autonomy – the crux of the UBCIC position – but preferred to amend the existing system rather than dismantle it altogether. The Caribou Tribal Council in the Williams Lake District also requested to have some of its member bands' capital and revenue funds transferred for band administration and implemented its own interpretation of the UBCIC's mandate in its communities.[31] The council's insistence on the need to "remove ourselves from the heavy hand of the Great White Father syndrome" and to follow the "principle of Indian helping Indian, Band helping Band" spoke to its continued dedication to pan-Indigenous unity and its own sovereignty.[32] Through this position, the council demonstrated its dedication to both local autonomy and provincial unity.

Highlighting its position to allow each band to opt into this decision via a band council resolution (BCR), the council forwarded resolutions from half of its bands to the DIA.[33] These innovative strategies demonstrated the flexibility of pan-Indigenous unity and the importance of local autonomy, but not every community sought full grassroots approval. This lack of consent, along with government discomfort with the decision, prompted intervention on the part of Ottawa.

In May 1975, Buchanan – citing concern over individual hardship on reserves and a lack of democratic decision-making – called on his regional director, Larry Wight, to ensure that band membership fully agreed with the funding rejection.[34] Buchanan had received multiple letters from band members upset about the funding decision and asking Buchanan to intervene.[35] He obliged by requesting that band and tribal councils forward their BCRs outlining the results of their referendums, so that he could understand the wishes of each community and adapt policy accordingly. Buchanan's request exposes the complexities and contradictions inherent in Indian Affairs whereby the minister was acting on requests to intervene while drawing on and preserving problematic department paternalism that the UBCIC was trying to reject. Such complexities meant that the situation across British Columbia was not easily divided into "allies" and "enemies."

Some communities in the Caribou District used department intervention and services strategically to register their political refusal of UBCIC mandates and even of their own Caribou Tribal Council. In a letter to Buchanan, Alexandria band councillor Mary Stamp explained the internal band and tribal council politics that were dividing the people on the question of funding rejection and the devolution of department services to the bands. Stamp noted that the Caribou Tribal Council was not fully representing the wishes of the member communities and explained that it was unsupportive of her community's decision to continue accepting government funding.[36] In her appeal to Buchanan, she deliberately integrated government involvement into the political practices of her community, directly challenging the competing politics of her tribal council and the UBCIC. The Alexandria Band refused the UBCIC's funding decision, choosing instead to use district- and community-based unity and a degree of government recognition to propel pan-Indigenous unity and Indigenous sovereignty according to its own agenda. Here, there is evidence of several forms of politics and articulations of unity. At the tribal council level, the communities supported the general decision of the UBCIC to reject government programs, but they continued to accept band funding in order to take control of their own programming. At the band level, communities decided for themselves whether they should accept band funding or not.

These qualified community-level refusals were not limited to the Caribou Tribal Council. Many districts, including the West Coast, Lakes, and Kootenay-Okanagan, upheld the principle of band autonomy, and several communities throughout the spring and summer of 1975 returned to government funding.[37] For instance, in June and July the Clayoquot, Ucluelet, Hesquiat, and Uchucklesaht Bands sent telexes to the Department of Indian Affairs stating that they were "not in agreement on the rejection of government funds by UBCIC," and "that they will be accepting all government funding and continuity of programmes."[38] In the case of the Hesquiat, the telex came from band council members, who noted that their chief had not consulted his people before voting "on such an important decision," and therefore that they were challenging his choice. In addition, less than one month after the Ucluelet Band returned to government funding, they passed a BCR withdrawing from the West Coast District Council. The community rejected district-level tribal unity and UBCIC pan-Indigenous unity, but united with other like-minded communities engaged in similar resistances. In contrast, the Osoyoos Band specifically used the UBCIC's own mandate of non-community intervention to urge the Department of Indian Affairs to investigate the true level of support for the rejection of funding and for the UBCIC itself.[39] Chief Stelkia argued that the UBCIC was not only ignoring its own directive of non-intervention in community affairs, but that it did not have community support to legitimize its actions. Taken together, these assorted responses illustrate how community refusals varied according to community political frameworks, ideologies, and resources.

Gendered Refusals

Generally, political refusals were also gendered, and women's organizations such as the British Columbia Homemakers' Association (BCIHA) were especially vocal in their opposition to the UBCIC's funding decision – although they were forced to work within the limited political spaces available to them. Occupying informal political channels in auxiliary organizations, the BCIHA used its political frameworks, which included politicized motherhood, community caretaking, and concern with the political outcomes regarding land claims and Indigenous rights, to demand more inclusive interpretations of unity than the UBCIC proposed. As a reserve-based women's organization representing status and non-status First Nation women, the BCIHA had been lobbying for improved housing, education, health, and child welfare since its inception in 1968.[40] The organization had also worked in conjunction with the UBCIC to pressure government for changes to policy, but the funding decision caused a rift between the two groups. The BCIHA disagreed with both the practical implications of funding refusal and its theoretical underpinnings, which, it argued, privileged grand political gestures over preserving community well-being.

Characterizing the UBCIC's decision as a political ploy, the BCIHA lamented that it was "weary mothers, little children and the disabled [who were] being caught in the cross fire between the politics of the department of Indian Affairs, the provincial government, and their own insensitive leaders."[41] Ts'ishaa7ath (Tseshaht) member and foster mother Agnes Dick accused leaders of "putting the children on the front lines of [the] battle to force a settlement," by rejecting funds that, among other things, "were necessary for the thirty-eight foster children on her reserve including seven in her own home."[42] At a meeting of the Ts'ishaa7ath Homemaker Foster Parents group, attendees, including Dick, criticized their West Coast District Council, local leadership, and the UBCIC for not exempting funding for foster children from their political mandate.[43] Like many other BCIHA members, Dick politically supported the land claim issue but, while UBCIC chiefs viewed the funding decision as a bold expression of sovereignty and an effective political move to pressure the land claim, Indigenous women felt the impact of these lost resources at home and refused to quietly acquiesce. Mobilizing women's accepted roles as mothers and community caretakers, BCIHA members argued that they had a duty to protect Indigenous families against poverty, and more importantly, that they deserved the political voice to do this.

The UBCIC's limited democratic structure had not made it easy for Indigenous women to participate in provincial politics. At the first UBCIC meeting in 1969, Chief Clarence Jules had emphasized political debate as a fundamental democratic right, but women's exclusion from band membership and their relegation to auxiliary "social" roles exposed an alternate reality. BCIHA members had a broader interpretation of "politics" and "democracy," and communicated these using the tools and forums available to them. This was nowhere more apparent than with respect to the 1975 funding decision. Reporting on the 1975 BCIHA conference, Rose Charlie used strong language with respect to the UBCIC decision: "We firmly believe that this ultimatum issued by these irresponsible leaders is an encroachment of those in power on the grassroots level of native people to be at liberty to choose whether or not they wish to refuse government funding. We firmly believe their actions to be an abridgement of the freedom of the individual to have a voice in the decisions that directly affect their children's lives."[44] Unlike UBCIC leaders who believed that effective politics required risk taking, sacrifice, and strong political gestures (that they alone were capable of making), the BCIHA suggested activists needed to consider community opinions and conditions above all else.[45] Beyond this consideration, it was clear that not everyone was in a position (economic or otherwise) to take such a political stand. Charlie continued, "We feel that these women [protesting the UBCIC decision] were only speaking out for something they feel is right. Their deep concern as mothers and women was very evident at [the BCIHA] conference. Every person in this country has a right to speak their mind ... And there is no reason in the world that they should be pushed into a corner, verbal or otherwise."[46] As an established and respected woman on the provincial political scene, Charlie was one of few who could have made such strong statements in defiance of the UBCIC. Recognizing the gendered nature of politics and democracy and women's resulting social and political oppression, Charlie and others incorporated Indigenous feminist resistance into their political agenda of social welfare and family cohesion.

The BCIHA was the most organized and consistent voice of opposition against the funding decision and successfully encouraged dozens of bands to ignore the UBCIC directive and restore funding to their communities. By rejecting funds and asking bands and other organizations to do the same, many believed that the UBCIC was ignoring its mandate to preserve the political autonomy of existing bodies. Of course, the UBCIC did not compel others to reject funding, but some communities felt pressured to do so.[47] At least one Homemakers' Association chapter, Stoney Creek, declared its support of land claim issues while concurrently accepting government funding.[48] Stoney Creek president Sophie Thomas made it clear that the BCIHA's lack of support for the UBCIC decision did not mean that the women disagreed with the wider aims of the political movement. In fact, the women still believed in the value of pan-Indigenous unity to achieve land claims and Indigenous rights, but, unlike the UBCIC, they were not willing to pursue these at all cost.

Several bands agreed with the BCIHA's political position and, in offering their support, further affirmed the organization's growing political authority. These communities not only publicly opposed the UBCIC mandate but also officially aligned themselves with the BCIHA. Several West Coast District communities attended the BCIHA's annual conference in June 1975 (where the organization discussed the UBCIC's funding decision) and made a statement that they officially "support[ed] [the] Indian Homemakers' Association of BC on their stand in not rejecting government funds."[49] Sympathetic organizations such as the Westcoast Fishermen also demonstrated support of the BCIHA and its decisions regarding funding by sending correspondence to DIA outlining their position on the question.[50]

More than simply disagreeing with the UBCIC's strategy and suggesting it was counterproductive, the BCIHA took a stand against the union by continuing its operations as before and stepping up to provide services that the UBCIC could not.[51] To accomplish this, the BCIHA needed a stable financial base and therefore continued to accept government funding. Beyond the practical consideration of being able to continue its political work, the BCIHA overtly noted the political significance in its decision, not only as a strong refusal against predominant UBCIC politics but also as a way to expose UBCIC hypocrisy. But providing services was challenging, particularly because the BCIHA was working with a level of funding far below what the UBCIC had received. In part, this discrepancy was because the UBCIC had a broader representative base, but it also spoke to the masculinist nature of politics, which saw women's organizations as apolitical. Despite the BCIHA's continued involvement in lobbying for community rights, government agencies continued to view the organization as tied wholly to women's social issues. Combatting this view in a letter to Indian Affairs in which she enclosed the BCIHA's 1976–77 budget, Charlie insisted that "our work is not confined to domestic problems." She argued that, in addition to "striving to solve the critical and urgent problems of Native Indian women, families, and communities in the areas of health, education, welfare, child care, nutrition, housing, and also employment and training," the BCIHA did advocacy work for Indigenous inmates, helped community members seek legal aid, and advised people on their rights of citizenship. Charlie maintained that Indian Affairs should provide adequate resources for this work, but that the BCIHA "have had very little financial assistance from Indian Affairs."[52]

The BCIHA budget Charlie submitted reflected the association's unequal political positioning when compared to the UBCIC, and subsequent margin notes, which reduced the original proposal from $53,760 to $35,160, re-inforced these differences. Before the revisions, the BCIHA president's monthly salary of $1,200 per month was comparable to that of the members of the UBCIC executive committee, at $1,500 per month, but the BCIHA figure was amended on the document to a stipend of $4,000 per year. A Department of Indian Affairs official likely made these revisions, as the budget document was in the department's archival records, and the hand-writing on it matched handwriting on other department documents in the file. These revisions appear to have had an impact, as a similar budget sent to the same office one month later proposed a $1,000 per month salary for the BCIHA president along with $500 per month for the first and second vice-presidents.[53] That these proposed salaries were significantly lower than those in the original budget indicated both the low levels of financial and moral support the BCIHA received from Indian Affairs as well as the women's adaptability in the face of such realities. While the UBCIC had access to political tools and benefits denied to the BCIHA, the women continued to use any available resources to aid their communities.

One of the BCIHA's primary goals during the funding debacle was to secure necessary resources for families. Because bands administered welfare and other payments, communities that had refused funding in solidarity with the UBCIC eliminated the sole access point of state support for com-munity members. While the Williams Lake, Lakes, and West Coast District examples proved that multiple political frameworks and refusals enabled districts and communities to implement their own interpretations of the funding decision, not every community member agreed with local leader-ship decisions, and gender was often a strong predictor of one's position. In the South Island District, for example, Margaret Point – a young mother of two – confronted members of her Nanaimo Band when she attempted to access welfare payments at the Nanaimo Department of Indian Affairs district office. Her community had rejected government funds in solidarity with the UBCIC, and, as in many other communities in May 1975, members were occupying the office to register their protest. When demonstrators refused to allow Point into the building, she turned in vain to the province and then to the city for aid, hoping they would bypass her community's authority and administer funds to her directly.[54] As a grassroots woman with little formal political influence, Point was not able to override her band's decision or its imposed economic barrier. Yet she knew to turn to the BCIHA and apply the experience they provided. Situations such as Point's fuelled the BCIHA's growing opposition to male-dominated politics. Point's experience was not uncommon, and individuals faced with financial uncertainty increasingly turned to the BCIHA for help. Using its limited resources, the BCIHA held conferences, published newspaper articles, and petitioned the Department of Indian Affairs and Secretary of State to re-instate funding. The organization continued to pursue its well-established social welfare agenda – drawing political legitimacy from women's accepted roles as community mothers – but explicitly, and unapologetically, crafted pan-Indigenous unity in terms of gender equality and family protection.

The BCIHA overtly linked community hardship to shortcomings in male leadership and positioned its membership as strong leaders, willing and able to direct the Indigenous movement in new ways. Implementing the same strategy as dissenting communities, the BCIHA incorporated an alliance with Indian Affairs into its political strategies, writing a series of telexes, letters, and reports to department officials Judd Buchanan and Larry Wight, and to Prime Minister Pierre Trudeau between May and July 1975. Labelling the UBCIC's decision to reject funding "irresponsible," and circumventing the organization's proclaimed provincial authority, the BCIHA insisted it was the federal and provincial governments' responsibility to ensure Indigenous communities received essential funds and services. Many Indigenous communities were facing health crises; in June 1975, Agnes Dick wrote to Buchanan to "urgently request funding for the less fortunate foster children on our reservation who have been denied proper diets as a result of the recent land claim issue." Under the banner of the UBCIC mandate – which denied funding to foster parents – Ts'ishaa7ath Chief Adam Sewish and band manager George Watts refused to sign food vouchers for the children.[55]

Outside the foster system, similar food insecurities prompted Charlie to report that "we are receiving calls from concerned families, where children are hungry and are stealing food in order to feed themselves."[56] Charlie demanded an immediate investigation by the department to address this specific issue, but the BCIHA also proposed broader structural changes to Indian policy that would minimize DIA involvement and allocate greater administrative powers to the BCIHA. In addition to demanding continued federal and provincial funding for Indian education and the transfer of financial responsibility for Indigenous foster children from Indian Affairs to the Department of Human Resources, the BCIHA also requested that departments such as Health and Welfare, Housing, Education, Fisheries, Water, Environment, and Community Development negotiate directly with the BCIHA (not Indian Affairs or the UBCIC) to ensure services remained in place for Indigenous communities.[57] This demand, which would fundamentally alter established political roles and relationships, caught Indian Affairs' attention.

In late June 1975, Charlie sent a concise and strongly worded telex to Buchanan demanding immediate financial assistance for needy families on Vancouver Island. She demanded government representatives be on hand later that same day to allocate resources, and the language left little room for negotiation.[58] Buchanan responded immediately by calling on Regional Director Larry Wight "to do everything possible to see that individuals in need are given assistance." After months of tense interactions with the UBCIC, Buchanan increasingly valued a strategic alliance with the BCIHA and BCNWS that would allow the department to reassert the status quo. Buchanan also replied to the BCIHA's suggestions regarding foster care, education, and assistance, and not only agreed with the women's assessment of the socio-political barriers for Indigenous families but called on the BCIHA to pressure chiefs and councillors to put the BCIHA objectives into action.[59]

Ironically, after generations of politically dislocating and dispossessing Indigenous women in favour of Indigenous men, the Department of Indian Affairs expected women to redirect the UBCIC. Despite the department's proclaimed change of heart (which was not accompanied by policy change) and women's long-standing resistance to their de-politicization, Indigenous women continued to face structural challenges to political autonomy. For example, women's membership status continued to ensure the precariousness of their political position, as did patriarchal attitudes about women's limited political capabilities. Yet, through its interactions with government and the UBCIC, the BCIHA insisted on expanding conceptions of Indigenous politics to include its activities and concerns, and the women used strategic political refusals and alliances to accomplish this.

The BCIHA's partnerships sent a clear message to the UBCIC rejecting politics as usual. While UBCIC members often envisioned the BCIHA as a direct extension of their organization – frequently referring to the

Homemakers as "our women" – Indigenous women did not always view this relationship in a positive light. The UBCIC phrase could denote unity, but it was also indicative of the political (not to mention social and economic) domination Indigenous women experienced at the hands of Indigenous men; the phrase "our women" was just as easily grounded in patriarchy and unequal power dynamics as in familial affection and political unity. BCIHA activities developed with these tensions in mind, but as association members spoke out against the UBCIC and male leadership, they were criticized and, at times, even threatened with violence.[60] Dick reported being bullied by younger political men in her community who – in response to her criticism of UBCIC politics – accused her of compromising the entire BC Indigenous political movement because she disagreed with the UBCIC. Some equated the union with "the movement" when, in reality, the Indigenous rights movement in BC had many different expressions. In response to these threats, the West Coast District Homemakers' Foster Parents group encouraged Dick and the other women to "speak out their feelings." Noting the generational dynamic between the women speaking out and the men opposing them as well as the need to use traditional teachings in the political efforts, the group insisted that older women like Dick should "not [let] the young bully them, but demand the respect due to an elder."[61] The group did not mention the gender dynamic apparent in the exchanges, but the underlying assumption was that women should stay out of UBCIC political matters.

Chemainus BCIHA member Irene Harris was also threatened with violence when she used band funds – in defiance of her band's funding position – to attend a BCIHA conference. These widespread threats prompted BCIHA president Rose Charlie to request police presence at the organization's annual conference in June 1975.[62] There the women spoke of being afraid to return home to their communities, concerned that critics would physically harm them.[63] Of course, male leaders had also been criticized for their political decisions, but these oppositions were not rooted in a deep history of gendered violence or the repression of political identities.[64] Such intimidation overtly challenged women's political identities and their perceived gendered transgression from community caretakers to an internal pressure group willing to criticize both Indigenous men and the settler state. Fears surrounding gendered violence add another layer to our understanding of women's reluctance to identify as political actors, justifying women's tendency to frame their work in the context of motherhood and community protection.

Operating from disadvantaged political positions, the BCIHA gained political capital through new alliances and its changing political platform, which no longer identified the UBCIC as allies in community service but instead relied on women's own confidence and capabilities. In this sense, the BCIHA not only refused the UBCIC decision and its political priorities, but also expressed an interest in taking over the UBCIC's former role as a service provider. While this was a strong political act of resistance and vote of non-confidence in the UBCIC, the BCIHA also perhaps inadvertently preserved existing gendered divisions within BC Indigenous politics, where macro-political concerns such as sovereignty and land claims were men's political domains and community health issues, including education and social services, were women's concerns. It is noteworthy that the BCIHA and BCNWS did not criticize the UBCIC's capabilities with respect to its original mandate to address the land claim or Indigenous rights but focused instead on its inadequacies in the arena of protecting communities. Indigenous women, the Homemakers' Association argued, could do a better job at the latter. Speaking to the "separate problem of [the] land claim," a resolution at the BCIHA conference insisted, "The UBCIC executive can only reject funds in their realm" and had *"no right to* require the Indian families in poverty to forego welfare."[65] The UBCIC was transgressing its role and encroaching on the territory of Indigenous women. There are no easy categorizations here. Indigenous women both accepted and defied their established roles by maintaining their gendered political mandates while crafting greater political authority.

Divergences among Indigenous Women

The BCIHA and BCNWS did not represent a universal Indigenous female political voice. Like the wider BC Indigenous movement (and mainstream feminism), Indigenous women's politics experienced degrees of multiplicity across organizations, communities, and positions – and these were evident in varied reactions to the funding decision. But Indigenous women, regardless of their political stance, mobilized motherhood to support their positions. In other words, women framed their political responses around their positions as mothers in order to assert their authority and speak on community matters. For instance, a group from the Okanagan calling themselves "interested mothers and grandmothers" appealed to Indian

Affairs to alleviate the hardship wrought by the UBCIC funding decision, explaining, "There are a lot of women on this reserve and grandmothers that are looking after their grandchildren."[66] Framing their political refusal of the UBCIC decision in terms of motherhood and familial protection, these women were not seeking a position in the political arena, like members of the BCIHA and BCNWS were, but they registered complaints in a similar manner. Women not involved in women's organizations also called on the UBCIC to respect their roles in communities as caretakers by rescinding political decisions that threatened these roles. Such positions exposed strong continuities in women's socio-political roles and priorities and demonstrated how everyday concerns were intensely political regardless of whether gender roles were mobilized strategically or not. A comparable letter came from Secwépemc women in BC's Interior, who used their political awareness and authority as mothers, as well as strategic alliances with Indian Affairs, to circumvent the authority of their chiefs and council and the UBCIC, and to appeal for financial help.[67] Motherhood and women's accepted gender roles, then, were significant sites of political work. Not everyone agreed with opposing the men, but all agreed motherhood was politically purposeful.

Others used this form of politicized motherhood to support the UBCIC funding decision. Casting Indigenous mothers as individuals responsible for ensuring the success of the UBCIC's grand political statement, an unidentified woman at the 1975 UBCIC meeting averred, "As mothers we are closest to ... children and we are the ones that are going to have to be the backbone for this movement. We are going to have to be the ones that are going to provide if someone else can't provide for us." She acknowledged the added strain the UBCIC's decision placed on mothers but emphasized their capacity to carry the weight of the decision to ensure the movement's success: "Don't let the fear of what this motion that was passed is going to mean to you mothers, because if we break down, everybody else will break down."[68] Here, she accentuated the power of Indigenous women but carefully crafted her comments as supportive rather than critical of Indigenous men. Sensitive about delegates interpreting her comments as part of a wider feminist dialogue, she explained, "I am not a women's libber although sometimes I sound like one."[69] Refusing to identify as a feminist – which many understood as antithetical to the collective Indigenous rights movement – this woman was attuned to how Indigenous women's goals of sovereignty, land claims, and maintaining Indigenous lifeways were not on the radar of the mainstream "women's libbers." Yet she also eschewed the type of Indigenous feminism the BCIHA and BCNWS practised, because, while she valued the role women played in the Indigenous rights movement, she did not incorporate a critique of gender inequality into her sovereigntist narrative. Ultimately, although this woman and the women's organizations agreed on the value and role of motherhood in women's politics and daily life, this woman maintained strong gendered alliances with male leadership, while the women's organizations willingly transgressed accepted boundaries of gendered politics.

Ultimately, during the 1975 funding decision, Indigenous women – from positions of unequal political power – used their accepted roles as mothers and community caretakers to rebuke or support political gestures of male-dominated organizations. In the process, some women developed feminist ideologies while others explicitly rejected any connection to the wider feminist movement. Yet, regardless of their ideological stance, each response was an attempt to preserve the welfare of communities and vulnerable people, as well as an effort to redirect the Indigenous movement.

By the end of the Chilliwack meeting of the UBCIC in 1975, the new leadership suggested that grassroots mobilization and the rejection of government funding provided solutions to, respectively, the dominant political authority of the chiefs and unwanted government intervention into UBCIC politics. These strategies were well situated within broader changes in the global Indigenous rights movement – particularly the growth of Red Power in the United States. Generational divisions in the movement, dissatisfaction with bureaucracy, and failed attempts at diplomacy motivated many groups and organizations to shift towards grassroots and direct-action approaches. The UBCIC strategy used the politics of refusal to identify funding and government-directed bureaucracy as damaging to unity, and recast the post-1975 UBCIC as a grassroots organization within a people's movement. Yet, amid this declared transformation in UBCIC politics, little actually changed. The structure of the organization remained the same, with a three-person executive and voting membership limited to band chiefs and councillors; thus, the bulk of political authority remained in the hands of band and UBCIC leadership. The funding decision itself was also short lived, with most communities returning to funding by the fall of 1975 and the UBCIC doing the same by the spring of 1976. Aside from increased community involvement in politics through direct action in late 1975, the people's movement envisioned by the executive never fully materialized. Yet the organization's drastic push against bureaucracy, government involvement, and unequal political authority was significant in outlining changing ideals of unity and the practical challenges to achieving these principles.

5

PROTEST

Direct Action through "militant May"

AFTER THE FUNDING ISSUE, the second part of the Union of British Columbia Indian Chiefs' two-pronged strategy developed in Chilliwack in April 1975 involved coordinating occupations, blockades, and strategic law-breaking for one month beginning on 1 May 1975. This shift was in line with the broad trajectory of the Red Power movement in the United States and Canada, which saw the 1972 Trail of Broken Treaties March end with the occupation of the Bureau of Indian Affairs office in Washington, DC, and protests at several strategic federal sites including Mount Rushmore, the Nike Missile sites, and the town of Wounded Knee, South Dakota. Across Canada, activists followed suit – taking up the political tools available to them to occupy Anicinabe Park near Kenora, Ontario, and Indian Affairs offices in the Prairie provinces. But perhaps nowhere was this shift towards radicalism more apparent than in the concentrated month of direct action in British Columbia. At the first public demonstration after the Chilliwack meeting, the executive emphasized how this break with government expanded the focus and influence of the UBCIC beyond the administrative walls of the organization into the communities where the organization would hear the voices of the people. "We're no longer the executive of an organization," declared Philip Paul to a gathering of land claim demonstrators preparing for a protest at the Victoria Legislature. Instead, he insisted, "we're the executive of an Indian movement. [And] this movement would shake the very bones of this country." The decision to engage in such direct action was an unprecedented one for an organization that was far from radical and had always sought change through policy papers and mediated discussions. Choosing to abandon these political methods in favour of direct action and rejecting government funding, and the relationships that accompanied them, represented a significant change in the Indigenous political movement in British Columbia.

THE SUMMER OF 1975 witnessed unprecedented direct action across the province, in what *Vancouver Sun* reporter Ron Rose would term "Militant May."[1] Rose's categorization came after the intense 1975 UBCIC meeting that agreed to adopt "a month of action" to protest stalled land claims negotiations. In a complete re-evaluation of its political goals, the UBCIC, which had once sought state-recognized political authority, now demanded political independence and asked the communities to stand in solidarity – which they did. Throughout the summer, Indigenous peoples blocked transportation corridors, including rail lines, highways, and logging roads, occupied offices of the Department of Indian Affairs, and protected their territories and resources from outside incursion by government agencies, non-Indigenous individuals, and resource industries. This coordinated burst of action was influenced by generations of Indigenous resistance, local politics, and global social movements.

Militant May represented another layer of political refusal whereby the UBCIC was refusing not just government money but also settler politics, governance, and dominance in British Columbia. Adding further nuance to the notion of everyday political refusals, the multiple political expressions practised by UBCIC member communities present political refusals as flexible pan-Indigenous phenomena. Communities incorporated direct-action protest against Canadian governments and industry as a pan-Indigenous strategy to maintain unity and express independence. The decision to pursue militant May was influenced by complex political encounters between the grassroots and leadership, Indigenous organizations and government agencies, moderate and militant activists, the young and the aged, and men and women. Each situated their own goals within the larger dialogue of pan-Indigenous unity, land claims, and Indigenous rights, resulting in co-ordinating and, at times, competing political activities. State officials and members of the mainstream press (influenced by Red Power militancy in the United States) also used the language of unity in their assessment of direct action by casting Indigenous participants as radicals brainwashed by American Indians who were corrupting the entire British Columbia movement. Throughout this period, militant May activists were homogenized through stereotypical images of Indigenous politics as foreign, masculine, youth-dominated, and militant. Of course, such characterizations did not reflect the reality of BC politics, where local concerns motivated action; women, children, and the elderly were ever-present; and "militancy" took the form of peaceful demonstrations and occupations.

This chapter demonstrates the flexibility of Indigenous politics. In British Columbia in 1975, direct action was an unexpected decision, but one that made sense considering the wide constituency of the UBCIC, the autonomy of Indigenous communities, and the continued organizing authority of the UBCIC. For militant May to be successful, however, the UBCIC needed to be an effective organization – one that people looked to for communication and direction; but it also needed communities and individuals with experience in direct action and with the desire to be more radical than the UBCIC had been. That militant May was sustained for such a long period of time, and succeeded in a few of its goals, tells us that it was part of a perfect political storm, where the conditions necessary for political change – in terms of both what was achieved and how the organization would act afterwards – were present in BC Indigenous communities.

Red Power

Militant May emerged out of a specific set of circumstances where the politics of global social movements, the UBCIC, and its member nations converged. In British Columbia, social movements like Red Power developed in unique locally inspired ways. A "decade-long Indian activist movement," Red Power is conventionally described as an American movement that began with the occupation of Alcatraz Island by the pan-Indian group the Indians of All Tribes in 1969 and ended with the Longest Walk in July 1978.[2] This limited temporal and geographic definition of Red Power ignores the ways in which radical ideologies and people moved across borders and reshaped the movement. Sherry Smith described Red Power in more nebulous terms, suggesting it was a "pan-Indian movement that demanded recognition of treaty rights, tribal sovereignty, and self-determination for native people."[3] Smith rejects the strict periodization adopted by others but generally agrees that Red Power coincided with the rise of other social and global decolonization movements. Many point to the 1961 creation of the National Indian Youth Council (NIYC) – a breakaway group from the more conservative

National Congress of American Indians (NCAI) – as a pivotal moment for the Red Power movement, with the term *Red Power* first used by NIYC members in 1964 and by Vine Deloria Jr. in 1966.[4] The Puget Sound fish-ins of the mid-1960s to mid-1970s are, then, generally considered part of the Red Power movement, as tribes centred around the Nisqually River drew on the terms of the western Washington treaties signed in the mid-1800s as proof of their continued right to fish, undisturbed, in their traditional territories.[5] Pre-dating Alcatraz, the fish-ins blur the strict timeline of Red Power. By the 1968 creation of the American Indian Movement (AIM) in Minneapolis, Minnesota, Red Power was firmly entrenched. Concentrated first in the Twin Cities (Minneapolis and St. Paul), where urban Indigenous peoples sought to combat police brutality, poor housing and employment opportunities, and underlying racism, AIM adapted models from the Black Panther Party to initiate an "Indian Patrol" (to protect against racial targeting by police); survival schools (to provide safe cultural education); cultural programming; new policies for state health, education, and child welfare; and legal defence systems.[6] The movement quickly spread outside the Twin Cities as Indigenous peoples across northern North America saw AIM programming and unity as a solution to their shared grievances. In addition to programs focused on cultural pride and support, AIM, like the Black Panthers, also proved willing to take up arms to engender change.

In Canada, activism had a similar trajectory, with much cross-fertilization between movements and across the borders of settler states. Métis activist Howard Adams, for instance, was heavily influenced by the revolutionary ideals of Malcolm X. Adams agreed with revolutionary violence in principle – as a way to free subjugated peoples from the shackles of colonialism – but he was convinced that Canadian Indigenous peoples could overcome colonial oppression using a non-violent strategy of radical nationalism, which involved raising collective consciousness of oppression and directing a cultural revolution. His tendency away from violence was, in part, an ideological split from global Third World leaders but also resulted from Canada's unique status as a settler colonial nation, which necessitated alternative strategies for combatting continued colonialism.[7] The burgeoning American Indian Movement was also visible in Canada, with notable American AIM members such as Dennis Banks and Vernon Bellecourt travelling north to support their peers in direct-action pursuits.[8]

In British Columbia, Red Power took the form of urban youth movements, such as the Native Alliance for Red Power (NARP), a Vancouver-based youth organization established in 1967, and AIM, which had chapters throughout the province after 1968.[9] According to former NARP member Ray Bobb (Stó:lō), the group solidified through the actions of two Indigenous women in Vancouver who were concerned about the mishandling of a case in Williams Lake against three white settlers charged with the rape and murder of an Indigenous woman. With no formal organizations or channels to turn to, the women organized a meeting in Vancouver in 1967, and participants decided to protest. Predating AIM by almost a year, the resulting organization, NARP, looked for inspiration to the Black Power movement in the United States – specifically the Black Panther Party – as well as other New Left and anti-war organizations operating around the city at the time.[10] Red Power was therefore largely community-based and limited to small organizations such as NARP and particular Indigenous communities such as the Syilx Penticton Band, where an AIM chapter was located, and the Stó:lō Cheam Band, which was actively involved in militant direct-action to protect their fishing rights. Red Power also built on centuries of resistance in Indigenous communities.

The UBCIC and Red Power

The UBCIC did not identify as a part of the wider Red Power movement. In part, this was because many delegates viewed Red Power as a militant direct-action movement, which was at odds with the UBCIC's more diplomatic and bureaucratic focus. Yet discussions about the potential role of Red Power in the UBCIC emerged almost from the beginning: at the inaugural UBCIC meeting, student delegate and NARP member Henry Jack addressed the delegates, suggesting that the negative definition of Red Power as a militant ideology had overshadowed its true purpose. Jack rejected this mischaracterization and proposed instead that Red Power could be expressed through the gathering of the chiefs and the people. He insisted the two could co-exist because, like the UBCIC, Red Power was about unity.[11] For Jack, like many others involved in the Red Power and AIM movements, direct action was merely one part of a broader political strategy and was no more important than efforts for cultural revival, treaty and rights recognition, and improved employment and education opportunities. Yet, while cultural, spiritual, and language programming and changes to legislation were underway across northern North America under the auspices of AIM and Red Power, so too were rumblings of the Alcatraz occupation, which would see the pan-Indigenous group the Indians of All Tribes stage a takeover of the former federal penitentiary on Alcatraz Island from 20 November 1969 until late June 1971.[12] The shift in political strategy away from cultural programming and local "Indian patrols" (originally devised to protect against police brutality near the bars along Minneapolis's Franklin Avenue) to occupations would put Red Power on the map, searing it into public consciousness as a radical militant (and thus homogeneous) movement.[13] By the time AIM members occupied the town of Wounded Knee in 1973, Red Power had become synonymous with militancy. Although Jack embraced elements of Red Power that suited the political mood of BC Indigenous peoples, others were suspicious of the movement, including Nuu-chah-nulth Ts'ishaa7ath Chief George Watts, who argued that Red Power had nothing to do with Indigenous politics in British Columbia. Over the course of just a few years, however, this resistance and suspicion began to change, particularly as AIM chapter representatives, including Secwépemc St'uxwtews Chief Ken Basil, simultaneously took part in the UBCIC. By 1975, the influence of AIM on the UBCIC was difficult to ignore, as approximately thirty members of the movement actively took part in the union's conference.[14] These members, who came from West Coast and Interior communities, and from other provinces such as Ontario, focused on dispelling myths about the militancy of AIM and insisted that they supported the land claim and stood ready to help.[15]

In fact, many AIM members were focused principally on the spiritual and welfare-oriented aspects of the movement. This was especially apparent in AIM's work at the Nasaika Lodge in Vancouver, which provided accommodations and support for urban Indigenous peoples, and at the "spiritual and survival" camp near Penticton, where members provided cultural and spiritual revival practices as well as accommodation and guidance to urban and rural Indigenous peoples struggling with poverty and addictions.[16] Jacob Kruger of Penticton spoke out in favour of the work young people in AIM were doing and not only implored delegates to consider supporting their cause but also asked them for donations for the spiritual and survival camp.[17]

The Red Power movement was certainly making waves among youth in the communities and in the UBCIC. Former UBCIC staff member Janice Antoine noted that the political mobilization of marginalized populations around the world influenced university students like her. "The Red Power movement, Black Power, [and] the women's movement were all a part of, or starting to be a part of, my consciousness," Antoine explained. "And," she continued, "the situation of our people and our communities, you know, probably like many of our generation, we just found it really unacceptable."[18] For Antoine, her then husband Chief Joe Mathias, and their friends, Red Power provided an opportunity for change, and, by the mid-1970s, more young people were turning to a variety of such channels to further develop their politics. This shift was part of a larger trend towards radicalism within the BC Indigenous movement, where, drawing influence and strength from the Puget Sound fish-ins and the Wounded Knee standoff in the United States, and blockades and sit-ins across Canada, the UBCIC and BC Indigenous activists became more amenable to direct action. Young activists, in particular, attended rallies and conferences, and, in many cases, their politicization got them involved in band governance, which granted them membership in the UBCIC.[19] In many ways, this infusion of youth and move towards direct action mirrored the shift (and ultimately schism) that took place between the NCAI and the NIYC in the United States, which saw youth splinter off in frustration with leadership's ineffective bureaucratic and democratic processes. Still, within British Columbia, Indigenous peoples found room for change (and radicalization) within their existing political organizations.

The prevalence of youth in activism also paralleled the patterns in global social movements. "Challenging bourgeois culture's values and beliefs in progress, order, achievement, and established authority," Smith explained, "the youthful counterculture advocated freedom from discipline and convention."[20] Outlining the transformative effect of the 1960s on Canada's "rebellious youth," Palmer likewise cast young people in central roles in the counterculture and in New Left movements such as the Student Union for Peace Action (SUPA) and the Front de Libération du Québec (FLQ).[21] The attention given to youth in sixties literature is warranted; youth did participate in new political, cultural, and economic dialogues, and this involvement captured the imagination of mainstream society in unprecedented ways. Youth similarly occupied the minds of Canadian government officials and the mainstream press in British Columbia, who agreed young radicals had spearheaded much of the direct action overtaking the province.[22]

Still, within the UBCIC, and the Red Power movement more generally, intergenerational relationships (including real and fictive kinship bonds) and political cooperation played important roles. As Donna Hightower Langston reminds us, "at a time when white student groups advised against trusting anyone over 30, American Indian youth actively pursued bonds with their elders and looked to them for cultural knowledge and leadership."[23] Young activists worked closely with older leaders, the young and the aged came together for demonstrations and political gatherings, and intergenerational connections were apparent through affective connections of family, community, and friendship. Delbert Guerin, for example, spent much of his time during UBCIC meetings with older leaders and mentors, and his contemporaries often teased him for this tendency. Nonetheless, Guerin insisted that the older leaders had significant experience and skills to pass on to the newer generation.[24] He also credited Andrew Paull with getting him involved in politics when he was a young boy, explaining that he used to deliver newspapers to Paull's house and Paull would tell him stories about Indigenous politics in an attempt to groom him for political work.[25] Many others, like Janice Antoine, had strong familial connections in the Indigenous rights movement. Antoine explained that her grandfather, father, and uncles served on the band council of her community and that her aunties, including Evelyn Paul, were involved in the Homemakers' Association. Antoine therefore grew up with a strong awareness of Indigenous political issues that was then intensified by global social movements in the 1960s and 1970s.[26]

The politics of youth did not develop in isolation. As children and teenagers, Clarence "Manny" Jules Jr. and his sisters Jeanette and Freda were present at UBCIC meetings and meetings of auxiliary women's organizations such as the BC Native Women's Association, which they attended with their father, Chief Clarence Jules and their mother, Delores. Like many others with strong political genealogies, for the Jules, Indigenous politics was a long-standing family affair.[27] In the case of Sioliya (June Quipp), her father, Albert Douglas, was involved in the Fraser East meetings in the lead-up to the creation of the UBCIC before he died tragically in 1969. Her mother, Edna Douglas, was involved in the Homemakers' Clubs and local politics. And former UBCIC staff member George Saddleman is the nephew of Chief Victor Adolph (one of the original UBCIC members).[28] Antoine, Guerin, and Don Moses also spoke of established leaders such as Andrew Paull, James Gosnell, and James Sewid meeting with their families and communities around kitchen tables and in community halls to discuss political issues, another clear link between activists in the 1960s and those of previous generations.[29] Such experiences within the Indigenous movement disrupt the view of the sixties as a moment of intense transformation and rupture from the politics and culture of previous eras. UBCIC politics suggest that the decade did not simply see the replacement of older political trends and actors with a giant influx of youth; rather, youth (and particularly young leaders) who entered the fray and shaped the movement were already influenced by family connections, community relationships, intergenerational political mentorship, and awareness of shared struggles across the globe.

It is also important to understand the generational groupings of UBCIC activists (and their ancestors) and their broad characteristics. Those active during the formative years of protest against settler state expansion, including John Celestin Chilaheetza, John Tetlenitsa, Basil David, and Clexléxqen (Petit Louis), relied on missionaries, settler lawyers, and other non-Indigenous people to translate their political goals and grievances from their own languages into petitions and political forums legible to the settler state. In later generations, their grandsons and great-grandsons would take up the fight, building new networks of cross-cultural understanding through their experience in residential schools, including the learning of English, and bringing both continuity and new political methods to the continued fight for Aboriginal title. Men such as Andrew Paull, James Gosnell, James Sewid, Forrest Walkem (descended from Tetlenitsa), Clarence Jules (descended from Clexléxqen), Delbert Guerin, and Gordie Antoine were of a generation that was deeply entrenched in its language and culture but could also operate as strong intermediaries between settler and Indigenous structures.

The first generations of UBCIC activists, then, mentored those who came after – a group of educated thirty-something men and women, many of whom were deeply connected to family politics, and some of whom were just getting their start. George Saddleman (descended from Chilaheetza), Adam Eneas, Don Moses, Percy Joe, Janice Antoine, and others may have remembered their parents and grandparents speaking Indigenous languages in their homes and at political meetings. Many of these individuals were the first in their families to continue past residential school to attain university degrees. Members of this generation took on band leadership positions in great numbers and participated in the UBCIC, but they were active in other political arenas as well. These relationships between the new generation and their forebears were at the forefront of British Columbia Indigenous politics.

Such cross-generational relationships and even fictive kinship bonds could bridge the ideological and relational gap between the UBCIC and Red Power. This was evident at the Chilliwack meeting, where Stó:lō community member Matilda "Tillie" Gutierrez used the language of motherhood and kinship or broadly defined family bonds to support the activities of AIM members. Emphasizing the vulnerability of youth, specifically of young men in AIM, an organization that was still not widely accepted in the UBCIC, Gutierrez appealed to union members for help. "There is something here I would like to say ... speaking as a mother to our children out here," Gutierrez began. "For five days I have been here, and there are about thirty young men that belong to the AIM. I know they are hungry, and none of us are doing anything about it." She continued, "These are the kids that wake up the white man, and they wake up the Indians because they do something about it. They wake us up: both sides of the fence are awakened when they make a move." She pleaded with the assembly, "Now, let's help these kids. We are going to pass a hat around for a little silver collection. This is what I want to do for these children because they are our children."[30] Gutierrez emphasized cross-generational links, connecting politics to kinship, and identified these young men as pivotal political actors who needed support to reach their full political potential. She did not mention the specific activities of AIM but focused on the effect the young activists had on the political community as well as their vulnerable positions as young people away from their home communities. Although Gutierrez supported how these AIM members "wake us up," she focused on relationships and kinship responsibilities to justify why members should provide financial and emotional support, insisting, "They are our children." Appealing to widely accepted notions of youth, family, unity, and community, Gutierrez cautioned against allowing differences in opinion to fracture the movement. Instead, she focused on the positive impact AIM was having, on the concept of familial support, and on a vision of pan-Indigenous unity that bridged ideological gaps. AIM would go on to play a crucial role in militant May, and Gutierrez's generational focus, while in part erasing Indigenous women's presence in AIM, did help combat prevailing stereotypes about the supposedly radical Indigenous activism.

This shift did not go unnoticed. Just three days later, George Watts suggested that, while the UBCIC did not identify with or fully accept AIM, political unity should take precedence. He explained: "A couple of years ago, if the American Indian Movement came to our conference they would have been thrown out. [Today], we don't have to stand up and say we belong to the American Indian Movement[. W]e have to take the position that we've got to align all the Indian people that have the ultimate goal in mind[;] we've got to take all our forces together and put them into some kind of workable situation that's going to bring about a solution to the land claims issue."[31] It was increasingly difficult for the UBCIC to ignore AIM or pretend it did not affect the chiefs' organization when, in fact, many of UBCIC leaders and delegates were also AIM members, and AIM's presence (for better or worse) was impossible to ignore in the United States. Overall, by the end of the meeting in 1975, the primacy of political unity amid strong ideological differences revealed a willingness to compromise for the good of the movement.

Community Radicalism

Histories of radicalism in several Indigenous communities across British Columbia also motivated the UBCIC's new focus. Throughout the 1970s, with fishing protests and the Cache Creek blockade in the summer of 1974, the Osoyoos, Penticton, and St'uxwtews bands reminded the UBCIC that diplomacy and bureaucracy were not the only ways to achieve political change. While the union remained on the periphery of these actions – supporting but not participating in them – over time, there was a discernible shift. In 1970, the UBCIC supported peaceful local protests and illegal action with the Deep Creek fish-in, which attracted over 150 participants from Indigenous communities around the province. The fish-in took place on 4 October to dispute the federal ban on taking spawning kokanee salmon. Osoyoos and Penticton community members explained that they had been fishing for kokanee in Deep Creek for over a thousand years and disputed the mainstream press's insinuation that the Indigenous fishery was responsible for destroying spawning fish. Instead, they argued that sport fishing and recreational swimming had led to declining fish stocks.

Syilx Osoyoos Chief James Stelkia, outlining the intention by Indigenous peoples to rebuff government restrictions and exercise their resource rights, argued, "The fish and game people say we have not got the right to go fishing. We say we do. We are doing what God gave us to do – and not the God of the government. I don't believe in him."[32] Fishing in contravention of state laws had long been a primary means to protest and circumvent fishery regulations, and these tactics intensified in the 1970s (alongside the

Puget Sound fish-ins in Washington State).[33] Placing Syilx cosmologies in direct opposition to settler political frameworks, Stelkia used the politics of refusal to explain the fish-in without indicating that he was seeking settler permission or legitimation of Syilx ideals. In fact, in refusing to "believe in" the "God of the government," Stelkia co-opted a time-honoured settler tactic of delegitimizing Indigenous ideologies and cultural beliefs, turning the tables on the settler state to prove that recognition worked both ways: Indigenous people needed to recognize settler political modalities for them to have any effect. By refusing to accept the settler state's authority over Indigenous peoples through fish and game laws, Stelkia made a strong case for Indigenous sovereignty. Stelkia invoked Indigenous rights defined by Indigenous peoples and motivated other communities to join the fish-in.

Demonstrators arrived not only to support the Osoyoos and Penticton communities and their cause but also to oppose widespread patterns of state intervention in Indigenous economies.[34] Although provincial fish and game laws had been unilaterally introduced and, at times, militantly enforced (a phenomenon not limited to British Columbia or Canada), state restrictions had deepened as the province began to embrace aggressive resource development under W.A.C. Bennett's Social Credit government. Socred initiatives, including the expansion of railways, highways, and bridges, and the creation of Crown corporations throughout the late 1950s and 1960s, complemented similar advances in private resource industries.[35] This forceful expansion and development disregarded Indigenous resource rights, and the economic downturn of the 1970s created challenging conditions for those Indigenous peoples who struggled to simultaneously participate in wage labour and traditional hunting and fishing pursuits.[36] Protests such as the one at Deep Creek, then, offered critical commentary on Indigenous rights issues, including the inherent right to resources as determined by the Creator, and on the current economic conditions on reserves – as well as the settler state's role in perpetuating these.[37]

By April 1974, the UBCIC was taking clearer steps to support community direct action, and to actively engage in it. The organization was clearly drawing strength from the actions of more radical communities as well as the continued efforts of Red Power activists in the United States who publicized dissatisfaction with broken treaties through the 1972 Trail of Broken Treaties caravan to Washington, DC, where activists would attempt to present President Nixon with a twenty-point position paper decrying the treatment of Indigenous peoples. When the president refused to meet with them, activists decided to occupy the national office of the Bureau of Indian Affairs to publicize their cause.[38] In February 1974, the Osoyoos Band blockaded Highway 97 at Okanagan Falls to protest the decision through the McKenna-McBride Commission in 1919 to eliminate reserve land, and, in April, Chief Stelkia made a motion at the UBCIC general assembly for province-wide demonstrations. Other leaders – frustrated with the lack of progress on Indigenous issues – supported his motion, leading George Watts to declare that the UBCIC had "agreed to *become radical*."[39]

Four months later, the armed Cache Creek blockade would test the limits of the UBCIC's decision to "become radical" and find it wanting.[40] The UBCIC's shift in mentality and hypothetical willingness to become radical did not yet match that of the Cache Creek Native Movement (CCNM) – a group of local community members, including many young radicals who were beginning to align with AIM – which proved willing to engage in both direct action and armed struggle, if necessary. The Cache Creek blockade began in August 1974, when Secwépemc St'uxwtews Chief Ken Basil led an armed obstruction of the local highway to protest substandard housing conditions on his reserve. After calls to build twenty new houses went unanswered, St'uxwtews members escalated their tactics. From their protest base camp at Two Springs on the Bonaparte Reserve, demonstrators handed out information pamphlets and charged a five dollar toll for cars in order to raise awareness about their housing crisis. When this strategy also failed to produce results, protesters initiated an armed blockade, shutting the highway down completely. Explaining this strategic turn, Basil noted, "We have tried many ways of communicating our problems to both provincial and federal governments ... but the only thing that gets any attention is the use of force."[41] Of course, Indigenous conflicts rarely begin with violence, and Cache Creek was no exception. It escalated only after all reasonable avenues were explored. The CCNM organized the blockade, but the three-week event also attracted supporters from Vancouver as well as American and Canadian activists involved in the 1969 Alcatraz occupation and the 1973 siege at Wounded Knee.[42]

Although this protest was local and based on concerns of an individual community, it was also highly representative of the conditions Indigenous peoples across Canada experienced, and this motivated others, including members of AIM, to participate. This participation illuminated the communication and cross-fertilization happening between local, national, and transnational movements, as ideas and individuals converged at Cache Creek to propel this local cause and the global social justice movement forward. Near the end of the conflict, Ed Burnstick, national coordinator for the Canadian chapter of the American Indian Movement, explained that 3,000 AIM members were poised to join the blockade if needed (a common response from AIM, which had a strong reputation for responding to community calls for assistance).[43] This blockade not only solidified AIM's involvement in British Columbia but also reinforced the broader turn towards radical politics.

The mainstream press was quick to criticize the presence of AIM and weapons at Cache Creek (citing the potential for violence), and it blamed CCNM members for compromising the "integrity of the Indian reform movement."[44] Indigenous unity, according to this interpretation, required complete uniformity. Thus, Indigenous activists were faced with unrealistic expectations that they all maintain similar political outlooks. Some reporters also blamed Indigenous peoples for their own difficulties; the *Province* argued that Indigenous militancy rather than government apathy was responsible for the Cache Creek protest, implying that, had St'uxwtews followed the proper political channels, the government would have met their demands.[45] Of course, this was not true – St'uxwtews members had been trying (in vain) to reach a peaceful and diplomatic solution by lobbying Indian Affairs for increased housing – and the media's inaccurate assessment of the situation prompted the UBCIC to respond.

Balancing its mandate to respect community autonomy while promoting unity and distancing itself from violent political activities, the UBCIC vociferously defended St'uxwtews, explaining that the community had gone through the proper administrative and diplomatic channels before resorting to direct action. Forrest Walkem, Nlaka'pamux Cook's Ferry Chief and the chairman of the UBCIC's executive committee, contended that armed insurrection at St'uxwtews was unavoidable. "As far as the Union and the Kamloops district council are concerned," Walkem began, "we did everything we could to try and avoid this situation." He declared, "We've gone to Ottawa to put our housing proposals together and they've been falling on deaf ears."[46] Walkem emphasized unity when defending CCNM actions. He conceded that militant direct action was not an ideal political device but averred that it was a legitimate last resort when state departments refused to hear valid concerns.

And yet this statement of support also confirmed the UBCIC's position as gatekeeper and official representative for the Indigenous rights movement.

It was not enough for Canadians and state officials to hear Chief Basil and St'uxwtews members justify the blockade. As we have seen, these individuals could be (and were) easily dismissed as rogue members of the Indigenous rights movement. The UBCIC, on the other hand, had an established reputation as a legitimate political organization, and its support at Cache Creek interrupted state attempts to discredit the CCNM as isolated radicals. The UBCIC's support, then, might have been enough to legitimize the Cache Creek protest had it not been for the accidental shooting of seventeen-year-old David James Robert (a visitor from Ontario) at the Two Springs camp.[47] Thereafter, the danger of armed protest became real and unacceptable to the UBCIC; it quickly withdrew its moral and media support. The increasing pressure from the press and the lack of support from the UBCIC took a toll at Cache Creek, and Basil ended the blockade 2 September 1974.[48] It was an anti-climactic end to the event. Yet, while St'uxwtews members were unable to achieve their political goals by the end of the blockade, many UBCIC member nations increasingly found themselves willing to pursue direct action. For the UBCIC as a whole, however, the Cache Creek blockade tested its radical limits and revealed its relative moderateness. The UBCIC's decision "to become radical" would not come to fruition until the following summer.

Militant May

In spring 1975, the report of the UBCIC's Action Committee on the McKenna-McBride Cut-Off Lands provided a specific framework for direct action tactics and brought the UBCIC one step closer to radical politics. The Cut-Off Lands Committee was tasked with researching the lands withdrawn from reserves during the McKenna-McBride Commission in 1919, and – once the issue was researched and communities consulted – with developing a strategy for redress.[49] In the face of the provincial government's refusal to compensate bands for lands divested after the commission, the committee (comprising chiefs and council members) recommended taking direct action. It advocated "a multi-phased coordinated plan that combines a number of tactics ... depending on the willingness of any one Band to be involved." The committee emphasized using "different levels of militancy," and insisted on solidarity between the UBCIC and protesting communities, noting that "this means supporting any Band that takes action, however militant, on the cut-off lands. SOLIDARITY means support, even if this is only verbal support. SOLIDARITY means support, even if your Band does not feel it can take similar action. SOLIDARITY means *not* criticizing any Band's actions in public. SOLIDARITY means *not* playing the white man's game of 'divide and rule.'"[50] The committee also suggested types of direct-action activities for communities: occupying and using the cut-off lands, and engaging in demonstrations, sit-ins, and blockades. It even outlined suggested locations for these activities; these included specific places on major highways, such as "Highway 16 where it goes through Seton Lake," and government buildings.[51] This strategy of targeting transportation routes and federal lands and buildings aligned with trends across northern North America, where Indigenous peoples occupied parks and landmarks including Mount Rushmore and Anicinabe Park, federal buildings such as Indian Affairs offices and the former penitentiary at Alcatraz, and places of great symbolism such as Wounded Knee (the site of the 1890 massacre). As militant May took hold, many Indigenous peoples took up the detailed suggestions made in the report.

Until April 1975, direct action was a community-based strategy that the UBCIC could choose to support or reject according to its political ideologies. This changed at the Chilliwack assembly, where the UBCIC, through careful negotiation with its member nations, explicitly expanded its concept of unity to include direct action. Originally, the discussion began with a specific concern about protecting fishing rights, with Bill Lightbown proposing a motion for the Food Fish Committee to coordinate a fish-in. The motion called for "every Indian that is able to engage in their aboriginal rights to fish even if it contravenes with the white man's law."[52] Penticton Chief Adam Eneas quickly supported the motion, asserting, "We are the only ones who can protect that right and if that means going to jail then we'll go to jail."[53] Others were more cautious, and, at times, disagreement about civil disobedience and direct action followed clear regional economic patterns. For instance, the West Coast nations that depended on commercial fishing for their livelihoods were wary of flouting Department of Fisheries laws and risking having their boats and commercial licences confiscated. Kerry Frank of the Kwawkewlth district explained: "All our fishing is done with a seine boat. We don't fish the rivers. It's fine to put sticks and spears on the line, but if we get busted we [lose] a $300,000 boat and it's a little hard to put that up."[54] Strategic law-breaking had a distinctly local and industry-based component. It did not mean the same thing to everyone or have the same implications; thus, it was challenging to come up with a collective strategy.

Recognizing the economic diversity of Indigenous peoples, George Saddleman asked to hear opinions on civil disobedience with respect to hunting rights from the Williams Lake District and "the north people who live on moose." These delegates spoke in favour of practising their Indigenous rights regardless of state regulations. As a result, the original fishing rights motion was approved and was later expanded to include a month of general direct action.[55] However, delegates' uneven responses prompted the UBCIC to approve and support law breaking but not mandate it.[56] Although some communities would later suggest that the UBCIC did not adhere to its policy of non-intervention, officially, communities were encouraged, through UBCIC authorization and support, to use direct action if they desired, and delegates promised not to condemn political activities regardless of their level of militancy. The UBCIC provided the framework and support needed to promote unity through direct action. As a cross-generational and heavily negotiated phenomenon, militant May employed pan-Indigenous unity and political refusal against settler-state agencies, authority, and presence in British Columbia.

Department of Indian Affairs Occupations

True to the UBCIC's promise that demonstrations and land and building seizures would "explode all over B.C. on May 1," the first day of the month saw community members, leaders, and UBCIC members participate in the simultaneous occupations of three Department of Indian Affairs district offices in Kamloops, Williams Lake, and Vernon (and quickly expand to others in Bella Bella and Nanaimo).[57] The occupations, which were organized by local activists but supported and advertised by the UBCIC, were meant to continue until the federal government agreed to negotiate the land claim and the Department of Indian Affairs permanently closed its offices and ceased to exist. In an act of Indigenous sovereignty, activists proposed to take over department services and programming, and refuse government funding, which would effectively render the DIA redundant.[58] This proposal sent a clear message that Indigenous peoples did not need Indian Affairs money or expertise to run their own affairs.

As the BC occupations began, the *Vancouver Sun* reported that hundreds of people entered the offices when they opened on 1 May and stayed in an attempt to pressure movement on land claims. The widespread participation in the occupations revealed strong opinions about the department's role in the communities. The Kamloops demonstration, led by Tk'emlúps te Secwépemc Chief Mary Leonard, attracted 100 supporters from approximately 25 bands in the Thompson-Nicola region, while the Williams Lake office occupation drew 160 activists from the 15 Indigenous communities in that area.[59] The occupations were a local response to the ways in which Indian Affairs was structured and operated in British Columbia communities but also drew strength from the occupation, in 1972, of the Bureau of Indian Affairs office in Washington, DC, and solidarity with the labour movement in British Columbia.[60]

Those at the Kamloops occupation capitalized on a growing alliance between labour and Indigenous groups, and employed a class-based strategy to shut the office down. As in other districts, Thompson-Nicola community members initially occupied the DIA office without disrupting operations or placing limitations on staff; instead, they discouraged community members from conducting regular business in the offices.[61] After two days, the Kamloops occupiers decided to move outside the building and set up a picket instead, which prevented department employees (who were members of the Public Service Alliance of Canada) from entering the office.[62] Participants used the picket to reject the welfare-style funding programs administered to Indigenous peoples by officials in the DIA, and called on department staff members to support them. The success of the picket relied on department employees recognizing the picket as legitimate, and, when they did so, this gesture of support was significant. Through this alternative strategy, participants quickly achieved their goal of closing down the district office, forcing officials to consider alternatives. As early as 23 June 1975, DIA Regional Director Larry Wight, unconvinced that the situation could be resolved, was arranging to retrain district staff and relocate them to other government agencies.[63] Solidarity between Indigenous peoples and labour was not limited to Kamloops. In fact, later that month organizations within the northwestern BC labour movement, including the Terrace, Kitimat, and Prince Rupert Labour Councils, had lent their official support for Nisga'a blockades against logging companies in the Nass Valley. The labour movement, which had previously supported Indigenous peoples' actions on an ad hoc basis, emphasized the need for "unity across the races" to fight multinational corporations bent on exploiting Indigenous peoples' natural resources and working-class labour.[64]

The UBCIC also supported a range of militant May activities through press releases and member participation, but these were not explicitly constructed as UBCIC events, exposing the complex political interplay between the organization and communities. *Nesika* reported on all the Department of Indian Affairs occupations, as well as on road and railroad blockades by communities including Westbank, Gwawaenuk (Port McNeill), and Tl'azt'en (Stewart-Trembleur).[65] UBCIC special bulletins encouraged groups to report on their activities and at times even called out directly to specific communities: "Hey! You Bella Coolas! Are you still occupying D.I.A.? We haven't heard from you!"[66] Scw'exmx Chief Percy Joe explained that, while many of the actions taken by communities during the summer of 1975 were locally organized and executed, the communities knew the UBCIC supported them. He suggested that sometimes this support took the form of a physical presence at protests or occupations, and at other times it was a moral presence that was communicated through *Nesika* and the UBCIC bulletins or through phone calls and word of mouth.[67] The certainty with which Joe explained his community's knowledge of UBCIC support is significant and highlighted the stability of UBCIC backing. The UBCIC publicity supported direct action and demonstrated the importance of disseminating information about these actions across the province. It is also noteworthy that BC Indigenous peoples did not rely on the UBCIC as the sole political framework for direct action, and this adaptability and independence sent a strong message to government about the power of Indigenous communities and politics.[68]

For the most part, the occupations were well received by district employees and Minister of Indian Affairs Judd Buchanan. A report by Williams Lake District supervisor Eric Underwood stressed the well-organized and peaceful nature of the sit-in in his district. The broad participation of community members in the demonstration, and consistently positive communications by district staff to Judd Buchanan, also brought sympathy for and acceptance of the occupation. On 19 June 1975, six weeks into the initial occupation, Chiefs Tony Meyers and Frank Boucher from the Stone and Quesnel communities, respectively, added their names to the Caribou Tribal Council's call for "the immediate closure of the Williams Lake District Office."[69] The tribal council's telex from two days earlier had demanded the immediate and permanent closure of the office and asserted that the current occupation would continue until Indian Affairs met these demands.[70] These communications provided an additional strategy of political refusal towards department intervention by providing written demands alongside direct action, and this strategy was effective. Asked to comment on the sit-ins, a DIA spokesperson declared, "These people do represent a good cross-section of the bands in their areas and the department attitude is that if there is a good representation and they want to stop Indian Affairs from working, they have a mandate to do that."[71] Buchanan agreed, and, in his correspondence to communities, Larry Wight, and officials from other agencies, including Human Resources, he emphasized his dedication to follow through with community wishes. He wrote to the West Coast District chiefs, asking if the closure of the Nanaimo district office reflected their wishes or if they preferred to have services restored.[72] The following day, communities in the South Island District stated unequivocally that they wanted community control of policies and services that affected them. [73]

Still, Indigenous communities did not universally approve of the occupations. In the South Island District, several communities such as the Cowichan and Qualicum were unhappy with the closure of the department office and the resulting reduction of services. To protest the actions of their district, the Cowichan Band passed a band council resolution requesting that the department move all relevant Cowichan files from the Nanaimo office to Duncan and, further, that it "provide ... services from a location on our reserve." Interestingly, the Cowichan Band did not criticize the occupiers or the UBCIC for denying the band access to funds and services but instead blamed Indian Affairs for "abandon[ing] its obligations and responsibilities by its delivery of the office to those in occupation."[74] The Qualicum Band, making similar demands, contended that, if Indian Affairs could not meet these requests, its staff in the South Island District should resign.[75] Cowichan and Qualicum seemed to accept the diverse political agendas of other communities in their districts and followed the UBCIC directive of not speaking out against the activities of individual communities. These bands therefore continued to preserve and enact pan-Indigenous unity even through their refusal of South Island and UBCIC directives.

Navigating these reactions to the occupations as well as to the question of funding proved difficult for Buchanan and other DIA officials, who, despite their stated willingness to follow community wishes, remained paternalistic in their handling of the occupations and the demands to eliminate Indian Affairs.[76] Department regional planner A.M. Cunningham implored Wight to ensure that community members and leadership "have full knowledge of the consequences" of closing the district offices and that the decisions "rest on a majority decision from the constituent Bands within a DIA district."[77] Although Indian Affairs had good reason to second guess the actions of the communities (considering opposition from women's organizations and several communities), its continued intervention into communities that were protesting this very kind of interference proved how deeply entrenched, normalized, and veiled paternalistic attitudes were, especially given the department's stated intentions to respect community wishes.

While not universally accepted or practised, the Department of Indian Affairs district office occupations reflected and promoted pan-Indigenous unity, in that they were widespread and lengthy political actions. Most of the occupied offices, including Vernon, Kamloops, Bella Coola, and Williams Lake, remained closed long into the summer months. The occupiers in Kamloops and Vernon succeeded in permanently closing the offices by September 1975, when Indian Affairs transferred services to the thirty respective band councils throughout the Thompson River and Kootenay-Okanagan Districts.[78] The occupations and resulting disruptions to DIA programming also allowed many BC Indigenous communities to envision their politics unfettered by department considerations, and this was a powerful boon for sovereignty.

The Black Tower Occupation and the American Indian Movement

Occupations extended to the regional Department of Indian Affairs office in downtown Vancouver, where Indigenous activists, including UBCIC executive member Bill Wilson, members of the Cut-Off Lands Committee, and one hundred AIM members came together to shut down the "Black Tower" (the colloquial name for the tall, black glass building that housed the regional headquarters of Indian Affairs in downtown Vancouver).[79] *Vancouver Sun* reporter Ron Rose described the Black Tower occupation as noisy but peaceful and outlined how an AIM security force maintained order by allowing department staff to move freely, banning drugs and alcohol from the premises, and restricting the occupation to department offices only.[80] Like the other district occupations, the Black Tower action had a strong and well-articulated political goal. Drawing on the ideologies and physical presence of AIM, occupiers designed the action to last until the 25 June land claims meeting between the province and Indigenous peoples, arguing that the occupation would increase the pressure for a suitable agreement and encourage the department to turn over its budget to the bands.

Unlike the other district occupations – where some department officials took activists' goals seriously – the Vancouver occupiers faced intense opposition by Indian Affairs, particularly Regional Director Larry Wight. Wight quickly dismissed the action as the work of foreign radicals who, he argued, had co-opted the BC Indigenous movement and did not fully represent it. This was a common accusation across social movements at the time. In 1973, when Cowichan members on the Quamichan Reserve participated in a fish-in to protest Department of Fisheries' attempts to ban their traditional fishing weirs, members of the mainstream press tried to undermine the validity of the protest by connecting Quamichan protests to Indigenous radicalism in the United States. Reporters asked demonstrators if they were militants inspired by the 1973 standoff at Wounded Knee between the Oglala Lakota, their allies in the American Indian Movement, and agents of the Federal Bureau of Investigation.[81] One article from *Nesika* also intimated that the Canadian government was drawing connections between Indigenous protest in British Columbia and the 1970 FLQ crisis. The paper reported, "The RCMP used to consider French Separatists and the FLQ as the main threat to national stability, but recent actions by native people, particularly in B.C. have changed that ranking. Although their report stated that native militants are not out to overthrow the government, they are certainly fearful of another kidnapping similar to the Pierre LaPorte [sic] kidnapping in 1970, this time by Indian militants."[82]

It is true that many demonstrators at Quamichan had connections to their American counterparts through family ties, mobility, or shared ideologies, and some of these American activists may have participated in this and other Red Power actions. Certainly outside forces motivated activists in British Columbia, yet the connections made by media between American and Canadian activists served to undercut Indigenous community members' right to fish for food by highlighting the supposed indoctrination of community members by outside militant ideologies.[83] In the case of the correlation between radical Quebec sovereigntists and activists in British Columbia, some, rather than taking offence, framed the government's concern and interest as a source of pride, noting that Indigenous activists had surpassed all other groups currently under government surveillance for radicalism. As the author cheekily exclaimed, "We're number 1!"[84] Nevertheless, in Vancouver, where participants orchestrated and publicized the Black Tower sit-in as an AIM event rather than a protest by surrounding local communities, department officials began to question whose goals the occupiers were pursuing.[85] Wight disregarded the ways in which activists transposed AIM into local conditions and developed their own unique political expressions.

There were AIM chapters in Vancouver and Penticton by the mid-1970s, though Paul Chaat Smith and Robert Allen Warrior have argued that chapters across the United States and Canada had little interaction with headquarters and pursued their political aims autonomously.[86] UBCIC executive member Philip Paul also highlighted this in his conversations with the media in May 1975, when he insisted that Canadian AIM members were inherently different from their American counterparts. Noting that AIM members active in British Columbia were genuinely concerned with helping communities, Paul emphasized the organization's dedication to unity, support, community, and spirituality rather than militancy.[87] In part, Paul's support was fuelled by pointed discussions between UBCIC and AIM members at the 1975 assembly in Chilliwack. Responding to criticism that AIM did not share the same political vision or strategies as the UBCIC, and therefore might compromise the movement, Ken Basil called on members of the Vancouver and Penticton AIM chapters to introduce themselves and outline their political ideologies. Basil hoped to disrupt public perceptions of AIM by explicitly connecting it to the UBCIC and British Columbia politics. Through a series of speeches, six AIM members expressed their support for the land claims and the cut-off land actions, and, after outlining the shared political goals of the UBCIC and AIM, Basil attempted to set critics' minds at ease. "I'd like to explain the policy of AIM," Basil began. "We don't go into areas until we are invited," he noted cautiously. "If you want us to act on our own, then we will. But we look for total participation. And that [is in] regards [to] demonstrations, sit-ins, or fishing and hunting rights ... We don't claim to represent the people but we speak out on issues that confront us, issues that have to be dealt with."[88] This was also the case in the United States, where AIM intervened when invited by locals.

Through his address, Basil carefully and intentionally stressed that AIM promoted community support rather than the militancy and violence often associated with the movement. Basil, like Henry Jack in 1969, presented

AIM and Red Power as integral to UBCIC political frameworks and pan-Indigenous unity. Furthermore, because Indigenous resistance movements were transnationally connected but not identical, AIM chapters in British Columbia drew influences from elsewhere while reacting to local issues and concerns, as evidenced by national AIM coordinator Ed Burnstick's offer of AIM support at Cache Creek in 1974.[89] Political movements and organizations also promoted cross-pollination, and individuals such as Ken Basil and Adam Eneas were involved in both the UBCIC and AIM concurrently.

Wight's support of the UBCIC and condemnation of AIM ignored activists' multi-sited political positions and, at least in his own mind, isolated Indian rights organizations from each other. The result was that he incorrectly dismissed the Black Tower occupation as unrelated to BC concerns, when it was anything but. The Black Tower protest was local. It was motivated by distinctly British Columbian political goals – that is, Indigenous peoples wanted independence from the Department of Indian Affairs and the elimination of the department altogether. It was also directly tied to UBCIC politics, and, in fact, the organization continued to play a pivotal role in the coordination and ratification of community-driven direct action strategies. UBCIC executive member Bill Wilson was a critical actor within the occupation, and the union used its newspaper and special bulletins to disseminate information about the occupation and lend its support.[90] Although the UBCIC described the occupation as an AIM event, it insisted that the UBCIC and other organizations were supporting the effort.[91]

The continued importance of the UBCIC was obvious to AIM regional director and UBCIC member Ken Basil when he drew on the union's approval to legitimize the occupation in the eyes of Indian Affairs.[92] Basil named the UBCIC as a contact in AIM's occupancy regulations; thus, the union maintained its status as a centralized political authority that facilitated and supported local initiatives.[93] This status supports the UBCIC's insistence that it was "no longer the executive of an Indian organization" but "an executive of an Indian movement," as AIM and other communities continued to use the union's strong reputation with government to push their agendas.[94] When the department confronted AIM and the UBCIC about their relationship with respect to the occupation, both agreed that they mutually supported each other. Although the relationship between the UBCIC and AIM was uneasy, the organizations were united in their opposition to Indian Affairs, and this, along with the participation by key

UBCIC members in the Black Tower occupation, further facilitated unity and promoted local aims. Just as Indigenous peoples had agreed to put aside their differences in 1969 to form the UBCIC, the organization consciously placed unity and Indigenous solidarity above all other considerations during the summer of action and, in this moment, incorporated AIM into its political agenda as best it could.

Radical Images

In addition to disregarding the Black Tower occupation as foreign and non-representative of the BC Indigenous movement, Wight also framed his opposition in gendered terms, with reference to a threatening radical masculinity. Soon after the action began, Wight called on the police to move in and clear the offices, citing concern for the safety of young female secretaries working in the department.[95] This preoccupation with the threat posed by Indigenous men not only erased the presence of female occupiers but equated direct action with masculine violence. This is not to say that such violence was impossible (as we have seen, Indigenous women were threatened with violence in their own communities), but there was no evidence to support Wight's concerns at the Vancouver office specifically. AIM members such as Derek Wilson and UBCIC officials who had offered their support noted that no violence or threatening behaviour occurred during the sit-in, by any parties, including Indigenous men.[96] Perhaps the 1972 occupation of the Bureau of Indian Affairs Headquarters in Washington, DC, was on Wight's mind, and he feared the same level of destruction of property and records that was experienced there. But it seemed Vancouver occupiers were not interested in directly replicating the Washington experience, but rather in adopting similar tactics that, at least in Washington, had proved effective for achieving some long-term goals such as the ultimate end of American efforts to legislatively "terminate" Native American nations – known as the "termination era."[97] In Vancouver, as police arrived, the occupiers left the offices quietly in what Bill Wilson reported was a "gesture of responsibility" and began an information picket outside the building instead.[98] The occupiers did not use violence or force to escalate their tactics but, rather, continued to employ the same types of direct action used in the districts. The presence of AIM, then, made little difference in terms of the occupation's goals and tactics, but it did make a significant difference in terms of how the department evaluated it.

Members of the mainstream media also played a role in emphasizing radical masculinity. Mainstream papers transmitted highly gendered understandings of militant politics by printing photos of stern-looking young men with long hair and dark sunglasses that emphasized militant threat and undercut public sympathies. This trend was not limited to the Black Tower occupation: during the 1974 Cache Creek blockade, images surfaced portraying young men with guns aimed at the camera lens.[99] Likewise, at the fishing protest on the Quamichan Reserve in 1973, a reporter for *Nesika* noted that "stories in the dailies talked about unsmiling Indians insolently cleaning their fingernails with machetes."[100] These intimidating portrayals rarely included references to women or children, who were ever-present at demonstrations and occupations and who were involved in AIM, and they likewise ignored the strong cross-generational component of Indigenous activism.[101] Like Wight's criticisms, such reporting served to undermine the legitimacy of Indigenous concerns.

This radicalization was a well-established but oft-resisted trend. As the plan for militant May was coalescing, Adam Eneas critiqued the mainstream media's portrayal of the recent Indian Affairs occupation in Vernon in an address to the UBCIC general assembly. The occupation, which began a few weeks before militant May, drew on Eneas's recommendations in the Action Committee on the McKenna-McBride Cut-Off Lands, a plan he had promoted to the UBCIC assembly in April. Commenting on the media's labelling of the occupiers as "young hotheads" – a phrase that both essentialized and dismissed activists as young men incapable of meaningful political action – Eneas called on those involved in the occupation to come forward. As five female Elders made their way to the front of the assembly, the imagery of young male Indian radicals dissipated. The women – Helen Alec, Mary Paul, Angeline Eneas, Susan Kruger, and Louise Gabriel – took turns addressing the delegates, often in their Indigenous language, to explain their support for the occupation and the need for rights recognition.[102] Drawing on oral histories of traditional use and occupation of the land and their determination to protect what the Creator gave them, these women grounded contemporary radicalism in long-standing political and cultural practice and, by doing so, disrupted mainstream ideals about what Indigenous politics – and particularly direct action – looked like.[103]

These women were not unique in their participation in political action, but they were highly underrepresented in the media, department conversations, and perhaps even in the minds of Indigenous community members themselves. In fact, although Eneas was clearly taking aim at the mainstream media present at the Chilliwack assembly, the extra flourish he gave to the presentation of these women suggested that he also expected UBCIC delegates to be surprised by the women's presence. Working to define their own political images, the women resisted the erasure of their radicalism and involvement in direct-action strategies. They subverted stereotypes of radical masculinity in an attempt to disrupt entrenched masculinist and youth-oriented conceptions of political activism and to demonstrate the intergenerational and gendered cooperation on the ground.

Indigenous Masculinities

But changing perceptions was an uphill battle. Some Indigenous men actively embraced images and practices of radical masculinity and incorporated these into their political agendas. Often these not only excluded female political participation and expression but also erased multiple expressions of masculinity and were distinctly heteronormative. Clothing played a central role in the construction and dissemination of AIM's image. Participants wore "uniforms" of jackets emblazoned with the AIM crest, sunglasses, bandanas, and long hair. As the reputation of AIM grew, members were easily identifiable by their appearance, and the AIM uniform became synonymous with radical Indian politics, although these clothing choices were similar to those of other male-dominated radical organizations, including the Black Panther Party and the Brown Berets. Yet, the unitary images of AIM jackets and bandanas and a Cache Creek Native Movement warrior with his gun fixed at the camera did not adequately capture the multiple expressions of Indigenous masculinities. On the ground, activists behaved according to current circumstances. At the Cache Creek occupation, AIM and CCNM members constructed themselves as masculine warriors who were not averse to armed struggle if necessary. At the Black Tower occupation, on the other hand, Basil and the other AIM members were rational risk-takers who enacted masculine authority through cautious, calculated, and ultimately peaceful political movements.[104] Demanding order, sobriety, and professionalism, and the ability to quickly reconsider political strategies according to local conditions, AIM members hoped their protest would be difficult to critique and dismiss.[105] In addition, as noted earlier, at UBCIC meetings, some AIM members emphasized spirituality and political legitimacy by appealing to rationality, moderation, and community well-being.[106]

These men managed their image and their actions according to their relationship with other organizations such as the UBCIC, their interaction with government agencies, and their own shifting ideas of what political strategies would be most effective in any given circumstance. In other words, multiple images were presented, according to shifting politics. AIM members were not unitary or static. They occupied multiple political, community-based, and gendered positions, but the most visible images of AIM – constructed internally and externally – obscured these gradations and over-simplified Indigenous masculinities and politics.

Non-radical male activists managed their masculinities in similar ways. Unlike AIM masculinities, which were often premised on risk taking and militancy, UBCIC masculinities were related to status, privilege, and political authority as a result of members' roles as organizational and community leaders. These masculinities converged and deviated according to status-based and racial hierarchies as UBCIC leaders interacted with grassroots membership and government officials. Before the 1975 funding decision, UBCIC executive members expressed their Indigenous masculinities through administrative interactions with governments, whereby leaders sought equal footing with those with whom they were liaising. Many leaders reasoned that, in order for government officials to take them seriously as Indigenous leaders, they had to speak the same political language as state representatives and maintain the same stature.[107] Wealth also played a significant role in this identity construction. Moreover, like AIM, clothing was pivotal to UBCIC masculinities. Activists such as Adam Eneas recalled how, following the suggestion of Bill Wilson, the executive began wearing matching navy blazers embellished with the UBCIC crest. Wilson reasoned that the executive should be both recognizable and dressed respectably, and that this would solidify their authority.[108] Oral interviews, however, reveal that the blazers could actually alienate UBCIC leadership from their constituents by advertising the wealth and political privilege many community members lacked.[109]

These varied expressions of Indigenous masculinities have a historical colonial context. Scott Rutherford argues that the direct political protest within the Red Power movement provided a way for young Indigenous men to reclaim masculinities that colonial encounters had altered.[110] Indeed, historic expressions of Indigenous masculinities in leadership, economic production, and cultural exchange were implicated in relationships with colonial actors and the emerging state, particularly with the advent of surveillance and control by Indian agents on reserve.[111] These containment and regulation strategies through the transition to reserves, limitations placed on mobility and traditional resource economies, the supremacy of the Indian agent, and residential schooling all disrupted traditional expressions of Indigenous manhood.[112] In nineteenth-century British Columbia, Indigenous men deployed multiple strategies to preserve their socio-economic and political status, including strategic uses of modern and traditional economic activities and pluralistic expressions of cultural exchange.[113]

By the 1970s, many of these approaches to containing Indigenous masculinities continued and weighed heavily on Indigenous men. Thus, political activism – particularly high-risk forms of direct action – provided a channel through which men could reaffirm and reshape their masculinities. As Kim Anderson, John Swift, and Robert Innes explain, "There are hundreds of Indigenous societies worldwide, all with their own particular traditional views of masculinities. They have all been affected by colonization, which means that Indigenous men in downtown Winnipeg, northern Yukon, southwest United States, or in Christchurch have succumbed to the hegemonic white patriarchal masculinity to varying degrees, accompanied by the dispossession of traditional masculinities."[114] The collision of Indigenous and Euro-Canadian cosmologies was transformative and led to the creation of alternate forms of Indigenous masculinities, many of these expressed, but not acknowledged, in political narratives. These and other challenges came to a head during militant May, directly impacting the political trajectory of the UBCIC in later years.

The Turn to Local and Nation-Based Politics

The UBCIC had difficulty recovering from the Chilliwack decision to relinquish funding and take part in local protests. One of the consequences of these actions was that many communities turned inward to develop local solutions for their struggles. The summer of 1975, in many ways, became a test run for nation-based and regional politics (also called tribal politics or tribalism), and many communities found they could accomplish more for their people outside the UBCIC than they could within it. By the late 1970s, this turn to tribalism resulted in the re-emergence of nationally rooted discourses of sovereignty.[115] In some cases, nation-based politics built on pre-existing tribal councils, including the Nisga'a, Nuu-chah-nulth, and

Caribou, but engagements with the UBCIC strengthened some of these after 1975.[116]

By May 1975, the desire for political and economic independence reached its pinnacle in BC Indigenous communities, and many drew on the UBCIC's funding decision to pursue sovereignty. In the Williams Lake District, this took the form of a more robust local body – its name changed from the Williams Lake District Council to the Caribou Tribal Council to emphasize nation-based rather than colonial identities.[117] The tribal council members no longer wanted to associate themselves with Williams Lake, as this was where the Department of Indian Affairs district office was located, and it served as a centre for department policymaking and a symbol of colonialism. Through the tribal councils, the UBCIC and Indigenous communities were practising new political expressions that specifically and concurrently incorporated nation-based and pan-Indigenous identities. We see Indigenous communities articulating and enacting sovereignty through the reorganization of local political schemes. The move towards tribal councils generated new articulations of Indigenous politics and unity with a renewed emphasis on local sovereignty and governance as a principal goal of Indigenous communities. By May 1976, this trend had come at a significant political cost to the UBCIC and highlighted one of the key tensions in the history of the organization – the conflict between local autonomy and provincial politics.

The UBCIC struggled to realize its hope of becoming a "peoples' organization," as participants were either frustrated with what many viewed as inadequate attempts to dismantle the union's hierarchy or became more interested in nation-based organizations. The 1976 annual general assembly was proof of this struggle, as it had the lowest attendance rates of any conference in the UBCIC's history, despite the union's advertising it as a people's conference in the hopes of attracting large numbers of delegates. The executive wanted to use the assembly to highlight important structural changes to the organization, notably, the inclusion of all delegates in the election processes. After months of solid direct action and political involvement at the community level, conference organizers held high hopes for the assembly, projecting 1,500 attendees.[118] Many were shocked when only 110 of the 192 voting delegates and approximately 200 observers arrived in Courtenay, and they were further dismayed that these numbers fell short of the quorum of 128 chiefs needed to conduct official business.[119]

In part, this historic low can be explained by the financial impact of the Chilliwack decision, which had crippled the UBCIC and many communities. Before May 1975, in the burgeoning era of professional politics, UBCIC chiefs and councillors could expect honorariums, travel funding, and per diems to offset the cost of attending meetings. In 1976, however, in the absence of funding, many leaders and delegates simply could not afford to attend the UBCIC meeting (or refused to do so on principle). In many cases, the districts with the lowest attendance levels (including Williams Lake and the Lakes Districts) were those that had publicized their economic challenges during the funding decision. The Nazko, Kluskus, Toosey, Alexis Creek, and Quesnel Bands were noticeably absent at the assembly, leaving the two districts (Williams Lake and the Lakes) underrepresented. These communities were ones that had passed band council resolutions opposing the funding decision.[120] The fact that these communities justified accepting government funds in terms of economic need rather than political disagreement with the UBCIC is significant. And their underrepresentation at the 1976 conference points to the financial challenges of attending UBCIC meetings, particularly in a year when they were still recovering from the funding decision.

In addition, the activities of 1975 fostered local political growth and independence, which enabled many tribal councils to turn back to local initiatives with the realization that, while there was strength in pan-Indigenous unity, negotiating a single political strategy was challenging. For example, from the outset of the UBCIC, communities had clashed over the decision to negotiate a single land claim covering all of British Columbia instead of pursuing individual claims tailored to each community or beginning with the clearly defined (if geographically limited) cut-off claim cases for the twenty-three communities that lost land after the McKenna-McBride Commission.[121] Leaders similarly struggled to determine if they should seek compensation for lands taken and resources lost before embarking on negotiations for land claims and Indigenous rights. Given communities' multiple historical experiences and divergent opinions, it is not surprising that activists made little progress in formulating a single concrete plan. Nation-based politics offered a solution by enabling communities to make decisions through tribal councils, which were more attuned to local problems and less weighed down by bureaucratic considerations than the UBCIC. This was an important shift: national politics was not just about the result of rights recognition and the land claim, but also about the process of achieving strong governance and expressions of national sovereignty.

BY THE LATE 1970S, the context of competing nationalism was intensified by Ottawa's attempts to repatriate the Canadian Constitution and by changes to the UBCIC, which included the introduction of a new presidency under George Manuel. It was in this highly complicated context that Indigenous activists negotiated Indigenous sovereignty. Ultimately, militant May demonstrated the power of pan-Indigenous refusals as Indigenous communities shifted their political strategies to incorporate direct-action tactics. The summer of action also reflected the continued importance of unity as Indigenous peoples protested resource extraction, government inaction on land claims, and unresolved Indigenous rights. It brought UBCIC politics into the communities, where individual bands could direct their political goals accordingly, but members struggled against media and government images of youth and radical masculinity that undercut the legitimacy of protest and erased women's political contributions. The new political strategies adopted by the UBCIC and the communities, however, would prove useful as the Indigenous political movement prepared to tackle its next major challenge, the patriation of the Canadian Constitution.

6

SOVEREIGNTY

"If you really believe that you have
the right, take it!"

ON 18 FEBRUARY 1980, George Manuel, a Secwépemc leader and Union
of British Columbia Indian Chiefs president, attended an Indigenous
sovereignty workshop at Canim Lake, British Columbia. There, he told
participants, "Sovereignty is the supreme right to govern yourselves, to rule
yourselves. Indians used to be able to control and exercise that right, now
we have to work to get that right back."[1] In contrast to settler colonial legal
understandings of Indigenous rights and title within the Canadian state,
Manuel's statement suggests a philosophical notion of Indigenous rights as
stemming from the inherent pre-colonial sovereignty and nationhood of
Indigenous peoples.[2] His declaration came as discussions of Indigenous
sovereignty intensified during debates on the patriation of the Canadian
Constitution, reignited years earlier by Prime Minister Pierre Trudeau. Yet
Indigenous peoples' concepts of sovereignty, rights, and title predated constitutional conversations, and Manuel's announcement reflected determination to fully implement these.

THE UBCIC's EXPRESSIONS of and purposes for unity had changed over
time and continued to do so within the patriation debates. Between 1975 and
1981, Indigenous peoples in British Columbia altered their political strategies while maintaining an emphasis on Indigenous oral traditions, histories
of sovereignty, and pan-Indigenous unity. The UBCIC and its member
nations pursued sovereignty according to tribally specific understandings,

local conditions, provincial and national relationships, gender dynamics, as well as fluid political epistemologies and legal possibilities. Continuing to reconfigure recognition and refusal along Indigenous axes of power, the UBCIC positioned itself as a political authority from which tribal councils, UBCIC member nations, and Indigenous women had to be recognized in order to receive political recognition within the Canadian Constitution. In other words, the UBCIC, as the representative organization in British Columbia, determined the parameters of Indigenous sovereignty, including who was encompassed in that concept and who wasn't. This was not a new position for the UBCIC, but it was intensified during the patriation process, where political stakes were high. Using the language of unity, the UBCIC acted as a gatekeeper to determine acceptable forms of sovereignty, which often ignored local nation-based expressions and excluded women by rejecting their citizenship. In this chapter, I explore the UBCIC's oscillating deployment of recognition and refusal with the Canadian state, where, at some times, it constructed sovereignty within the framework of the settler state and, at others, refused to engage with that state. These interactions contribute to *Assembling Unity*'s overall argument – that concurrent and ever-changing political frameworks fuelled internal and external recognitions and refusals that followed political, status-based, and gendered lines. Ultimately, all of this was done under the guise of unity and sovereignty.

The concept of Indigenous sovereignty – which I define as the processes by which Indigenous people outline and execute their own political strategies, institutions, and customs according to local and historically specific circumstances – is worth considering here.[3] Indigenous peoples have always understood themselves as sovereign nations and, in the late 1970s to the early 1980s, were central players in discussions of sovereignty and the Canadian Constitution (even as they encountered state resistance). Most historical scholarship downplays Indigenous sovereignty, relegating it to the sidelines.[4] Here I situate long-standing Indigenous discussions of sovereignty within a specific historical context to understand sovereignty as lived and expressed by communities in British Columbia. By looking closely at the patriation debates, we can better understand how Indigenous peoples discerningly intervened to demand recognition of their sovereignty and rights using millennia-long political traditions, including oral histories, which explained their historic relationship to the land, and Canadian political systems, which assumed Canadian sovereignty over Indigenous lands.

Oral Traditions and Sovereignty

Indigenous sovereignty predates the arrival of others to these lands, and understanding its deep roots in pre- and post-contact political bodies, inter-tribal relationships, and oral traditions is essential to late twentieth-century patriation debates. While "pre-contact" and "post-contact" are a false di-chotomy in many respects, and quantifying pre-contact belief systems, politics, and relationships is challenging across British Columbia (and elsewhere), I will highlight a few salient examples that serve to disrupt the notion that Indigenous sovereignty is a "colonial" issue, intervention, or response. These examples are by no means exhaustive, but they are illustra-tive. Indeed, every Indigenous community had its own systems of processes for maintaining lands and resources, as well as socio-political organization and autonomy. Every nation understood itself as independent and sovereign, and oral traditions as well as historical and archaeological evidence support this. Through these traditions and evidence, we can see aspects of trade, mi-gration, warfare, resource use, and community creation and dissolution.

Secwépemc peoples, for instance, whose traditional territories are in the interior of British Columbia, maintain oral traditions of Sk'elép's (Coy-ote's) laws, which explain that each nation holds exclusive rights to its homelands and resources. Stseptekwle (Secwépemc oral tradition) also note how Secwépemc interacted with bordering tribes, including Syilx, Stó:lō, Nlaka'pamux, and Dakelh, according to their tribal laws.[5] Warfare, accord-ing to ethnologist James Teit, was not uncommon. Marianne and Ron Ignace explain that "the oral histories of 'wars' that [Teit] heard from Secwépemc consultants contain accounts of raiding parties of outsiders including St'át'imc, Lil'wat (Lower Lillooet), Sekéwemc (Cree), and Sekani, who in each case entered Secwépemc country, trying to occupy fishing locations or hunting areas, and in other cases raided for women."[6] Secwépemc raiding parties, according to Teit, were often unleashed against the Okanagan in the 1700s, culminating in a final battle at Balancing Rock near Kamloops Lake, with Secwépemc victory.[7] Teit also discussed the long-standing rivalry be-tween the northern Syilx and Secwépemc over territory between their respect-ive lands and noted that, after years of war, the two groups reached an agreement to end the conflict.[8] Likewise, the Stó:lō of the Fraser Valley look to sxwōxwiyá:m (Stó:lō oral tradition) of Xexá:ls's transformations of people, animals, and the environment as proof of their rights and responsibilities to their territory.[9] Although Indigenous expressions of sovereignty changed over time, they remained rooted in Indigenous knowledge of the past.

Indigenous peoples also upheld their own political structures after contact and sought to affirm sovereignty by resisting colonization.[10] Stseptekwle reveal that, after contact, Sk'elép continued to protect Secwépemc sovereignty rights in multiple ways, including meeting with the queen of England to assert Secwépemc sovereignty over their lands.[11] Oral traditions ground contemporary politics as well. As the first ancestor of the Syilx, Coyote is a central trickster figure in Okanagan oral history, and, although these oral histories are located in the myth age or early contact times, political actors such as Upper Nicola Chief George Saddleman look to these stories to make sense of their current political world. For example, the traditional oral history of Coyote and Fox explains how the Big Chief (or God in some stories) gave Fox the ability to heal Coyote if he was injured or killed during his antics. Fox merely had to jump over Coyote four times, and, even in the direst situation where only a hair or bone fragment remained, Coyote would come back to life. These stories remain deeply ingrained in Indigenous peoples' lives and can be adapted according to the political needs of any given time. Saddleman uses this story of Fox and Coyote today to illustrate the continued need for strong inter- and pan-Indigenous relationships, explaining that, when some leaders are struggling, others can lift them up and save them like Fox did for Coyote.[12]

The settler state has often refused to recognize the existence and continued importance of traditional political models and ideologies. According to Splatsín te Secwépemc Chief Wayne Christian, interactions with the state prompted Indigenous communities to modify existing vocabularies of sovereignty to present their political practices in terms the state would understand. In doing this, Indigenous peoples were not adopting settler concepts of sovereignty based on Western Enlightenment ideas of land ownership; rather they were simply trying to explain notions of sovereignty that they already knew and practised.[13] We see evidence of this in the early twentieth century, when Indigenous peoples used petitions and delegations to affirm their sovereignty. Secwépemc, Nlaka'pamux, and Syilx chiefs asserted their unequivocal sovereignty over the lands and resources of their territories in the 1910 Laurier Memorial, a letter they presented to the prime minister as he made his way through their territories.[14] Indigenous peoples also used this strategy in response to both the 1912–16 Royal Commission on Indian Affairs for the Province of British Columbia (commonly known as the McKenna-McBride Commission) and the 1969 *Statement of the Government of Canada on Indian Policy* (commonly known as the White Paper). Between the late nineteenth and mid-twentieth century, BC Indigenous peoples mastered colonial political practices and, when appropriate, used those forms to advance their assertions of sovereignty.

Constitutional Debates

Given millennia-long traditions of Indigenous sovereignty and centuries of challenging settler colonialism, it is not surprising that Indigenous peoples were highly critical of plans to patriate the Canadian Constitution. Their principal concern was that they might lose their "special status" that had been codified by the Royal Proclamation of 1763, which outlined the Crown's process for negotiating control over Indigenous lands through treaties, and the 1867 British North America Act, which affirmed the federal government's legislative responsibility for Indigenous peoples and their lands.[15] Indigenous interests were at stake in constitutional revisions, but this was not reflected in emerging discussions about patriation.[16]

As the patriation processes advanced, the UBCIC adapted its discussions of sovereignty, highlighting the organization's capacity for strategic compromise and political flexibility. At the 1979 UBCIC general assembly, President George Manuel, speaking about Indigenous rights, had declared, "If you really believe you have the right, take it! Indians need to get away from the belief that big things only happen in Ottawa under the authority of White people."[17] Asserting the importance of recognizing Indigenous rights internally, Manuel and the UBCIC challenged communities to reject settler state recognition as a precondition for legitimizing Indigenous rights. Indigenous peoples simply had their own rights and did not need the state to verify or define these. Yet this firm and straightforward position would soon falter. Within a year, Manuel declared a "state of emergency" at the UBCIC assembly, arguing for immediate action to have Indigenous rights and governance (as expressions of sovereignty) entrenched in the constitution.[18] The resulting 1980 *Aboriginal Rights Position Paper* directly tethered Indigenous rights and governance to constitutional structures, noting, "Aboriginal rights means that we as Indian people have the right *within the framework of the Canadian Constitution* to govern through our own unique forms of Indian Governments (Band Councils)."[19] This recognition of

Canada as a legitimate polity in which Indigenous rights could be situated contrasted sharply with the UBCIC's previous position.

Yet recognizing that the window for including Indigenous rights in the constitution was limited and that the federal government was intent on preserving Canadian unity, the UBCIC offered a strategic compromise that grounded these rights within state-recognized structures. As an experienced and established organization, the UBCIC framed Indigenous self-government – termed "Indian government" – within the broader Canadian socio-political context, which, in 1980, included unstable French-English relations and a Quebec referendum. Conscious of Trudeau's concerns about special group rights, the UBCIC purposefully constructed Indigenous self-government as preserving rather than threatening liberal multiculturalism and the Canadian nation-state. The organization asserted, "In our quest for self-determination, we should not be called separatists. The tensions between the English and the French have led governments to refuse to even listen to our position. We are committed to a strengthening of Canada for we have more at stake in this country than anyone else."[20]

Still, the UBCIC rejected Trudeau's proposal to erase Indigenous-Crown relationships and to transfer federal responsibility for Indigenous peoples to the provinces. Although section 24 of the proposed constitution recognized "Native rights and freedoms as they presently exist," the UBCIC argued that this section failed to capture Indigenous understandings of rights, eliminated Indigenous peoples' fundamental connection to the British Crown, and denied Indigenous involvement in shaping constitutional definitions of "Native rights."[21] Manuel declared, "We have no objection to the decolonization of Canada. What we are objecting to is [that] during the course of decolonization, the obligations by the Royal Proclamation of 1763, and many other treaties will automatically be repealed or deleted." He continued, "As I see it, once the Constitution is patriated, the Queen will just be a figurehead. I see our rights that *we presently hold* and the governing authority which *we hope to increase* to generate self-determination will go out the window."[22]

Seeking compromise, the UBCIC suggested creating a third level of government equal to the federal and provincial governments but run by and for Indigenous peoples within constitutional federalism. The organization argued that such trilateral federalism would ensure that Indigenous rights would be "recognized, expanded, and entrenched within the British North America Act" and would not be subject to intervention.[23] It proposed twenty-four areas in which Indian governments would have jurisdiction, including citizenship regulations, management of reserve lands, waterways, resources, education, and health and welfare. It also outlined a type of confederacy to unite local Indian governments within this system.[24] In recommending this framework, the UBCIC sought to entrench in the Canadian Constitution the types of Indigenous governance bands were already practising, without conceding to the Canadian state the validity or genesis of Indigenous sovereignty and governance.

The *Aboriginal Rights Position Paper* also provided illustrative examples, pointing to the Splatsín te Secwépemc's 1980 Indian Child Caravan and child welfare bylaw as proof of existing Indian government and Indigenous sovereignty.[25] Organized to protest the high rates of child apprehension (by settler society's social service organizations) in Splatsín communities, the "caravan" secured the signing of a bylaw that gave the Splatsín nation exclusive jurisdiction over its children.[26] The UBCIC also found evidence of strong Indian government in a bylaw passed by the Mowachaht Band of Gold River and members of the Nuu-chah-nulth Tribal Council to restrict pollution from a pulp and paper mill in their territory. These actions, according to Manuel, codified tribal law into Canadian law and validated Indian government.[27] Recognizing the coexistence of settler colonial and Indigenous sovereignties, this political pluralism resembles, but does not mirror, Audra Simpson's concept of "embedded sovereignties." Simpson notes that the Kahnawà:ke Mohawk community "possess[es] a consciousness of itself as a nation in spite of its location in the place and space of the reserve and as a nation within the place, space, and present time of Canada – as a sovereignty within multiple sovereignties."[28] The UBCIC's position paper created space for such embedded sovereignties, but it did so through a framework of strategic settler recognition rather than the outright refusal of state recognition, which Simpson regards as a fundamental aspect of embedded Indigenous sovereignties.

Several Indigenous groups contested the UBCIC's definition of Indigenous sovereignty and governance, its calculated alliance with the settler state, and its assumption that it had the authority to impose its views on all Indigenous communities in the province.[29] Although Manuel referenced the importance of Indigenous peoples' "own unique forms of Indian Governments" and agreed that, philosophically, Indian government was inherent to Indigenous peoples and could not be undermined, he insisted that, to guarantee protection, it should be contained within Canadian political paradigms.[30] Yet, even as a deliberate strategy of compromise, this move legitimized Canadian authority by binding Indigenous sovereignty to recognition by the settler state. Several Indigenous communities, especially in Nuu-chah-nulth and Haida territories, rejected this stance, arguing that Indigenous people had a natural or inherent right to sovereignty and that they simply needed to exercise it.[31] This philosophical dispute highlighted the profound challenges of pan-Indigenous representation and the seemingly impossible decision (common in most resistance movements) of whether to work within a system to challenge it (thus recognizing the system as legitimate) or to refuse that system outright and seeking change from the outside.[32] Determining the response put Manuel and the UBCIC in an un-enviable position during the patriation debates, but it was a question the union had been weighing since 1969.

The constitutional debates also exposed the extent to which embedded and multiple sovereignties were contemplated and contested internally among Indigenous peoples and between Indigenous peoples and the settler state. Indigenous sovereignties reflected the continuity and flexibility of BC Indigenous political thought and practice. Yet the UBCIC, by dictating what Indian government should look like (with respect to band governments within the constitution), also reproduced the unequal power dynamics of political recognition that Coulthard argued have plagued Indigenous-state relationships within the Indigenous political movement as a whole.[33] Serving as the "final word" on sovereignty, the UBCIC's decision contradicted the flexibility the union proclaimed in its early definition of Indian government. Indigenous peoples in British Columbia, then, had to navigate the landmines of political recognition by the settler state and by the UBCIC.

Indigenous Women, Citizenship, and Sovereignty

The fraught relationships between the male-dominated Indigenous organizations and the British Columbia Indian Homemakers' Association and the British Columbia Native Women's Society also intensified as the patriation debates pressured Indigenous leaders to solidify state-recognized Indigenous sovereignty within the limited window for patriation. These time constraints did not bode well for gender equality, and male leaders – who had earlier participated in conversations about women's status under the Indian Act – increasingly shifted their focus away from the act and women's political status and towards the constitution, denying their inherent interconnectedness.[34] For their part, most Indigenous women supported sovereignty and constitutionally protected Indigenous rights, but many were concerned by the ways in which narrow state-defined concepts of Indian status and political agency (which many of their leaders accepted) excluded them and their families from citizenship and sovereignty. In response, they sought gender equality and family inclusivity as a cornerstone of sovereignty and unity, and they pressured the UBCIC to do the same. Such an approach would have required revisiting the question of political rights and women's status in the Indian Act, however, and the UBCIC – convinced that gender equality was, at best, irrelevant to the sovereignty question and, at worst, a destructive distraction to the Indigenous rights movement as a whole – was uninterested in doing this.[35]

The UBCIC's argument for Indigenous sovereignty (realized through band control of membership) continued to rest on colonial policy and ignored the reality that the masculinist socio-political construction of the "band" excluded many women. Citizenship and sovereignty, then, took on a "hyper-masculinist" character, where men enjoyed stable citizenship and political authority, while women's political presence (both physical in terms of membership status, and conceptual in terms of political concerns) was relegated to the margins.[36] The UBCIC positioned itself as the gatekeeper to both, epitomizing a broader trend in Indigenous politics, according to Jo-Anne Fiske: "In the course of their struggle for 'Indian Rights,' that is, rights perceived to be inherent Indigenous entitlements as well as rights of statute and treaty, Indigenous women have had to respond to two antagonistic discourses: that of the state and that of their own male leadership."[37] This dual challenge was not well recognized in organizations like the UBCIC, where many men failed to see the sexism that existed within their ranks, or, if they did see it, failed to think it important.

Instead, women's social support roles (which often saw them in subservient roles as kitchen and administrative staff) were seen as separate but equal and were further defended as "traditional" – in line with how Indigenous communities had always acted. "Our political leaders are usually men; women play the support roles," Tsimshian activist Val Dudoward observed.[38] When Indigenous men constructed this supporting role as a positive affirmation of women's positions, they could distance themselves from sexism, which many believed to be a colonial construction and problem, not an Indigenous one. At UBCIC meetings, leaders would talk about the empowered and respected positions of "our women," noting that they were "mothers

of the nation" and the backbone of communities. This view not only legitimized women's continued marginalization but perpetuated problematic
and often inaccurate tropes of "traditional" Indigenous communities, and
some women refused to accept this reasoning.

Dudoward and others argued that male leaders also often used non–
tribally specific references to "tradition" to legitimize their political and
cultural authority and drew on hereditary chieftainships and customary
relationships and roles to undermine women's positions.[39] Typically, these
references pointed to men's long-standing roles as leaders and community
representatives, and they revealed the extent to which pan-Indigenous organization could, at times, conveniently obscure tribal specificity. In response, some women exposed the contradictory ways in which male leaders
used the language of motherhood to politically empower women as "mothers
of the nation" – valued caretakers of families and communities – while at
the same time ignoring their subjugated status and refusing to include them
in discussions of sovereignty and politics. Indigenous women increasingly
asked how they could be "mothers of the *nation*" when many were refused
citizenship within their nations. The reality of women's experiences in politics, according to Dudoward, did not fit the respectful and women-centred
attitudes many leaders claimed to have.

Part of this male dominance stemmed from the underrepresentation of
female chiefs, which remained well into the 1980s – and remains even today
– yet, even when the UBCIC opened the proceedings to community members for debate, female delegates' voices remained muted. Dudoward noted
that, when women's opinions emerged, they were on "women's issues" such
as childcare and education. Rose Charlie lamented women's exclusion from
work on the cut-off claims and in housing development, employment, and
consultations concerning revisions to the Indian Act. And, not only were
women cordoned off to speak on "gender appropriate" issues, but ultimately,
even in these so-called women's areas, the final decisions rested with the
men. This deep-seated practice led to continued misconceptions of women's
political capabilities and also broadened the mandate and scope of women's
organizations. Frustrated, Charlie explained, "The Indian Homemakers' Association of British Columbia ... [has] not only the responsibilities of
representing and expressing the needs, wants, and deprivations of the Indian
women and families, but for all the Indian people of this province." She
continued, "We have been working for many years to correct the deficiencies and to propose plans of action and to represent our Indian people to

governments and organizations."[40] Implicit here is the notion that Indigenous women's political work was being blocked.

In British Columbia, many women refused to accept gendered political oppression and used feminist critiques even as they continued to construct their politics as inherently maternal. BCIHA members Rose Charlie and Karen Fish, for instance, openly discussed sexism and patriarchy in interviews, articles, and exchanges with other women and activists.[41] Many folded their roles as Indigenous mothers, and the accompanying political responsibilities, into their feminism. For instance, Charlie insisted the BCIHA and Indigenous women "are making Native male leaders realize their power lies in the strength of their women and the women are the backbone of the family and the community."[42] This was simply one expression of Indigenous feminist thought among many, however. Dudoward took up the language of gender discrimination separate from discussions of motherhood and suggested, "The defense of non-action taken by political leaders, phrases like 'we can't separate our struggle by recognizing only the struggles of women' or 'we have to stick together' or 'we have to make sure of what we're doing before we change the Indian act' have become jaded code-words of procrastination."[43] Indeed, some male leaders recognized women's oppression in and exclusion from Indigenous politics, sovereignty, and nationalism, but rationalized that Indigenous peoples' eventual decolonization (through the current Indigenous rights movement) would effectively end sexism.[44]

The belief that the success of the movement would eliminate sexism was a common assumption in many global rights movements, where women were expected to bury their concerns for the good of the movement. Movements such as Red Power and Black Power not only collapsed sexism into racism, insisting that decolonization and racial equality would solve both problems, but actively perpetuated sexism in their political activities.[45] The assumption that gender did not matter as much as the other causes within a movement privileged the male experience as universal, representative, and, ultimately, more important. As a consequence, resistance against male-centric definitions of sovereignty was increasingly common in women's Indigenous movements outside of Canada as well. Outlining Indigenous women's understandings of the interconnectedness of tribalism, race, gender, and nationalism, the American Indigenous scholar Renya Ramirez astutely suggests, "Sovereignty can no longer mean that Native men have the right to control Indian women's lives. It can no longer simply mean separation and independence. It must also involve respect, interdependence, responsibility, dialogue, and engagement with indigenous women's rights and claims."[46]

The gendered nature of politics and membership divided Indigenous communities and organizations. The National Indian Brotherhood (NIB) was notorious for its stance against the Indigenous women's movement – particularly regarding Indian Act status and the potential reinstatement of tens of thousands of women and children to band nominal rolls. In response to fears of what this influx would mean for the political, social, and economic status quo (disregarding, of course, the negative impact status losses had for families and communities), NIB spokesmen blamed feminism (rather than Indian Act policy) as the problem. Taking up broad understandings of the feminist movement as concerned with individualistic rather than collective rights, the NIB and their allies saw these "women's libbers" as traitors to the communal nature of Indigenous communities and, thus, to Indigenous sovereignty. Many characterized activist women's criticism as akin to colonial-style attacks on Indigenous rights and decried the women as "anti-Indian."[47] Dudoward, for one, would not let such accusations stand. She and others saw their struggle as a communal one – concerning their families and nations – and thus framed Indigenous women's rights in collectivist terms, calling on Indigenous leaders to take seriously the concerns of 50 percent of their community members or risk losing their movement altogether. By continuing to allow Indian Act dispossession, she argued, Indigenous men were not capitalizing on women's political potential.[48] Dudoward insisted that rampant sexism – not calls for gender equality – was hampering the Indigenous rights movement.

Approaches such as Dudoward's helped foster unity between Indigenous and non-Indigenous female activists. In the early 1970s, sixty-five representatives from regional Indigenous women's organizations came together under a National Steering Committee of Native Women, where delegates discussed funding gaps between male and female Indigenous organizations, the feasibility of women organizing on a national level alongside existing local and provincial organizations, and shared issues affecting all Indigenous women.[49] Representatives from the BCIHA also attended conferences such the Status of Women Council of British Columbia conference in 1973: the group received financial assistance from the council for its advocacy work and, on 22 October 1973, attended a national day of mourning – organized by the council – where women could grieve the loss of the *Lavell* case.[50] That same year, the BCIHA annual report highlighted the methodical deprivation of Indigenous women through the Indian Act as well as the support received by the Status of Women Council. Although this support was not solicited by Indigenous women or the BCIHA and BCNWS, the council's work specifically, and Indigenous women's alliance with mainstream feminists generally, promoted the Indigenous women's cause.[51] Of course, support worked both ways: the BCIHA disseminated relevant information from mainstream women's organizations to its constituents, including a lengthy *Indian Voice* article outlining Kathleen Jamieson's report on women and the law in Canada. This report, which was part of a larger report from the Canadian Advisory Council on the Status of Women, outlined a broad survey of Indian policy and revealed the "double-edged irony" of the Indian Act, under which Indigenous women were "the most disadvantaged minority in Canada today, a citizen minus," through gender, economic, and racial discrimination.[52]

Such cooperation and overlap between Indigenous and non-Indigenous women's movements, however, were cautious: these gendered partnerships included a keen awareness of the unique racial and gendered biases Indigenous women faced. BCIHA member Karen Fish was critical of wholesale gender solidarity because "Indian women face obstacles in their struggles for change that the white middle class women's movement has never had to deal with." She continued, "Indian women are discriminated against because they are Indian, because they are women, and more than either of these, they are discriminated against because they are Indian women."[53] Members of the Indigenous women's movement recognized how other frames of experience and structural inequalities fragmented their womanhood in ways that non-Indigenous women did not experience. Nonetheless, through these partnerships, the BCIHA and BCNWS incorporated a number of political influences into their politics to promote gender equality as well as Indigenous rights, thus shaping Indigenous feminist debates about the multiplicity and historicity of women's experiences.

In 1973, Indigenous women's efforts led to the creation of the Native Women's Association of Canada (NWAC), a national organization representing Indigenous women, which brought together thirteen existing Indigenous women's associations from across the country, including the BCIHA and BCNWS, and helped coordinate efforts towards gender equality. NWAC member organizations (of which the BCIHA and BCNWS were part) held conferences (to which they invited government officials and representatives from male-dominated organizations), conducted community surveys, and published materials on Indigenous women's rights in an attempt to secure stable political, social, and economic positions for women.[54] New national organizations like NWAC placed increasing pressure on the federal government to address Indian Act sexism (among other gender inequalities), but government officials did not quickly take these issues up. In part, Ottawa's sluggishness stemmed from deeply entrenched patriarchal attitudes within federal agencies, which had historically resulted in policy-level gender discrimination, as well as dismissive attitudes towards Indigenous women's political organizations. In the 1970s, many federal agents could identify sources of overt gender discrimination (such as the Indian Act), but they were less mindful of normalized discriminatory structures (such as band leadership), as well as how these two strands interacted. Thus, while officials were interested in pursuing changes to the Indian Act, they also respected band autonomy, which many failed to understand in gendered terms. In 1977, after a series of debates in the Commons Standing Committee on Justice and Legal Affairs (focused on Bill C-25, the Canadian Human Rights Act), Justice Minister Ronald Basford expressed concern about the violation of Indigenous women's human rights in the Indian Act.[55]

Other parliamentarians shared Basford's concerns, and some, including Conservative Member of Parliament Gordon Fairweather, suggested eliminating section 12 altogether – a move that had been widely supported by Indigenous women's organizations. Basford insisted, however, that any changes must come from band governments and not the Department of Indian Affairs. Dismantling colonial mentalities was important to the department, as it attempted to recraft its image and promote limited Indigenous self-government. Mindful of the optics of imposing top-down change and outlining the precarious relationship between the government and Indigenous leaders, Basford noted, "the Government has made a commitment to Indian leaders not to change the Indian Act until consultations were completed and Mr. Fairweather's amendment would jeopardize the 'good-faith working relationship' the Government has with Indian representatives."[56] These officials had good reason to be reluctant about making unilateral changes to the Indian Act under the guise of "protection," considering the disastrous White Paper policy attempt, but they failed to see the gendered implications of the decision to cede responsibility to the band governments. This strategy was costly – any refusal to listen to Indigenous women's demands to eliminate section 12, along with the failure to acknowledge how privileging band authority further entrenched male political power and priorities, came at the continued expense and erasure of Indigenous women's rights and political inclusion.

Ultimately, Indian Affairs agreed with the women pressing for change, and, notwithstanding opposition from Indigenous male leadership, on 17 July 1980, Indian Affairs Minister John Munro declared a moratorium on discrimination against Indigenous women who married white men.[57] While, in this noteworthy moment, the DIA turned against its policy of gendered assimilation, it simultaneously embraced band council authority more thoroughly – a move rife with contradictions. Announcing the position of Indian Affairs on membership provisions, Munro explained that each of the five hundred bands across Canada would have to ask him to introduce the moratorium in order for it to come into effect.[58] The idea was to avoid unilateral department decision-making and preserve band control over membership. This move was highly welcomed by communities that rejected department intervention and those that feared the financial and political ramifications of altered membership. Yet giving bands a choice preserved women's precarity. In the end, most refused to implement the moratorium. Given the significant resistance to reinstating non-status women, it is not surprising that by the end of 1980 only eleven bands had accepted the moratorium.[59] The British Columbia bands and the UBCIC were deeply implicated in this failure. Although the UBCIC general assembly took place a mere three months after Munro introduced the moratorium, the minutes do not mention it at all, making it, on the one hand, difficult to assess why bands ignored the mandate and, on the other, clear that gender equality in membership was not a priority.

Of course, there were also problems with DIA priorities. The moratorium appeared to preserve band autonomy, yet the undercurrent of state authority remained, with the department's strong declaration of their position against gender discrimination. Munro acknowledged the "paternalistic attitude of various state departments," but there was no overt recognition that the state had unilaterally codified this bias in its policies in the first place.[60] Instead, government statements, in an ironic "move to innocence," chastised male Indigenous leaders for allowing such inequality to persist in their communities.[61] The bureaucratic process of observing the moratorium was also problematic. Along with being sanctioned by the department, which in itself placed undue pressure on communities to fall in line with officials who controlled their funding and services, the process for eliminating section 12(1)(b) was administered through Indian Affairs rather than the communities. Communities could decide whether to follow the department's wishes, but the existing settler colonial frameworks still forced them to liaise with Munro in order for any changes to take place. The minister insisted that the communities had to ask him to make the changes, placing the ultimate authority in his hands. Paradoxically, this process preserved long-standing colonial political hierarchies and, as always, positioned the state as the "protector" of Indigenous women.

Disappointing results from Indian Affairs' moratorium did not deter Indigenous women, who increasingly relied on growing international attention to renew efforts regarding women's status. Despite the 1974 loss in *Lavell,* by the late 1970s pressure was mounting (particularly in the international arena) to address sexism in the Indian Act. In part, this pressure came from a Maliseet woman, Sandra Lovelace, who, after losing her status on marriage to a non-Indigenous man, petitioned the United Nations in 1978 to address Canada's sexist treatment of Indigenous women. This action placed the oppression of Indigenous women in Canada on the international stage.[62] Finally, in 1981, on signing the 1979 UN Convention on the Elimination of All Forms of Discrimination against Women (CEDAW), the federal government was forced to address gender discrimination in the Indian Act. Section 12(1)(b) of the act violated CEDAW, and the Lovelace case provided the opportunity to push for amendments. The ratification of CEDAW was a significant step towards recognizing Indigenous women's rights to membership, but it was not until 1985 that changes to the Indian Act were made to address gender discrimination. In British Columbia, while Indigenous women challenged Indian Affairs and the UBCIC's heteropatriarchal political ideals in the late 1970s and early 1980s, women's citizenship concerns would essentially be muted by male leaders' increasing preoccupation with constitutional patriation.

The Constitution Express

The UBCIC continued to pursue its own agenda with respect to membership and sovereignty, and it was not alone. By the fall of 1980, Indigenous political organizations across the country were poised to respond to government practices, as they perceived the federal government's constitutional patriation plans were, as George Manuel told reporters, "designed to make

Indian rights illegal."[63] Although Indigenous leaders were included in constitutional talks leading up to patriation, they were given only observer status within discussions. This failure to allow full and equal participation by Indigenous peoples prompted a series of Indigenous leaders' meetings as well as marches and demonstrations on Parliament Hill in spring 1980.[64] Addressing the extent of Indigenous involvement in a speech to leaders of the UBCIC, the National Indian Brotherhood, and other Indigenous organizations, Trudeau maintained that "you will continue to be involved in the discussion of constitutional changes *which directly affect you.*"[65] The assumption here, of course, was that potential constitutional amendments did not concern Indigenous peoples, and therefore the federal government was under no duty to consult. The UBCIC was still interested in entrenching Indigenous rights within the constitution, and members agreed that confronting the prime minister was the most effective way to have their voices heard. Cognizant of Trudeau's plan to seek patriation by 1 July 1981, the UBCIC proposed immediate political action.

In November 1980, the UBCIC hired two passenger trains to bring people from across Canada to Ottawa to protest constitutional content and processes. Reminiscent of a variety of earlier actions – including the "moccasin miles" that raised funds to create the UBCIC; the 1972 Trail of Broken Treaties caravan to Washington, DC; and even historic Indigenous delegations to Victoria, London, and Ottawa – the "Constitution Express" took Indigenous protest to the streets in a nationwide bid for recognition. In the lead-up to this initiative, the UBCIC published a series of bulletins on constitutional issues to raise grassroots awareness and support. It organized billets to house the participants along the way and in Ottawa, and it asked participants to bring drums and traditional dress to participate in songs and ceremonies.[66] Onboard the trains, members took part in constitutional workshops designed to educate them and prepare them for political engagement and protest in Ottawa. The express gained considerable momentum, attracting approximately one thousand participants to the trek to Ottawa.

In part because of past events that had ended in conflict – including the Trail of Broken Treaties march and the Wounded Knee occupation – organizers and participants were keen on keeping public opinion on their side. The UBCIC banned drugs and alcohol on the express and maintained strict rules for behaviour. Despite this concerted attempt to manage the express's image, however, the federal government worried that violent protest would ensue when the train arrived in Ottawa. To help quell this fear, RCMP officers stopped and searched the trains in northern Ontario. The RCMP claimed that it was responding to a bomb threat, but Robert (Bobby) Manuel, who was leading the delegation in his father's absence, was suspicious.[67] As the trains were evacuated and bags searched, Bobby Manuel was convinced the RCMP was looking for weapons, not bombs.[68] With no evidence of a bomb (or weapons), the police allowed the express to continue. When it reached Ottawa on 5 December 1980, George Manuel's other son, Arthur, who was there to meet the protesters (who included his wife Beverley, their children, and his brother), described the atmosphere as "electric." He explained that the "station [was] throbb[ing] with Indian music and with the excitement of arriving protestors."[69]

The Constitution Express reinvigorated activists, allowed Indigenous peoples to voice their concerns about the constitution and the patriation process, and enabled them to enact expressions of sovereignty they had been honing through debates and policy papers. The express also, unexpectedly, led leaders of the UBCIC to replace limited definitions of Indian government, and the goal of state recognition, with concepts of sovereign nationhood.[70] This shift reflected new attitudes towards and suspicions of the process of negotiating the constitution. After returning from Ottawa, George Manuel presented UBCIC supporters with this change in strategy. He explained that, because the federal government had not consulted Indigenous peoples about their definitions of Indigenous rights and governance, entrenching state definitions in the constitution would not only fail to guarantee these important rights but would actually compromise them.[71] Up until this point, the UBCIC had been open to strategic compromise that left room for state political structures and recognition, but it now viewed this negotiation as unproductive. According to *Indian World,* the Constitution Express "re-awakened our nations" and led Indigenous people to appeal to the international community to promote their visions of Indigenous governance, sovereignty, and nationhood.[72]

International Lobbying Efforts

Between 1980 and 1981, BC Indigenous leaders pressed their cause on the global stage. The UBCIC sent representatives to several international locations: to the Netherlands, to give testimony to the Russell Tribunal, a third-party organization that accepted cases in much the same way as a court; to the United Nations in New York; and finally, to the British Parliament in

London. The Russell Tribunal supported the call for Indigenous sovereign self-determination in a written decision in November 1980. In it, the tribunal denounced Canada's exclusion of Indigenous peoples from the patriation process and confirmed the right of Indigenous peoples to exist as distinct and sovereign nations.[73] Fortified by this decision, forty-one activists who had taken part in the Constitution Express to Ottawa turned to the United Nations to protest their treatment by the federal government and ask that the UN mediate between Indigenous nations, Canada, and the British Crown.[74]

The Russell Tribunal's decision was not only a noteworthy ideological victory for the UBCIC, it also influenced Canada's constitutional negotiations by extending the date for constitutional hearings from 8 December 1980 to 8 February 1981 so that the Constitution committee could hear from Indigenous groups across the country. In preparation for these consultations, Indigenous leaders met in Vancouver in January 1981 to develop a unified position and form a national provisional Indian government.[75] Participants negotiated clear definitions of important terminology, including *sovereignty, self-governance, self-determination,* and *nationhood.* Such precision and consistency would ensure a strong position from which to negotiate Indigenous protections. Unfortunately, the federal government showed little interest in safeguarding Indigenous rights and was even less interested in accepting Indigenous definitions of these concepts.

In November 1981, the constitutional agreement hammered out by Canada's first ministers dropped the language of Aboriginal and treaty rights that had been added to federal proposals the previous spring.[76] This move was an egregious violation of the federal government's stated commitment to take Indigenous claims seriously and reflected a fundamental misunderstanding of Indigenous concerns. Vigorous Indigenous protest yielded a bittersweet victory. Negotiators reinserted the clause recognizing and affirming Aboriginal and treaty rights, but they still declined to define those rights, so Indigenous politicians felt it offered little, if any, real protection.[77]

At the same time, another delegation of participants from the Constitution Express petitioned to British Parliament to refuse patriation of the Canadian Constitution until Indigenous peoples were duly and genuinely consulted. But the British Parliament declined to become involved in what it considered an internal conflict between Canada and its Indigenous nations. Britain's neutrality lent support to the Canadian government's position, but Indigenous leaders remained highly critical of the reinserted clause. One unnamed UBCIC activist held that the government's recognition of Aboriginal and treaty rights in the constitution did not capture Indigenous understandings of rights, which included sovereign self-government: "The Federal Government, which has not had a new thought about Indians in one hundred years, adopted the phrase and changed it to Indian self-government. The Federal Government's definition is very narrow while the Indians' definition encompasses our universe." By co-opting Indigenous terminology while ignoring the tribal and historical specificities of Indigenous sovereignties, the government was instantiating settler understandings of political epistemologies. As far as BC Indigenous activists were concerned, the government falsely equated "Aboriginal and treaty rights" with settler modes of "Indian government," and UBCIC activists balked at this misconception. As the unnamed UBCIC member insisted, "Indian Government defined by the Federal government can never be Indian Government."[78]

Patriation and Its Aftermath

With the critiques and concerns of Indigenous leadership still outstanding, settler Canadian politicians reached agreement on the patriation of the constitution in November 1982. Queen Elizabeth II travelled to Ottawa and, on April 17th of that year, proclaimed the new Constitution Act. As expected, Indigenous politicians had the opportunity to explicate the significance of their constitutional concerns at a first ministers meeting in March 1983. There, while BC Indigenous leaders again demonstrated that they shared a common goal and had similar discourses of sovereignty, rupture remained when it came to the Canadian state's ability to understand their language. Yet the Constitution Express, and the related international lobbying efforts it spurred, brought some measure of victory. They directly resulted in the Canadian government prolonging the constitutional debates. This was a significant accomplishment that paved the road for section 35(1), which "recognized" and "affirmed" the "existing aboriginal and treaty rights of the aboriginal peoples of Canada."[79] By failing to define these rights, however, section 35(1) ensured that further work would be needed to address Indigenous peoples' concerns.

By the early 1980s, Indigenous activists' dual and overlapping political engagements prompted an encouraging government response in the form of the 1983 *Report on the Sub-Committee on Indian Self-Government,* otherwise known as the Penner Report, for its chair, Liberal MP Keith Penner. UBCIC activists had worked closely with parliamentary committees and government officials to forward concerns about the patriation of the constitution, and the Penner Committee indicated a willingness to take Indigenous actors seriously. The recommendations Penner outlined in his final report seemed promising. Indeed, they came back full circle to the UBCIC's 1980 proposal for Indian government, revealing both the impact of UBCIC lobbying and the extent to which Penner understood Indigenous perspectives and the value of Indigenous solutions to the Indigenous rights issue. Like the 1980 UBCIC proposal, the Penner Report recommended a third level of government for status Indian bands, with a constitutional division of powers that would place them alongside the federal and provincial governments.

Penner's endorsement of the UBCIC's 1980 vision of Indigenous sovereignty was a noteworthy shift towards state affirmation of Indigenous government, yet the report remained problematic on two fronts. First, Penner's recommendations failed to address the criticisms the UBCIC faced from its constituents concerning its limited definition of Indian government, and it did not acknowledge how the organization's conceptions of Indigenous sovereignty had shifted after the Constitution Express. Second, Penner's individual willingness to reframe Indigenous-settler political relationships was not mirrored in the federal government response, which saw Penner's recommendations summarily shelved. Ultimately, even when a government official supported Indigenous rights, the settler state remained unwilling to accept the fundamental concept of Indigenous sovereignty on Indigenous terms.[80]

THE PATRIATION ERA OF Indigenous politics produced uneven results. On the one hand, the work done by Indigenous activists (including UBCIC representatives) was essential in ensuring Indigenous rights were included in the Canadian Constitution. Yet these rights, which were without clear definition and resided within Canadian state structures, did not represent the type of sovereign nationhood many UBCIC member nations (and, at one time, Manuel himself) idealized. This strategic compromise ensured debates around sovereignty and Indigenous rights would continue long into the future. Further, like many of the UBCIC's political mandates, the pursuit of sovereignty between 1975 and 1983 was understood in the broader context of pan-Indigenous unity. Yet sovereignty had multiple and often competing articulations that changed according to local Indigenous goals, UBCIC ideologies, gender dynamics, national political contexts, and internal debate. And the high stakes and high pressure situation of patriation did little to smooth out differences of opinion, particularly as communities and Indigenous women's groups resisted the UBCIC's definitions of membership, sovereignty, and unity, as well as its self-appointed role as the sole political authority required to bestow political recognition on others. As elsewhere in the UBCIC's history, Indigenous peoples continued to believe in unity as an ideal political framework but refused to have the terms of unity dictated to them by UBCIC leadership. Broadly speaking, this tells us that sovereignty (like unity) is broadly defined, yet is a historically and culturally specific phenomenon that is multiple, negotiated, contested, and highly adaptable.

REFLECTIONS

IT WOULD BE EASY TO conclude that the Union of British Columbia Indian Chiefs ultimately failed to achieve its original goals of settling the British Columbia land claim, achieving Indigenous rights recognition, and reaching true pan-Indigenous unity. But to evaluate success and failure in these limited terms would not only undermine the UBCIC's broad accomplishments between 1969 and today but would also devalue and dismiss the centuries of political work that came before. To do this would miss the point of Indigenous politics, resistance, and resilience, and would create a false paradigm whereby success can only equal concrete political gains and failure the inability to achieve these. But the history of the UBCIC tells us that the process of political organization was just as important as what was accomplished. And ultimately, the UBCIC and its allies and member nations succeeded in demanding a voice at the table. This voice was not always representative of women's or grassroots opinions, but marginalized interest groups never failed to remind UBCIC leadership of these inequities and demand better. By examining these processes, we can observe how the modern Indigenous rights movement in British Columbia changed over time. Indigenous women and grassroots folks demanded that their visions of unity, sovereignty, community, citizenship, political strategy, and economic development be represented, and, over time, the UBCIC acknowledged some of these perspectives (though some more than others). But, if it had not been for women's organizations like the British Columbia Indian Homemakers' Association and the British Columbia Native Women's Society, issues relating to women's status under the Indian Act, women's representation in the UBCIC, and community suffering under the Chilliwack decision to refuse government funding would not have been addressed. Likewise, grassroots people reminded their leaders that they did not have unchecked political authority. Of course, as this study has demonstrated, the division between grassroots and leadership was not definite or permanent, and many leaders also participated in critical work to achieve better representation.

While the UBCIC would never again reach its pre-Chilliwack popularity or representative base – with many communities content to pursue regional rather than provincial unity, and others having lost faith in the organization overall – the union remained a significant force. Its dwindling base, however, meant that other organizations, including the Alliance Bands, the Native Brotherhood of British Columbia (NBBC), the British Columbia Association of Non-Status Indians (BCANSI), and the United Native Nations (UNN), challenged the Department of Indian Affairs' recognition of the UBCIC as the representative provincial organization (and, with that, its large funding packet). In fact, as early as 1977, bands were withdrawing from the UBCIC and joining these other organizations, citing a lack of action and "true unity" within the province as justification.[1] That same year, the Alliance Bands, the NBBC, and the UNN came together under the auspices of the B.C. Coalition of Native Indians to "work jointly in the arena of Aboriginal rights and land claims," indicating that, while many appeared to have lost faith in the UBCIC as a vehicle for Aboriginal rights recognition, they still believed in political unity as the ultimate tool to achieve such recognition.[2] Healthy debate, then, was a cornerstone of the British Columbia Indigenous political movement.

Despite a tendency among critics to view debate and disagreement in Indigenous political circles as indicative of dysfunction and a lack of political capacity and capability, I argue instead that they demonstrate the robust nature of Indigenous political thought. They also challenge the impossible double standard facing Indigenous politics and political actors, which demands that they have levels of representation and agreement that no political organization or group could achieve. Such a standard ignores the heterogeneity of Indigenous peoples as well as their varied opinions and beliefs. By enabling Indigenous peoples involved in the UBCIC to tell their own stories, this study embraces the messiness that is political experience.

And, of course, it is important to remember that Indigenous political issues and the UBCIC are not simply in the past. They have continued currency today, especially as the UBCIC continues to pursue the yet unresolved Indian land question. Between 1983, when this study ends, and 2018, the UBCIC and the British Columbia Indigenous movement have undergone much change. A quick survey of this period is a useful way to cap off a study that has continually emphasized the long history of Indigenous politics. Just as I have extended the historical roots of the UBCIC, I must also consider the UBCIC beyond the scope of this research. Taking an uncompromising stance on Indigenous title and rights, insisting that any agreement with the settler state cannot result in the explicit or implicit extinguishment of Indigenous rights, the UBCIC has come up against the provincial government's current strategy: the BC Treaty Process. Created in 1992 under the auspices of an independent facilitating body, the BC Treaty Commission (BCTC), the treaty process helps negotiate land treaties between the provincial government and Indigenous peoples to achieve solutions to land ownership and Indigenous self-government.[3] The Treaty Commission evolved out of recommendations from the 1991 British Columbia Claims Task Force, which brought together representatives from Indigenous communities and the provincial and federal governments, including representatives from the emerging First Nations Summit, an organization of First Nations and tribal councils interested in developing a provincial treaty process.

The Treaty Commission also has roots in the context of Indigenous-settler relations in the 1990s, specifically the renewed period of direct action by Indigenous communities. Although direct action was a well-established political strategy used extensively across the province, especially in the summer of 1975, Nicholas Blomley notes that "the summer of 1990 saw the most extensive rounds of blockades ever."[4] The BC blockades were certainly influenced by the standoff between the Kahnawà:ke Mohawk and the city of Oka, Quebec, as Indigenous peoples across the nation expressed their solidarity with the Mohawk. Yet British Columbia activism was also intensely local.[5] Indigenous peoples in what is now British Columbia had negotiated for their rights to be recognized in the Canadian Constitution and had submitted formal land claims statements to the federal government throughout the early 1980s, but Ottawa continued to drag its feet, and the provincial government maintained its long-standing stance of not recognizing Indigenous rights. By 1990, tensions were high, and Indigenous peoples demanded action on Indigenous title and rights issues.

When the BC Treaty Process began, it attracted much interest from communities that had spent twenty years with the UBCIC, tribal councils, and other organizations trying to resolve the land question. As a result, the UBCIC saw much of its support siphoned off to newer organizations like the First Nations Summit, which supported the treaty.[6] The treaty process, however, has proven difficult. Many nations have become disillusioned with the lengthy and costly process, the political costs associated with gaining self-government on treatied land, and the relinquishing of their stake in the wider traditional territories. Some Indigenous peoples also reject the Treaty Commission's basic assumption that the British Crown owns the lands in British Columbia and that First Nations are expected to "regain" their title to it.[7] Today, the UBCIC has recovered some of its member nations who have abandoned the treaty process and believe that the UBCIC's ideology of non-extinguishment of title is the only path to take. Although, technically, the BC Treaty Process no longer demands that Indigenous peoples "cede, release, and surrender" their Indigenous title to the land not included in treaty – a requirement known as "certainty" – an undercurrent of the old perspective remains.[8] Today, "certainty" is cloaked in more acceptable terminology. Many First Nations view the treaty process as promoting real-estate agreements rather than nation-to-nation relationships, and for many, including the UBCIC, this approach is unacceptable.[9] In her study on alternatives to the BC Treaty Process, Nahumpchin (Jennie Blankinship) captures the sentiments of nations opposed to the treaty when she writes, "The BCTC process, emphasized by many Indigenous leaders, is a façade, a cynical manipulation that perpetuates the problems that negotiations are supposed to resolve; it is veiled as another form of domestication, an advanced form of co-optation, control, manipulation, denial and assimilation."[10]

In spite of growing hostility to the treaty process, the UBCIC has never regained the dominance it held between 1969 and 1975. Yet it remains an important organization both in the history of BC Indigenous politics and global Indigenous issues and in the context of current conditions. When asked to gauge the contributions or legacy of the UBCIC, activists have mixed opinions. Some point to the supposed "heyday" of UBCIC organizing in the early 1970s as evidence of a successful organization with much potential that ultimately let greed, power, and government intervention undermine its potential to enact real change. Others reject this "lost opportunity" interpretation and reason that, overall, the UBCIC has been a stable political organization through which advances in politics, education, health and welfare, and economic development have been achieved.

Yet, just as Chief Richard Malloway lamented the haltingly slow progress of Indigenous rights issues in 1975, in 2013 former Lower Nicola Chief Don Moses observed that activists today are still fighting the same battles he entered the movement to address fifty years ago.[11] Indeed, many of the activists I interviewed expressed their disappointment that, over the years, the faces around the table changed, the reports got longer, but the issues remained the same and the solutions seemed out of reach.[12] This problem is not unique to the UBCIC; other Indigenous organizations, including the Assembly of First Nations (AFN), have faced criticism from grassroots and resurgent activists about the purpose, direction, and accomplishments of Indigenous politics. For example, recently the AFN has been cast by Indigenous critics as a settler state–dominated body that simply reproduces colonial oppression, and the organization faces questions about its validity and its ability to speak for the nation's Indigenous peoples.

Amid this slow progress, however, is a glimmer of hope. As I have argued here, the settler colonial project remains incomplete, largely due to acts of resistance by Indigenous peoples, and, as a result, the dialogue between Indigenous and state actors is still ongoing. Today, the UBCIC has moved past the lexicon of treaties to pursue litigation and direct action, while many nations continue to take incremental steps towards rights negotiations, "negotiating for small pieces of the puzzle," as former UBCIC executive director Don Bain noted.[13] Unlike organizations, such as the First Nations Summit, that believe in beginning with Indigenous rights and title recognition from the reserve base first and then moving outwards, the UBCIC demands broad recognition from entire tribal territories.

Believing in the power of Indigenous sovereignty, the UBCIC and a growing number of Indigenous peoples are increasingly unconcerned with state interpretations, acceptance, or recognition of Indigenous rights, and continue to enact long-standing interpretations of sovereignty and strong traditions of activism in their daily lives. Bain noted that the UBCIC's original vision of the strength of unity remains today, and he argued, "It's not about collapsing goals in together, but standing together."[14] Pan-Indigenous unity, in other words, continues to be a dominant theme. The recent Idle No More movement demonstrates the strength of unity, and many are entering a stage of politics Glen Coulthard has termed a "resurgent politics of recognition," which is "premised on self-actualization, direct action, and the resurgence of cultural practices that are attentive to the subjective and structural composition of settler-colonial power."[15] Reflecting on the UBCIC's activities, including a willingness to become involved in direct-action strategies and the union's stance on non-extinguishment, Sto:lō Grand Chief Clarence Pennier suggested that the UBCIC embraces many of the same attributes as resurgent politics, and that this has the potential for transformative politics.[16]

The UBCIC remains on the front lines of the Indigenous sovereignty movement through engagements with government, anti-pipeline demonstrations, protests over missing and murdered Indigenous girls and women, and a myriad of other political issues. Therefore, understanding its history takes on new importance. Many activists that were involved in the UBCIC during the timeline of this study are still politically active today, and others continue to have a stake in the political outcomes of Indigenous rights. Many also spoke of their hope that the younger generations would learn this history and become motivated, as they did, to continue the fight. Xwisten Chief Saul Terry believes that "a lot of youth don't really know the real history of what has come to be now. And so they are quite oblivious of what their struggles were or continue to be."[17] Current and future generations need to understand the political histories of their ancestors, and I hope that *Assembling Unity* contributes to this knowledge transmission.

Appendix

Union of British Columbia
Indian Chiefs Districts, 1971

District name(s) and number of bands	Bands[a]
1. Williams Lake District (15 bands)	Alexandria, Alexis Creek, Alkali Lake, Anaham, Canim Lake, Canoe Creek, Kluskus, Nazko, Nomaiah Valley, Quesnel, Soda Creek, Stone, Toosey, Ulkatcho, Williams Lake
2. West Coast District (14 bands)	Ahousaht, Clayoquot, Ehattesaht, Hosquiaht, Kyuquot, Muchatlaht, Nitinaht, Nootka, Ohaiht, Opotchosaht, Sheshaht, Toquaht, Uchucklesaht, Ucluelet
3. Bella Coola District (4 bands)	Bella Bella, Bella Coola, Kitasoo, Oweekano
4. Lakes District – after 1979, Prince George District (13 bands)	Burns Lake, Cheslatta, Finlay River, Fort George, Fraser Lake, Lake Babine, McLeod Lake, Necolsie, Omineea, Stellaquo, Stony Creek, Stuart-Trembleur, Takla Lake
5. Lillooet-Lytton District (18 bands)	Anderson Lake, Boothroyd, Boston Bar, Bridge River, Cayoose Creek, Douglas, Fountain, Kanaka Bar, Lillooet, Lytton, Mount Currie, Pavilion, Samahquam, Seton Lake, Siska, Skookumchuck, Skuppah, Spuzzum
6. Fort St. John District (4 bands)	Fort Nelson, Fort St. John, Hudson Hope, Saulteau
7. West Fraser District – after 1979 united with East Fraser to become Fraser District (11 bands)	Burrard, Coquitlam, Homalco, Katzie, Klahoose, Musqueam, Sechelt, Semiahmoo, Sliammon, Squamish, Tsawwassen

District name(s) and number of bands	Bands[a]
8. East Fraser District (24 bands)	Aitchelitz, Cheam, Chehalis, Hope, Kwaw-kwaw-A-Pilt, Lakahahmen, Langley, Matsqui, Ohamil, Peters, Popkum, Scowlitz, Seabird Island, Skawahlook, Skulkayn, Skwah, Skway, Soowahlie, Squila, Sumas, Tzeachten, Union Bar, Yakweakwioose, Yale
9. North Coast District – after 1979, Campbell River District (7 bands)	Hartley Bay, Kincolith, Kitkatla, Masset, Metlakatla, Port Simpson, Skidegate
10. Kwawkewlth District[b] (14 bands)	Campbell River, Cape Mudge, Comox, Kwawkewlth, Kwawwawaineuk, Kwiakah, Kwicksutaineuk, Mamalillikulla, Nimpkish, Nuwitti, Quatsino, Tanakteuk, Tsawataineuk, Turnour Island
11. Kootenay-Okanagan District – after 1979, united with Thompson-Nicola to become Central District (12 bands)	Columbia Lake, Lower Kootenay, Lower Similkameen, Okanagan, Osoyoos, Penticton, St. Mary's, Shuswap, Similkameen, Spallumcheen, Tobacco Plains, Upper Westbank
12. Babine District – after 1979, Gitksan-Carrier District (8 bands)	Glen Vowell, Hagwilget, Hazelton, Kispiox, Kitsegukla, Kitwancool, Kitwanga, Moricetown
13. Terrace District – after 1979, Northwest District (6 bands)	Canyon City, Gitlakdamix, Greenville, Kitimaat, Kitselas, Kitsumkalum
14. South Island District – after 1979, Nanaimo District (19 bands)	Beecher Bay, Chemainus, Cowichan, Esquimalt, Halalt, Lake Cowichan, Lyackson, Malahat, Nanaimo, Nanoose, Pacheenaht, Pauquachin, Penelakut, Qualicum, Songhees, Sooke, Tsartlip, Tsawout, Tseycum
15. Thompson-Nicola District (18 bands)	Adams Lake, Ashcroft, Bonaparte, Clinton, Coldwater, Cook's Ferry, Deadman's Creek, High Bar, Kamloops, Little Shuswap, Lower Nicola, Neskainlith, Nicomen, Nooaitch, North Thompson, Oregon Jack, Shackan, Upper Nicola

a Band names appear as in the original document.
b Kwawkewlth is also spelled Kwawkwelth in the historical records.
Sources: Data from URC, Union of BC Indian Chiefs bylaws, and organization materials.

Notes

Beginnings

1 Recognizing the difficulties of labelling Indigenous communities according to geopolitical organization and socio-political realities, I will use the terms *Indigenous communities* and *bands* somewhat interchangeably. I acknowledge the politically and culturally problematic nature of equating Indigenous communities with settler-state-determined "bands," and, wherever possible, I avoid the latter term. In some cases, where Indigenous peoples used the term *band* or where the political structures of band membership are explicitly discussed, I will default to this term for clarity. I take the same approach to *reserves* and typically use the term *community* to refer to these geopolitical spaces.

2 The term *Aboriginal,* which is used in the Canadian Constitution, has strong political implications, including recognizing the legitimacy of the settler state to define Indigenous peoples. I have chosen instead to employ the term *Indigenous* to avoid the unnecessary adoption of settler-state paradigms and to follow my political inclinations to replace settler terms with Indigenous ones. Where possible, for cultural appropriateness, I name specific Indigenous communities using current iterations. At times, I place historic names in brackets for clarity.

3 Union of British Columbia Indian Chiefs Resource Centre (hereafter URC), Minutes of the Indian Chiefs of British Columbia Conference, 17–22 November 1969.

4 Clarence Jules interview, 12 June 2012.

5 Marge Kelly interview, 3 May 2012.

6 Don Moses interview, 11 June 2013.

7 Jeanette Jules, personal conversation, 12 June 2012.

8 Kelly interview; Moses interview.

9 Kelly interview.

10 Jules interview.

11 Ibid.; Kelly interview; URC, Minutes of the UBCIC General Assembly Held at Evergreen Hall, Chilliwack, BC, 21–25 April 1975. This type of collection was also common practice in early twentieth-century organizing. Manuel and Posluns, *The Fourth World,* 85.

12 Ignace and Ignace, *Secwépemc People, Land, and Laws,* 288–93.

13 Boldt, *Surviving as Indians,* 21; Cardinal, *The Unjust Society;* Miller, *Skyscrapers Hide the Heavens;* Tennant, *Aboriginal Peoples and Politics.*

14 Tennant, *Aboriginal Peoples and Politics,* 152; anonymous, interview with author, 25 June 2013.

15 Tennant, *Aboriginal Peoples and Politics,* 53; Jules interview; McFarlane, *Brotherhood to Nationhood;* URC, Minutes of the Indian Chiefs of British Columbia Conference, 17–22 November 1969.

16 This percentage corresponds to the population of the 140 bands present at the UBCIC meeting.

17 See Coulthard, *Red Skin, White Masks;* Simpson, *Mohawk Interruptus.*

18 Drake-Terry, *The Same as Yesterday;* Raunet, *Without Surrender, without Consent.* See also Carstens, *The Queen's People.*

19 Drees, *The Indian Association of Alberta;* Tennant, *Aboriginal Peoples and Politics.*

20 Drees, *The Indian Association of Alberta;* Tennant, *Aboriginal Peoples and Politics.*

21 For further select discussions on Indigenous politics and protest, see also Blomley, "'Shut the Province Down'"; Hodgins, McNab, and Lischke, eds., *Blockades and Resistance;* Lambertus, *Wartime Images, Peacetime Wounds.*

22 Eneas interview, 3 June 2013; URC, Minutes of the Union of BC Indian Chiefs General Assemblies, 1969–1983; *Nesika: The Voice of BC Indians,* 1972–77; *Unity,* 1970–71; P.C. Smith and Warrior, *Like a Hurricane.*

23 P.C. Smith and Warrior, *Like a Hurricane.*

24 M. Anderson and Robertson, "The 'Bended Elbow' News"; "Indians Continue Occupation of Downtown Gov't Offices," *Vancouver Sun,* 10 May 1975, 1 and 11; Ticoll and Persky, "Welcome to Ottawa"; Rutherford, "Canada's Other Red Scare."

25 Manuel and Posluns, *The Fourth World,* 243–45; Ware interview, 20 August 2012.

26 Wolfe, "Settler Colonialism," 388.

27 Alissa Macoun and Elizabeth Strakosch, "The Ethical Demands of Settler Colonial Theory," *Settler Colonial Studies* 3, nos. 3–4 (2013): 426–43; Coulthard, "Subjects of Empire"; Coulthard, *Red Skin;* Lyons, *X-Marks;* Simpson, *Mohawk Interruptus,* 12.

28 L.T. Smith, *Decolonizing Methodologies.*

29 Barkaskas, "The Indian Voice."

30 Fiske, "Carrier Women."

31 See Aroha Harris and Mary Jane Logan McCallum, "'Assaulting the Ears of Government': The Indian Homemakers' Clubs and the Maori Women's Welfare League in Their Formative Years," in *Indigenous Women and Work: From Labor to Activism,* edited by Carol Williams (Urbana: University of Illinois Press, 2012), 225–39, and Williams's volume more generally.

32 Kathryn Magee, "'For Home and Country': Education, Activism, and Agency in Native Homemakers' Clubs, 1942–1970," *Native Studies Review* 18, no. 2 (2009): 27–49.

33 Nickel, "'I Am Not a Women's Libber.'"

34 Maile Arvin, Eve Tuck, and Angie Morrill, "Decolonizing Feminism: Challenging Connections between Settler Colonialism and Heteropatriarchy," *Feminist Formations* 25, no. 1 (2013): 8–34.

35 Hughes, "Negotiating Ungovernable Spaces"; Nickel, "'You'll Probably Tell Me.'"

36 URC, Minutes of the Union of BC Indian Chiefs General Assembly Held at Evergreen Hall, Chilliwack, BC, 23 April 1975; UBCIC video recording of Union of BC Indian Chiefs General Assembly, Evergreen Hall, Chilliwack, BC, 23 April 1975.

Part 1: Pan-Indigenous Unity

1 Union of British Columbia Indian Chiefs Resource Centre (hereafter URC), Minutes of the Indian Chiefs of British Columbia Conference, Kamloops, BC, 17–22 November 1969.

2 Ibid. The UBCIC represented the status Indian population through the band councils, but non-status and Métis individuals also had some representation through the British Columbia Association of Non-Status Indians (BCANSI), which was present at UBCIC meetings.

3 URC, Minutes of the Indian Chiefs of British Columbia Conference, 17–22 November 1969.

Chapter 1: Unity

1   Boldt, *Surviving as Indians;* Miller, *Skyscrapers Hide the Heavens;* Tennant, *Aboriginal Peoples and Politics.*

2   Union of British Columbia Indian Chiefs Resource Centre (hereafter URC), "Resolutions," in Minutes of the Indian Chiefs of British Columbia Conference, 17–22 November 1969.

3   Ignace and Ignace, *Secwépemc People, Land, and Laws,* 292–94.

4   Bill Angelbeck and Eric McLay, "The Battle at Maple Bay: The Dynamics of Coast Salish Political Organization through Oral Histories," *Ethnohistory* 58, no. 3 (2011): 359–92; David M. Schaepe, "Rock Fortifications: Archaeological Insights into Precontact Warfare and Sociopolitical Organization among the Stó:lō of the Lower Fraser River Canyon, B.C.," *American Antiquity* 4 (2006): 671–705. Laich-Kwil-Tach has been written historically as "Lekwiltok."

5   Ronald Ignace (Stsmél'ecqen), "Our Oral Histories Are Our Iron Posts: Secwepemc Stories and Historical Consciousness" (PhD diss., Simon Fraser University, 2008), 116–17.

6   Saddleman interview, 7 February 2015.

7   Pennier interview with author, 25 July 2012; Ware interview, 20 August 2012; Zirnhelt, "The Caribou Tribal Council."

8   Zirnhelt, "The Caribou Tribal Council," 19.

9   Tennant, *Aboriginal Peoples and Politics.*

10 Charlie interview, 3 June 1998; Charlie, "Grand Chief Rose Charlie"; "Moccasin Miles," *Indian Voice* 1, no. 2 (1969): 8; "Moccasin Miles," *Indian Voice* 2, no. 4 (1970): 11.

11 Fiske, "Colonization."

12 Jamieson, "Sex Discrimination and the Indian Act." See also Sterritt, *Racialization of Poverty.*

13 Jamieson, "Sex Discrimination and the Indian Act," 117–18; Jo-Anne Fiske, "Native Women in Reserve Politics: Strategies and Struggles," *Journal of Legal Pluralism and Unofficial Law* 30/31 (1991): 121–38; Barker, "Gender, Sovereignty, Rights."

14 *An Act for the Gradual Enfranchisement of Indians, the Better Management of Indian Affairs, and to Extend the Provisions of the Act,* SC 1869, c 42.

15 Jamieson, "Sex Discrimination and the Indian Act," 112–36; Barker, "Gender, Sovereignty, Rights," 261–63.

16 Jamieson, "Sex Discrimination and the Indian Act," 117–25.

17 The records of the BCIHA reference this dislocation and its effects. Library and Archives Canada (hereafter LAC), RG 10, vol. 1, box 16, file E6417-2254, Indian Homemakers' Association of BC, 1983, notes for a speech by Hon. John Munro to the Indian Homemakers' Association of BC, 30 April 1981; Charlie interview; "Native Women's Rights Dominate Homemakers' Annual Conference," *Nesika: The Voice of BC Indians* 2, no. 6 (1973): 4.

18 LAC, notes for a speech by Hon. John Munro, 30 April 1981. For more information on this phenomenon across Canada and the United States, see Krouse and Howard, eds., *Keeping the Campfires Going.*

19 Jamieson, "Sex Discrimination and the Indian Act," 112–36; *An Act to Amend and Consolidate the Laws Respecting Indians,* SC 1876, c 18, 19–20.

20 Pennier interview with author, 25 July 2012; Voyageur, "Out in the Open"; Voyageur, "Female First Nations Chiefs."

21 Jamieson, *Indian Women and the Law;* Hawthorn, *A Survey of the Contemporary Indians.*

22 This is not to say that women were not involved in an official capacity in the male-dominated political organizations, although examples of this are sparse. For instance, Jane Cook was the only woman on the Allied Tribes executive when the Kwakwaka'wakw bands joined the organization in 1922. Leslie Robertson and the Kwagu'ł Gixsam Clan argue that Cook's

inclusion was because the bands wanted to send representatives who were "skilled in English and had an understanding of law who could communicate the organization's stand to villagers." Robertson and the Kwagu'ł Gixsam Clan, *Standing Up with Ga'axsta'las*, 257–58.

23 Milne, "Cultivating Domesticity," iii.

24 LAC, RG 10, box 1, file 987/24-5, Constitution and Regulations for Indian Homemakers' Clubs, Indian Affairs Branch, Department of Citizenship and Immigration, Ottawa, 1951, 6; Milne, "Cultivating Domesticity," 63n59.

25 Milne, "Cultivating Domesticity," 63.

26 Leger-Anderson, 37; Canada, Department of Mines and Resources, *Report of Indian Affairs Branch for the Fiscal Year Ended 31 March 1941*, 163.

27 LAC, RG 10, vol. 8482, file 1/24-5, reel C-13816, General – Homemakers' Club Correspondence, 1955–1958, memorandum to W from C. Roberts, Indian Affairs Branch, Department of Citizenship and Immigration, 10 April 1957; Homemakers' Clubs, Statement as of 1 August 1956.

28 LAC, RG 10, box 1, file 987/24-5, Homemakers' Club – Gen., 1973–1981, Constitution and Regulations for Indian Homemakers' Clubs, Indian Affairs Branch, Department of Citizenship and Immigration, Ottawa, 1951.

29 LAC, RG 10, vol. 11481, box 1, file 971/24-5, V84-85/288, Homemakers' Clubs, Homemakers' Club Bulletin, 1 October 1955.

30 Ibid.; LAC, RG 10, box 7, file 901/24-2-2254 (part 4), 1994–95/474, Indian Homemakers' Association of BC, Travel Information & Resource Unit Program, April 1, 1979–March 31, 1980, Indian Homemakers' Association (7/1968–2/1979); RG 10, vol. 11484, file 976/24-5 (part 2), V84-85/289, Homemakers' Clubs, 1967–1969; RG 10, vol. 13462, file 901-24-5-1, Homemakers' Club – Conventions, 1969/04–1970/09.

31 Kelly interview, 3 May 2012.

32 This trend is also visible in feminist analyses of women's activities, where women are resistant to speaking about their work in political terms. This tendency can present interpretive challenges. Krouse and Howard, eds., *Keeping the Campfires Going*; Nancy Janovicek, "Oral History and Ethical Practice after TCPS2," in *The Canadian Oral History Reader*, ed. Kristina Llewellyn, Alexander Freund, and Nolan Reilly (Montreal and Kingston: McGill-Queen's University Press, 2015), 78; Katherine Borland, "'That's Not What I Said': Interpretive Conflict in Oral Narrative Research," in *The Oral History Reader*, ed. Robert Perks and Alistair Thompson (New York: Routledge, 2006), 320–30.

33 Moran, *Stoney Creek Woman*, 135.

34 Marge Kelly, telephone conversation with author, 12 April 2012.

35 Strauss and Valentino, "Gender and Community"; Arndt, "Indigenous Agendas," in Krouse and Howard, *Keeping the Campfires Going*.

36 Jacqueline A. Rouse, "'We Seek to Know ... in Order to Speak the Truth': Nurturing the Seeds of Discontent – Septima P. Clark and Participatory Leadership," in Collier-Thomas and Franklin, *Sisters in the Struggle*, 96–97; Judi Bernstein, Peggy Morton, Linda Seese, and Myrna Wood, "Sisters, Brothers, Lovers ... Listen ..." (pamphlet) (Boston: New England Free Press, 1967); Kimberly Springer, "The Interstitial Politics of Black Feminist Organizations," *Meridians* 1, no. 2 (2001): 155–56.

37 LAC, vol. 11481, RG 10, box 1, file 971/24-5, V84-85/288, Homemakers' Clubs, 1947–1955, Homemakers' Club Bulletin, March 1955.

38 Indian Affairs Branch, Department of Citizenship and Immigration, *Indian News* 2, no. 3 (1957): 7.

39 Molly Ladd-Taylor, *Mother-Work*.

40 Collins, "Shifting the Center," 45.

41 Charlie interview.

42 Charlie interview; "Homemakers' Progress!" *Indian Voice* 1, no. 1 (1969): 1 and 6; LAC, RG 10-C-IV-7, box 1, file 901-24-1-10 (part 1), BC Native Women's Society, 1971–76; RG 10-C-IV-7, box 1, file 901-24-1-10 (part 2), BC Native Women's Society, 1971–1976, letter from Barbara Barr, administrative assistant, BC Region, to F.J. Walchli, director general, BC Region, 11 August 1976.

43 LAC, RG 10-C-IV-7, box 1, file 901-24-1-10 (part 2), BC Native Women's Society, 1971–1976, letter from Mildred Gottfriedson to F.J. Walchli, 19 October 1976. Sioliya interview, 25 June 2012; LAC, RG 10, vol. 11484, file 976/24-5 (part 2), Homemakers' Clubs, 1967–1968, letter from Mrs. Mildred (Gus) Gottfriedson to Mr. Duncan Clarke Re: Homemakers' Convention last year at Kamloops, 27 April 1968; RG 10-C-IV-7, box 1, file 901-24-1-10 (part 2), 1994-95/563 GAD, BC Native Women's Society, 1971–1976, letter from Barbara Barr, to F.J. Walchli, 11 August 1976.

44 LAC, RG 10, box 7, file 901/24-2-2254 (part 4), Indian Homemakers' Association, 1968–1979, Travel Information & Resource Unit Program, 1 April 1979–31 March 1980; "Indian Women Call for Prompt Action: Men Don't Understand," *Native Voice* 22 no. 5 (1968): 1–2.

45 LAC, RG 10, box 16, file E-6417-2255 (part 1), 1994-95/595 GAD, BC Native Women's Society, 1980/08–1981/02, "History from the Years 1968 to 1979"; RG 10-C-IV-7, box 1, file 901-24-2-5 (part 3), 1994-95/563 GAD, Indian Homemakers' Association of BC, 1977–78.

46 LAC, RG 10, vol. 11481, box 1, file 971/24-5, V84-85/288, Homemakers' Clubs, Homemakers' Club Bulletin, 1 October 1955; RG 10, vol. 11484, file 976/24-5 (part 2), V84-85/289, Homemakers' Clubs, 1967–1969.

47 LAC, RG 10, vol. 13462, file 901-24-5-1, Rose Charlie to regional director J.V. Boys, 3 July 1969, Homemakers' Club – Conventions, 1969–1970.

48 LAC, RG 10-C-IV-7, box 1, file 901-24-1-10 (part 1), BC Native Women's Society, 1971–76, BC Native Women's Society – Board Meeting, Chilliwack, BC, Board Members, 1970.

49 Indian Affairs Branch, Department of Citizenship and Immigration, *Indian News* 2, no. 3 (1957): 7.

50 Charlie interview; Charlie, "Grand Chief Rose Charlie"; "Moccasin Miles," *Indian Voice* 1, no. 2 (1969): 8; "Moccasin Miles," *Indian Voice* 2, no. 4 (1970): 11.

51 URC, "Summary of Proceedings, Chiefs' Conference, Kamloops, 1969," in Minutes of the Indian Chiefs of British Columbia Conference, 17–22 November 1969.

52 LAC, RG 10, box 2, file 978/24-2-12 (part 1), Union of British Columbia Indian Chiefs, 1973–1976, Union of BC Indian Chiefs, memorandum, 6 May 1971.

53 *Unity: Bulletin of the Union of British Columbia Indian Chiefs* 1, no. 2 (1970): 4.

54 The biggest change to the UBCIC occurred in 1977, when members elected George Manuel in the capacity of president, where previously no such position had existed. The structural change also resulted in the creation of four vice-presidencies, one for each major region: Southwestern, Northern, Central-Interior, and Coast. This channelled significantly more power into the hands of fewer leaders. URC, Minutes of the Union of BC Indian Chiefs 9th General Assembly, Prince George, 26–28 April 1977.

55 LAC, RG 10, box 2, file 978/24-2-12 (part 1), Union of British Columbia Indian Chiefs, 1973–1976, Union of BC Indian Chiefs, memorandum, 6 May 1971; Lowe, "A Strategic Analysis," 11.

56 Lowe, "A Strategic Analysis," 11.

57 For Prairie political organization, see Drees, *The Indian Association of Alberta*; F. Laurie Barron, *Walking in Indian Moccasins: The Native Policies of Tommy Douglas and the CCF* (Vancouver: UBC Press, 1997).

58 Tennant, *Aboriginal Peoples and Politics*, 17.

59 Ibid. Robin Fisher, *Contact and Conflict: Indian-European Relations in British Columbia, 1774–1890,* 2nd ed. (Vancouver: UBC Press, 1990).

60 Tennant, *Aboriginal Peoples and Politics,* 18; C. Harris, *Making Native Space,* 18–19.

61 C. Harris, *Making Native Space,* 19.

62 Some scholars such as Cole Harris and Paul Tennant have suggested that BC's treaty-making experience was limited by the fiscal restraints of the Crown, which refused to finance further treaties on the mainland during Douglas's tenure, and individual beliefs of colonial actors, who felt that purchasing Indigenous land was unnecessary, especially given the recent influx of white settlers after the 1858 gold rush. But it seems that, in spite of parsimonious or even racist attitudes, most white settlers and colonial policymakers agreed that the land belonged to the Indigenous peoples. Tennant, *Aboriginal Peoples and Politics,* 21–25; C. Harris, *Making Native Space,* 18–44. Harris suggests treaties were no longer practical after 1854, as Douglas had secured "all the land he thought he needed for colonization and could defend, and because treaty making had become a time consuming business that, at least for the time being, was not worth the trouble" (21). Other scholars insist that Douglas's attitudes towards treaties had shifted; whatever the reason, it is clear that the principal goal of the treaties was to remove Indigenous peoples from lands desired by settlers.

63 Lutz, *Makúk,* 70–79.

64 Ignace and Ignace, *Secwépemc People, Land, and Laws,* 434–39.

65 *An Act for the Gradual Enfranchisement of Indians, the Better Management of Indian Affairs, and to Extend the Provisions of the Act,* SC 1869, c 42; *An Act to Amend and Consolidate the Laws Respecting Indians,* SC 1876, c 18.

66 Guerin interview, 16 April 2013.

67 Foster, "'We Want a Strong Promise'"; Galois, "The Indian Rights Association"; Carlson, "Rethinking Dialogue and History"; Tennant, "Native Indian Political Organization"; Titley, *A Narrow Vision.*

68 Carlson, *A Stó:lō–Coast Salish Historical Atlas,* 170–73; Ignace, "Our Oral Histories Are Our Iron Posts."

69 Tennant, *Aboriginal Peoples and Politics,* 53.

70 Carlson, *A Stó:lō–Coast Salish Historical Atlas,* 173; Manuel and Posluns, *The Fourth World,* 81.

71 Carlson, "Familial Cohesion," 22–23.

72 Tennant, *Aboriginal Peoples and Politics,* 53.

73 Ibid., 85.

74 Foster, "'We Want a Strong Promise,'" 126; Mitchell, "The Allied Tribes of British Columbia," 22–23.

75 Mitchell, "The Allied Tribes of British Columbia," 22–23.

76 Tennant, *Aboriginal Peoples and Politics,* 55; Carlson, *A Stó:lō–Coast Salish Historical Atlas,* 170–75.

77 Ignace and Ignace, *Secwépemc People, Land, and Laws,* 462–63; Galois, "The Indian Rights Association," 6–7.

78 Carlson, "Rethinking Dialogue."

79 Foster, "'We Want a Strong Promise,'" 127.

80 Tennant, *Aboriginal Peoples and Politics,* 87.

81 Foster, "A Romance of the Lost."

82 Ignace and Ignace, *Secwépemc People, Land, and Laws,* 466–67; Foster, "A Romance of the Lost," 194–95.

83 "The Declaration of the Indian Chiefs in the Southern Interior of British Columbia, 1910," in Carlson, *A Stó:lō–Coast Salish Historical Atlas,* 176.

84 J.A. Teit, for the Chiefs of the Shuswap, Okanagan, and Couteau or Thompson Tribes, "Memorial to Sir Wilfrid Laurier, Premier of the Dominion of Canada," presented 25 August 1910, http://shuswapnation.org/wordpress/wp-content/uploads/2012/09/137543_Shuswap Nation_Bro.pdf.

85 Posluns, *Speaking with Authority,* 13.

86 Tennant, *Aboriginal Peoples and Politics,* 92.

87 Meetings with the Capilano and xʷməθkʷəy̓əm (Musqueam) bands produced discussions about reserve allocations and reductions from Douglas's original allotment. "Capilano Indian Reserve, 21 June 1915," and "Musqueam Reserve No. 2, 24 June 1913," *Report of the Royal Commission on Indian Affairs for the Province of British Columbia [McKenna-McBride Report]* (Victoria: Acme Press, 1916), vol. 2: 40–42.

88 See the following items in the *McKenna-McBride Report,* vol. 2: "Meeting with Coquitlam Band, 8 January 1915," 115–16; "Meeting with Langley Band, 9 January 1915," 131–32; "Meeting with Matsqui Band, 11 January 1915," 144; "Meeting with Upper Sumas Band, 11 January 1915," 154, 164–65; "Meeting with Chilliwack Band, 13 January 1915," 173–78; "Meeting with Harrison River Band, 10 January 1915," 231–33; "Meeting with Sliam-mon Band, 19 February 1915," 296; "Meeting with Kla-Hoose Band, 20 February 1915," 303–4; "Meeting with Homalco Band, 23 February 1915," 310; "Meeting with Cowtain Band, 17 August 1915," 335; "Meeting with Leeachan Band, 17 August 1915," 347; "Meeting with Cheakmus Band, 17 August 1915," 352; "Meeting with Peter Byrne of New Westminster Agency, 25 January–4 February 1916," 525–26, 534, 541; "Capilano Indian Reserve, 21 June 1915," 40–42.

89 Manuel and Posluns, *The Fourth World,* 84–95; Tennant, *Aboriginal Peoples and Politics,* 89. According to George Manuel, Paull had been involved in matching Indigenous labourers with work in the hop fields of the Fraser Valley and Washington State, and with fishing along the coast. Beyond working in this employment agency–type capacity, Paull went on to organize a fishermen's union in the 1920s to protect Indigenous interests.

90 Manuel and Posluns, *The Fourth World,* 84. See also Tennant, *Aboriginal Peoples and Politics,* 92–95.

91 Galois, "The Indian Rights Association," 6.

92 Foster, "'We Want a Strong Promise,'" 133n71.

93 Tennant, *Aboriginal Peoples and Politics,* 94–95, Foster, "'We Want a Strong Promise,'" 133–34.

94 Mitchell, "The Allied Tribes," 76–99.

95 Tennant, *Aboriginal Peoples and Politics,* 102; Wendy Wickwire, "'We Shall Drink from the Stream and So Shall You': James A. Teit and Native Resistance in British Columbia, 1908–22," *Canadian Historical Review* 79, no. 2 (1998): 199–236.

96 Mitchell, "The Allied Tribes," 92–102.

97 Ibid., 67–68; Parker, "'We Are Not Beggars,'" 21; Manuel and Posluns, *The Fourth World,* 95; Tennant, *Aboriginal Peoples and Politics,* 95–116.

98 Parker, "'We Are Not Beggars,'" 21.

99 Guerin interview, 16 April 2013.

100 For more information on the banning of Indigenous ceremonies and the Indigenous responses, see Douglas Cole and Ira Chaikin, *An Iron Hand upon the People: The Law against the Potlatch on the Northwest Coast* (Vancouver: Douglas and McIntyre, 1990) and Robertson and the Kwaguʼł Gix̱san Clan, *Standing Up with Gaʼaxstaʼlas.*

101 Parker, "'We Are Not Beggars,'" 22–31.

102 Guerin interview, 16 April 2013; "Brotherhood Urges Equal Education, Liquor Rights," *Native Voice* 14, no. 11 (1960): 2; "Lands Big Issue at Kamloops Meeting," *Native Voice* 8, no. 5 (1959): 1; "Native Brotherhood of British Columbia Holds Historic Convention at Kamloops

in March," *Native Voice* 14, no. 2 (1960): 24; Peter R. Kelly, "Steps to Equality," *Native Voice* 14, no. 2 (1960): 3 and 21.

103 "Brotherhood Urged to Be Native Voice," *Native Voice* 8, no. 1 (1959): 5.
104 Ibid.
105 Kelly, "Steps to Equality," 3 and 21.
106 Hon. Ellen Fairclough, "Native Indians Need Have No Fear of Losing Status or Rights by Vote," *Native Voice* 14, no. 2 (1960): 4.
107 Guerin interview, 16 April 2013; Saddleman interview.
108 Tennant, *Aboriginal Peoples and Politics,* 133 (emphasis added).
109 Ibid., 135.
110 "'Big 5' Fail to Carry Indian Vote," *Native Voice* 22, no. 1 (1968): 1 and 8; Tennant, *Aboriginal Peoples and Politics,* 134.
111 "'Big 5' Fail to Carry Indian Vote," 1 and 8.
112 "Meet Sets Sights on Full Unity," *Native Voice* 21, no. 1 (1967): 1.
113 Weaver, *Making Canadian Indian Policy,* 13.
114 For discussions on 1960s activism in Quebec, see Mills, *The Empire Within.*
115 Palmer, *Canada's 1960s,* 293–97.
116 Ibid., 259.
117 I. Adams, "The Indians."
118 Palmer, *Canada's 1960s,* 264–65.
119 Manuel and Posluns, *The Fourth World,* 236.
120 Ibid., 243–45.
121 Ware interview.
122 Manuel and Posluns, *The Fourth World,* 97.
123 Miller, *Skyscrapers Hide the Heavens,* 226.
124 Turner, *This Is Not a Peace Pipe,* 13–14.
125 Cardinal, *The Unjust Society,* 1.
126 Reuben Ware, email communication to author, 8 October 2012. Similar policy developments were occurring in the United States at the time. With the policy of termination, the US government terminated the status of American Indians in an attempt to assimilate them. Like the White Paper in Canada, this prompted strong protest from American Indian tribes. Cobb, *Native Activism;* S. Smith, *Hippies, Indians.*
127 Weaver, *Making Canadian Indian Policy,* 5.
128 Ibid.
129 McFarlane, *Brotherhood to Nationhood,* 108–9.
130 Charlie, "Grand Chief Rose Charlie."
131 Turner, *This Is Not a Peace Pipe,* 15.
132 Miller, *Skyscrapers Hide the Heavens,* 224; McFarlane, *Brotherhood to Nationhood,* 108–21.
133 Morris, *The Treaties,* 96. This phrase, which appears in the records of treaty negotiations between the Queen's representatives and Canadian First Nations, symbolizes the perpetual and binding relationship between the treaty parties.
134 Boldt, *Surviving as Indians,* 22. See also McFarlane, *Brotherhood to Nationhood,* 108–21; Miller, *Skyscrapers Hide the Heavens,* 222–24.
135 Turner, *This Is Not a Peace Pipe,* 15.
136 Various amendments to the act have been made since its inception in 1876, including intervention in band governance procedures (1884 and 1920); the prohibition of religious ceremonies (1885); and prohibiting Indigenous people covered by the act from hiring lawyers to pursue land claims (1927–51).

137 Cardinal, *The Unjust Society*, 1. Using this phrase to describe the ideology of Minister of Indian Affairs Jean Chrétien and Deputy Minister John A. Macdonald concerning Indigenous peoples, Cardinal was playing off General Phil Sheridan's statement on exterminationist American Indian policy: "The only good Indian is a dead Indian." This phrase is also reproduced in Wolfe, "Settler Colonialism," 397.

138 Weaver, *Making Canadian Indian Policy*, 5; Turner, *This Is Not a Peace Pipe*, 27; Miller, *Skyscrapers Hide the Heavens*, 230–35; Woolford, *Between Justice and Certainty*.

139 Weaver, *Making Canadian Indian Policy*, 3.

140 Guerin interview, 16 April 2013; Terry interview, 30 August 2012; Jules interview; Manuel interview, 14 August 2012; Saddleman interview.

141 Jules interview; Sioliya interview; Ware interview; Wahmeesh interview, 28 June 2012.

142 Hawthorn, *A Survey of the Contemporary Indians*.

143 Indian Association of Alberta, *Citizens Plus*, 2.

144 URC, Minutes of the Union of BC Indian Chiefs Second Annual Convention, 16–21 November 1970, Vancouver.

145 Union of BC Indian Chiefs, *A Declaration of Indian Rights: The BC Indian Position Paper*, 17 November 1970, https://d3n8a8pro7vhmx.cloudfront.net/ubcic/pages/1440/attachments/original/1484861419/3_1970_11_17_DeclarationOfIndianRightsTheBCIndianPositionPaper_web_sm.pdf?1484861419.

146 Ware interview.

147 Carlson, *The Power of Place;* Carlson, *A Stó:lō–Coast Salish Historical Atlas;* Ignace and Ignace, *Secwépemc People, Land, and Laws*.

Chapter 2: Authority

1 Union of British Columbia Indian Chiefs Resource Centre (hereafter URC), Minutes of the Union of BC Indian Chiefs General Assembly Held at Evergreen Hall, Chilliwack, BC, 21 April 1975; URC, video recordings of the Union of BC Indian Chiefs General Assembly Held at Evergreen Hall, Chilliwack, BC, 21 April 1975 and 23 April 1975.

2 URC, "Union of BC Indian Chiefs Constitution," Minutes of the Union of BC Indian Chiefs Second Annual Convention, 16–21 November 1970, Vancouver.

3 Library and Archives Canada (hereafter LAC), RG 10, box 2, file 978/24-2-12 (part 1), Union of British Columbia Indian Chiefs, 1973–1976, Union of BC Indian Chiefs, memorandum, 6 May 1971.

4 The male-dominated nature of Indigenous politics has been documented elsewhere. See, for example, Fiske, "The Womb Is to the Nation."

5 URC, Minutes of the Union of BC Indian Chiefs Second Annual Convention, 16–21 November 1970.

6 Ibid.; anonymous interview, 25 June 2013.

7 URC, Minutes of the Union of BC Indian Chiefs Second Annual Convention, 16–21 November 1970.

8 Rocky Amos, "Community Voices Too Seldom Heard," *Nesika: The Voice of BC Indians* 2, no. 8 (1973): 3.

9 URC, Minutes of the Union of BC Indian Chiefs General Assembly Held at Evergreen Hall, Chilliwack, BC, 21 April 1975.

10 University of British Columbia, Rare Books and Special Collections, box 5, file 5-1, Letters – Incoming to B.C. Native Women's Society and Native Women's Association of Canada, 1973–1976, letter from Hattie Ferguson, North West Indian Cultural Centre, to Kitty Maracle, 12 February 1974.

11 URC, Minutes of the Union of BC Indian Chiefs General Assembly Held at Evergreen Hall, Chilliwack, BC, 21 April 1975.

12 URC, Neskonlith Band Council, "Band Council Resolution," in the Information Kit from the Union of BC Indian Chiefs 7th Annual General Assembly, 21–25 April 1975.

13 URC, Minutes of the Union of BC Indian Chiefs General Assembly Held at Evergreen Hall, Chilliwack, BC, 21 April 1975.

14 Ibid.; URC, video recording of the Union of BC Indian Chiefs General Assembly Held at Evergreen Hall, Chilliwack, BC, 23 April 1975 (emphasis added); URC, video recording of the Union of BC Indian Chiefs General Assembly Held at Evergreen Hall, Chilliwack, BC, 21 April 1975. Walkem's use of the pronoun "he" to refer generally to the category of chiefs is telling. Female chiefs were still greatly underrepresented in 1975, but this term also affirms the dominance of male chiefs in Indigenous peoples' political imaginations.

15 On 23 April 1975, Ray Harris noted he was not part of any club and was not a chief or councillor, but wanted to speak. Likewise, Charles Chapman noted he was not a delegate and did not have voting rights. URC, Minutes of the Union of BC Indian Chiefs General Assembly Held at Evergreen Hall, Chilliwack, BC, 23 April 1975.

16 Ware interview, 20 August 2012.

17 "Indian Women Call for Prompt Action: Men Don't Understand," *Native Voice* 22, no. 5 (1968): 1–2; Sioliya interview, 25 June 2012.

18 Ouellette, *The Fourth World*, 30–31.

19 Jamieson, "Sex Discrimination and the Indian Act," 126.

20 "Membership Is a Band Affair," *Nesika: The Voice of BC Indians* 1, no. 5 (1973): 2. Concern over strained resources with the potential influx of reinstated women to communities was part of a wider trend. See Janovicek, "'Assisting Our Own,'" 59.

21 "Membership Is a Band Affair," 2.

22 Ibid.

23 "Native Women's Rights Dominate Homemakers' Annual Conference," *Nesika: The Voice of BC Indians* 2, no. 6 (1973): 4.

24 "Major Surgery Needed Now" (editorial), *Nesika: The Voice of BC Indians* 2, no. 7 (1973): 3 and 12.

25 URC, Kit Materials from the Union of BC Indian Chiefs 6th Annual General Assembly, 23–25 April 1974.

26 Ibid. (emphasis added).

27 Jamieson, "Sex Discrimination and the Indian Act," 126.

28 Charlie interview, 3 June 1998; Sioliya interview; "Homemaker President Urges Union of All Chiefs," *Indian Voice* 9, no. 6 (1977): 2–3; "Moccasin Miles," *Indian Voice* 1, no. 2 (1969): 8; "Moccasin Miles," *Indian Voice* 2, no. 4 (1970): 11; Charlie, "Grand Chief Rose Charlie."

29 LAC, RG 10, box 2, file 901/1-8, Indian Act, letter from Rose Charlie to Judd Buchanan, minister of Indian Affairs, 28 October 1974.

30 Jules interview.

31 Eneas interview, 3 June 2012; anonymous interview.

Chapter 3: Money

1 Guerin interview, 16 April 2013. For more information on Indigenous longshoremen in British Columbia, see Parnaby, "'The Best Men."

2 Manuel and Posluns, *The Fourth World*, 285.

3 Rouse, "'We Seek to Know,'" 96–97; Judi Bernstein, Peggy Morton, Linda Seese, and Myrna Wood, "Sisters, Brothers, Lovers ... Listen ..." (pamphlet) (Boston: New England Free Press, 1967).

4 Union of British Columbia Indian Chiefs Resource Centre (hereafter URC), Union of BC Indian Chiefs 5th Annual General Assembly Information Kit, 1973; URC, Minutes of the Union of BC Indian Chiefs Second Annual Convention, 16–21 November 1970.

5 Jules interview, 12 June 2012; URC, Minutes of the Indian Chiefs of British Columbia Conference, 17–22 November 1969; "Moccasin Miles," *Indian Voice* 1, no. 2 (1969): 8.

6 A few years later, when Marge Kelly became a councillor, she began receiving $35 per day as an honorarium from the UBCIC and subsidies for accommodations. These honorariums increased in the mid-1970s, a time that corresponded with the UBCIC's financial stability. Interestingly, Guerin recalled receiving money from his band, while Kelly explained that her band did not provide any funds. Kelly interview, 3 May 2012.

7 Manuel and Posluns, *The Fourth World,* 85.

8 Antoine interview, 5 June 2013.

9 "First Citizen's Fund," *Unity: Bulletin of the Union of British Columbia Indian Chiefs* 1, no. 1 (1970): 11–13.

10 Million, *Therapeutic Nations,* 18–19.

11 Tennant, *Aboriginal Peoples and Politics;* Drees, *The Indian Association of Alberta;* Coulthard, *Red Skin, White Masks.*

12 Ramos, "Aboriginal Protest," 76–77.

13 "First Citizen's Fund," 11–13; Clément, *Canada's Rights Revolution,* 33, 85–86.

14 Ware interview, 20 August 2012; Guerin interview, 16 April 2013; Tennant, *Aboriginal Peoples and Politics,* 168.

15 URC, Minutes of the Union of BC Indian Chiefs General Assembly, 1973–1975; Ramos, "Aboriginal Protest," 77.

16 Tennant, *Aboriginal Peoples and Politics,* 168.

17 Department of Indian Affairs, *Annual Report, Fiscal Year 1974–1975* (Ottawa: Information Canada, 1975), 33.

18 Ibid., 35.

19 Pennier interview with author, 25 July 2012; Eneas interview, 3 June 2012; Ware interview; Antoine interview. Pennier noted that one challenge to providing travel funding was that chiefs had to submit receipts for reimbursement. He explained that this was a foreign concept to many of them and caused some difficulties.

20 Manuel and Posluns, *The Fourth World,* 31.

21 Clément, *Canada's Rights Revolution,* 33, 85–86.

22 Eneas interview; Guerin interview, 16 April 2013; Saddleman interview, 7 February 2015; Terry interview, 30 August 2012; URC, Minutes of the Union of BC Indian Chiefs Sixth General Assembly, Williams Lake, BC, 23 April 1974. Andie Diane Palmer also discusses this general trend in the late 1960s of transferring services from Indian Affairs to bands. Andie Diane Palmer, *Maps of Experience: The Anchoring of Land to Story in Secwepemc Discourse* (Toronto: University of Toronto Press, 2005), 51.

23 Guerin interview, 16 April 2013.

24 URC, Lou Demerais, "1974 Annual Report as Presented to the Seventh Annual General Assembly, Chilliwack, 21–25 April 1975," in the Annual General Assembly Information Kit.

25 Pennier interview with author, 25 July 2012.

26 Mandell interview, 12 March 2012.

27 Million, *Therapeutic Nations,* 19; URC, Minutes of the Union of BC Indian Chiefs Annual Meetings, 1971–1974.

28 URC, Union of BC Indian Chiefs, *A Declaration of Indian Rights: The BC Indian Position Paper,* 17 November 1970, 8.

29 URC, Minutes of the Sixth Annual General Meeting, 1974, Williams Lake, BC, 24 April 1974.

30 Library and Archives Canada (hereafter LAC), RG 10, vol. 3, box 2, file 901-1-10, Indian Affairs Branch – Band Council Resolution, 3 March 1974, Liaison – Financial Advisory Services for Indian Bands, 1/1975–10/1976.

31 Ibid., letter from Chief Dan Michell to Larry Wight, regional director, 12 June 1975.

32 The UBCIC office moved quite frequently. Activists' accounts reveal that the offices were first established on the S̲k̲wx̲wú7mesh (Squamish) reserve in North Vancouver, then moved to West 12th Street and Arbutus in Vancouver, and then onto the xʷməθkʷəy̓əm (Musqueam) reserve. The offices also resided on the Coqualeetza grounds in Stó:lō territory, on West 4th in Vancouver, and today are located on Water Street in Gastown. Saddleman interview; Pennier interview with author, 25 July 2012.

33 Saddleman interview; Pennier interview, 25 July 2012.

34 Pennier interview with author, 25 July 2012; Saddleman interview.

35 Pennier interview with author, 25 July 2012.

36 Ware interview.

37 "First Citizens' Fund," 13–14; Bill Wilson, "Letter," *Unity* 1, no. 1 (1970): 14; Bill Mussell, "Chief's Council Meeting: 13–14 August 1971," *Unity: Bulletin of the Union of British Columbia Indian Chiefs* 1, no. 6 (1971): 5.

38 Chief Dennis Alphonse, "Letter to Minister of DIAND (Chrétien)," *Unity: Bulletin of the Union of British Columbia Indian Chiefs* 1, no. 1 (1970): 9; Bill Wilson, "Letter to Minister of DIAND (Chrétien)," *Unity: Bulletin of the Union of British Columbia Indian Chiefs* 1, no. 1 (1970): 9.

39 "Moricetown Canyon Fishing Ban," *Unity: Bulletin of the Union of British Columbia Indian Chiefs* 1, no. 1 (1970): 10.

40 Mandell interview.

41 "Reservations on Credit," *Unity: Bulletin of the Union of British Columbia Indian Chiefs* 1, no. 1 (1970): 8.

42 Ware interview.

43 Ibid.; Antoine interview; Zirnhelt, "The Caribou Tribal Council," 36.

44 Antoine interview.

45 Guerin interview, 16 April 2013.

46 URC, Minutes of the Union of BC Indian Chiefs Sixth Annual Meeting, Williams Lake, BC, 23 April 1974.

47 Guerin interview, 16 April 2013.

48 URC, Minutes of the Union of BC Indian Chiefs General Assembly Held at Evergreen Hall, Chilliwack, BC, 22 April 1975.

49 Indian Affairs Branch, Department of Citizenship and Immigration, *Indian News*, 1954–69.

50 URC, Minutes of the Union of BC Indian Chiefs, Annual General Assemblies, 1969–1976; Kelly interview.

51 Compiled from data in LAC, RG 10, box 2, Indian Homemakers' Association of British Columbia, file 901/24-2-5 (part 2), Basic Minimum Budget, 1976; box 1, file 901/24-24-1-12 (part 2), Union of British Columbia Indian Chiefs, Union of BC Indian Chiefs Budget Proposal, 1976.

52 Wahmeesh interview, 28 June 2012.

53 Ibid.

54 Sioliya interview, 25 June 2012.

55 Ibid.

56 G. McKevitt, "Women Leaders Emerge among Nootkas," *Nesika: The Voice of BC Indians* 3, no. 3 (1974): 7.

57 Kelly interview; Marge Kelly, telephone conversation, 30 April 2012.

58 Kelly interview.

59 Ibid. Kelly continues to hold this opinion even though she has been involved in community initiatives and organizations regarding Indigenous health and access to services.

60 Springer, "Black Feminists Respond"; Kimberly Springer, "The Interstitial Politics of Black Feminist Organizations," *Meridians* 1, no. 2 (2001): 155–56.

61 LAC, RG 10, box 1, file 901/242-12 (part 2), UBCIC Budget Proposal to the Department of the Secretary of State, 1976–1977.

62 Eneas interview; Guerin interview, 16 April 2013; URC, Minutes of the Union of BC Indian Chiefs, 1972–1975.

63 LAC, RG 10, box 1, file 901/242-12 (part 2), UBCIC Budget Proposal to the Department of the Secretary of State, 1976–1977. The $500 per month honorariums for the executive council were introduced in 1974 and lasted only until funding was rejected in April 1975. URC, minutes of the Union of BC Indian Chiefs General Assembly Held at Evergreen Hall, Chilliwack, BC, 23 April 1975. The operating budget for the UBCIC varied year to year according to levels of government funding. In 1971, the organization proposed a budget of $3.6 million, while in 1976 a mere $275,000. This gap resulted from the UBCIC's decision in April 1975 to reject government funding as a political strategy to achieve political and economic independence. LAC, RG 10, box 1, file 901/242-12 (part 2), UBCIC Budget Proposal to the Department of the Secretary of State, 1976–1977; URC, Minutes of the Union of BC Indian Chiefs, 1972–1975; Tennant, *Aboriginal Peoples and Politics,* 158.

64 Antoine interview; Eneas interview; URC, Minutes of the Union of BC Indian Chiefs, 1973–1975; Tennant, *Aboriginal Peoples and Politics,* 185.

65 Eneas interview.

66 Antoine interview; Eneas interview; URC, Minutes of the Union of BC Indian Chiefs, 1973–1975.

67 Antoine interview.

68 Antoine interview; Guerin interview, 16 April 2013.

69 URC, Minutes of the Union of BC Indian Chiefs General Assembly Held at Evergreen Hall, Chilliwack, BC, 23 April 1975.

70 Harmon, *Rich Indians,* 2–15.

71 Eneas interview; Christian interview, 4 June 2013.

72 Guerin interview, 16 April 2013.

PART 2: A PHILOSOPHICAL REVOLUTION AND COMPETING NATIONALISMS

1 Yakweakwioose is one of the six bands of the Ts'elxwéyeqw (Chilliwack) Tribe; the others are Skowkale, Skway, Soowahlie, Squiala, and Tzeachten. Carlson, "Indian Reservations," in *A Stó:lō–Coast Salish Historical Atlas,* 94–95; Ts'elxwéyeqw Tribe website, http://tselxweyeqw.ca/UXTZO/index.php.

2 The four ancestors are Th'eláchiyatel, Yexwéylem, Síyémches, and Wíli:léq.

3 Carlson, *You Are Asked to Witness,* 15.

4 Union of British Columbia Indian Chiefs Resource Centre (hereafter URC), Minutes of the Union of BC Indian Chiefs General Assembly Held at Evergreen Hall, Chilliwack, BC, 21 April 1975.

Chapter 4: Refusal

1 Union of British Columbia Indian Chiefs Resource Centre (hereafter URC), Minutes of the Union of BC Indian Chiefs General Assembly Held at Evergreen Hall, Chilliwack, BC, 22 April 1975.

2   Bradley G. Shreve, *Red Power Rising: The National Indian Youth Council and the Origins of Native Activism* (Norman: University of Oklahoma Press, 2011).

3   URC, Minutes of the Union of BC Indian Chiefs General Assembly Held at Evergreen Hall, Chilliwack, BC, 24 April 1975; Manuel interview, 14 August 2012; Ware interview, 20 August 2012; Tennant, *Aboriginal Peoples and Politics,* 179. The Grants to Bands program was also known as Band Core funding. URC, Lou Demerais, "1974 Annual Report as presented to the Seventh Annual General Assembly, Chilliwack, 21–25 April 1975," in the Annual General Assembly Information Kit; URC, Minutes of the Union of BC Indian Chiefs Sixth General Assembly, Williams Lake, BC, 23 April 1974.

4   Eneas interview, 3 June 2013; Saddleman interview, 7 February 2015; Manuel interview; Ware interview; URC, Minutes of the Union of BC Indian Chiefs General Assembly Held at Evergreen Hall, Chilliwack, BC, 24 April 1975; URC, Lou Demerais, "1974 Annual Report."

5   Manuel interview.

6   Kelly interview, 3 May 2012; Saddleman interview; Pennier interview with author, 25 July 2012; Terry interview, 30 August 2012; Guerin interview, 31 May 2013.

7   Tl'azt'en Nation was formerly known as the Stuart-Trembleur Band. The band is a member of the Dakelh (Carrier) tribal group and is located on the north shore of Stuart Lake near Tache River. Tl'azt'en Nation webpage, http://tlaztennation.ca, accessed 26 June 2018.

8   Library and Archives Canada (hereafter LAC), RG 10, vol. 1994-95/412, box 1, file 987/24-2-12, news release, Bulletin #3, 5 May 1975; URC, Minutes of the Union of BC Indian Chiefs General Assembly Held at Evergreen Hall, Chilliwack, BC, 24 April 1975.

9   URC, Minutes of the Union of BC Indian Chiefs General Assembly Held at Evergreen Hall, Chilliwack, BC, 24 April 1975.

10 Diitiid7aa7tx (Ditidaht) First Nation, also known as Nitinat, is a member of the Nuu-chah-nulth tribal group and is located on the west coast of Vancouver Island.

11 LAC, RG 10, vol. 1994-95/412, box 1, file 987/24-2-12, news release, Bulletin #3, 5 May 1975; URC, Minutes of the Union of BC Indian Chiefs General Assembly Held at Evergreen Hall, Chilliwack, BC, 25 April 1975; Tennant, *Aboriginal Peoples and Politics,* 168.

12 Pennier interview.

13 URC, Minutes of the Union of BC Indian Chiefs General Assembly Held at Evergreen Hall, Chilliwack, BC, 25 April 1975.

14 Ibid.

15 Kelly interview; Guerin interview, 31 May 2013.

16 Kelly interview.

17 Guerin interview; Eneas interview; Joe interview, 5 June 2013.

18 LAC, RG 10, vol. 1994–95/412, box 1, file 987/24-2-12 (part 1), Union of BC Indian Chiefs, news release, Bulletin #3, 5 May 1975; URC, Minutes of the Union of British Columbia Indian Chiefs Annual General Assemblies, 1972–1981.

19 URC, video recording of Union of BC Indian Chiefs General Assembly Evergreen Hall, Chilliwack, BC, 24 April 1975; URC, Minutes of the Union of BC Indian Chiefs General Assembly Held at Evergreen Hall, Chilliwack, BC, 25 April 1975. St'uxwtews (Bonaparte) First Nation is a Secwépemc community located near Chase, BC.

20 URC, Minutes of the Union of BC Indian Chiefs General Assembly Held at Evergreen Hall, Chilliwack, BC, 24 April 1975.

21 Ron Rose, "180 Indians Lose Jobs in Happy Mass Layoff," *Vancouver Sun,* 30 April 1975, 25.

22 Ware interview.

23 Ibid.

24 Pennier interview.

25 Saddleman interview.

26 Joe interview. Grand Chief Percy Joe has been chief of the Scw'exmx since 1971, when he was thirty years old.

27 "Philip Paul: You Can't Undue [sic] Life Time of Paternalism in Short Time," *Indian Voice* 7, no. 6 (1975): 10–11; LAC, RG 10, box 1, file 987/24-2-12 (part 1), Union of BC Indian Chiefs, 1972–1981, news release, Bulletin #3, 5 May 1975.

28 LAC, RG 10, box 1, Vol. 2, file 901/24-2-12 (part 2), Union of BC Indian Chiefs, 1975–77, news release, Bulletin #6, 11 June 1975.

29 *Owikeno* is also spelled *Oweekeno*. The Oweekeno are from Rivers Inlet in the Bella Coola District and today are known as the Wuikinuxv Nation.

30 LAC, RG 10, box 1, file 901/1-1-1-1 (part 1), Office Phaseouts, May–September 1975, telex from Owikeno Council of Chiefs to Judd Buchanan, minister of Indian Affairs, 16 May 1975 (emphasis added).

31 Caribou Tribal Council member bands are Alexandria, Alexis Creek, Alkali Lake, Anaham, Canim Lake, Canoe Creek, Kluskus, Nazko, Nemaiah Valley, Quesnel, Soda Creek, Stone, Toosey, Ulkatcho, Williams Lake. LAC, RG 10, box 1, file 901/1-1-1-1 (part 1), Office Phaseouts, May–September 1975, letter from Dave Somerville, Caribou Tribal Council administrator, to Judd Buchanan, minister of Indian Affairs, 22 June 1975.

32 Ibid.

33 The bands that forwarded BCRs demanding that Indian Affairs transfer control of capital and revenue funds included Nazko, Kluskus, Stone, Toosey, Alexis Creek, Quesnel, and Alkali Lake. See LAC, RG 10, box 1, file 901/1-1-1-1 (part 1), Office Phaseouts, May–September 1975 for the following BCRs: Kluskus Band, 21 May 1975; Nazko Band, 21 May 1975; Toosey Band, 6 June 1975; Stone Band, 22 May 1975; Alexis Creek Band, 27 May 1975; Quesnel Band, 18 June 1975.

34 LAC, RG 10, box 1, file 901/1-1-1-1 (part 1), Office Phaseouts, May–September 1975, letter from Judd Buchanan to Mrs. Mary Stamp, Alexandria band councillor, 17 July 1975, and letter from Dave Somerville, Caribou Tribal Council administrator, to Judd Buchanan, minister of Indian Affairs, 22 June 1975.

35 LAC, RG 10, box 1, file 901/1-1-1-1 (part 1), Office Phaseouts, May–September 1975, telexes from Rose Charlie, Indian Homemakers' Association, to Judd Buchanan, minister of Indian Affairs, 27 and 30 June 1975; telex from Louise Louis, Okanagan Indian Reserve, to Judd Buchanan, minister of Indian Affairs, 29 June 1975; and letter from Judd Buchanan to Rose Charlie, 28 July 1975.

36 LAC, RG 10, box 1, file 901/1-1-1-1 (part 1), Office Phaseouts, May–September 1975, letter from Mrs. Mary Stamp to Judd Buchanan, 24 June 1975.

37 LAC, RG 10, box 1, file 901/1-1-1-1 (part 1), Office Phaseouts, May–September 1975, telex from Chief Samson Robinson, Uchucklesaht Band, to Judd Buchanan, 3 July 1975; press release, Lakes District Council of Chiefs, 5 July 1975; and telex from Jim Stelkia, Osoyoos Band, to Judd Buchanan, 18 June 1975.

38 LAC, RG 10, box 1, file 901/1-1-1-1 (part 1), Office Phaseouts, May–September 1975, telex from Chief J. Lawrence, Ucluelet Band, to Judd Buchanan, 27 June 1975; telex from Chief Samson Robinson, Uchucklesaht Band, to Judd Buchanan, 3 July 1975; telex from Hesquiat Band Council to Judd Buchanan, 27 June 1975; telex from Chief Joe Frank and Howard Tom, Clayoquot Band Council, to Judd Buchanan, 27 June 1975.

39 LAC, RG 10, box 1, file 901/1-1-1-1 (part 1), Office Phaseouts, May–September 1975, telex from Jim Stelkia, Osoyoos Band, to Judd Buchanan, 18 June 1975.

40 LAC, RG 10, box 7, file 901/24-2-2254 (part 4), Indian Homemakers' Association, 1968–1979, Travel Information and Resource Unit Program, 1 April 1979–31 March 1980.

41 "Innocent Caught in Cross Fire," *Indian Voice* 7, no. 6 (1975): 13.

42 Ron Rose, "Leader of Indian Conference Asks Protection for Delegates," *Vancouver Sun,* 19 June 1975, 1–2.

43 LAC, RG 10, box 1, file 901/1-1-1-1 (part 1), Office Phaseouts, May-September 1975, minutes of the meeting of Homemaker Foster Parents, 21 July 1975.

44 "Rose Charlie against UBCIC Decision," *Indian Voice* 7, no. 6 (1975): 1–2.

45 Ibid.

46 "From the Editor's Chair," *Indian Voice* 7, no. 6 (1975): 4.

47 "Rose Charlie against UBCIC Decision."

48 LAC, RG 10, box 1, file 901/1-1-1-1 (part 1), Office Phaseouts, May-September 1975, telex from Sophie Thomas, Stoney Creek Homemakers' Club, to Judd Buchanan, 27 June 1975.

49 LAC, RG 10, box 1, file 901/1-1-1-1 (part 1), Office Phaseouts, May-September 1975, telex from Chief J. Lawrence Jack, Ucluelet Band, to Judd Buchanan, 27 June 1975; telex from Chief Samson Robinson, Uchucklesaht Band, to Judd Buchanan, 3 July 1975; telex from Hesquiat Band Council to Judd Buchanan, 27 June 1975; telex from Chief Joe Frank and Howard Tom, Clayoquot Band Council, to Judd Buchanan, 27 June 1975.

50 LAC, RG 10, box 1, file 901/1-1-1-1 (part 1), Office Phaseouts, May-September 1975, telex from Ernest David, Westcoast Fishermen, to Judy Sesullion, secretary of the minister of Indian Affairs, 27 June 1975.

51 "Rose Charlie against UBCIC Decision"; LAC, RG 10, box 1, file 901/1-1-1-1 (part 1), Office Phaseouts, 5/1975–9/1975, telex from Rose Charlie, president of Indian Homemakers' Association, to Judd Buchanan, minister of Indian Affairs, 30 June 1975.

52 LAC, RG 10, box 2, file 901/24-2-5 (part 2), Indian Homemakers' of British Columbia, letter from Rose Charlie to F.J. Walchli, director general of Indian Affairs, 10 November 1976.

53 Ibid., letter from Rose Charlie to F.J. Walchli, director general of Indian Affairs, 28 December 1976.

54 "Mother Given Run Around," *Indian Voice* 7, no. 6 (1975): 13.

55 LAC, RG10, box 1, file 901/1-1-1-1 (part 1), Office Phaseouts, May-September 1975, letter from Agnes Dick to Judd Buchanan, February 1975.

56 LAC, RG 10, box 1, file 901/1-1-1-1 (part 1), Office Phaseouts, May-September 1975, letter from Rose Charlie to Larry Wight, 31 July 1975.

57 LAC, RG 10, box 1, file 901/1-1-1-1 (part 1), Office Phaseouts, May-September 1975, telex from Rose Charlie, president of the Indian Homemakers' Association, to Judd Buchanan, minister of Indian Affairs, 27 June 1975.

58 Ibid., telex from Rose Charlie, president of the Indian Homemakers' Association, to Judd Buchanan, minister of Indian Affairs, 30 June 1975.

59 LAC, RG 10, box 1, file 901/1-1-1-1 (part 1), Office Phaseouts, May-September 1975, telex from Judd Buchanan to Rose Charlie, 28 July 1975.

60 "Rose Charlie against UBCIC decision," *Indian Voice* 7, no. 6 (1975): 1–2; "Homemaker President Urges Union of All Chiefs," *Indian Voice* 9, no. 6 (1977): 2–3.

61 LAC, RG 10, box 1, file 901/1-1-1-1 (part 1), Office Phaseouts, May-September 1975, minutes of the Homemakers' Foster Parents meeting, West Coast District, 21 July 1975.

62 Rose, "Leader of Indian Conference Asks Protection"; "From the Editor's Chair," *Indian Voice* 7, no. 6 (1975): 4.

63 Rose, "Leader of Indian Conference Asks Protection."

64 See Janovicek, "'Assisting Our Own.'" For additional information on Indigenous women and violence, see Culhane, "Their Spirits Live within Us"; Sherene H. Razack, *Race, Space, and the Law: Unmapping a White Settler Society* (Toronto: Between the Lines, 2002). Stó:lō activist Lee Maracle also has spoken about the prevalence of lateral violence within Indigenous communities as a result of colonization. Explaining her own feminist awakening in the early

1980s, Maracle spoke of finally recognizing the internal colonization of Indigenous women by their men, who saw them as "vessels for male gratification" and stoic targets for male violence. Lee Maracle, *I Am Woman*.

65 LAC, RG 10, box 1, file 901/1-1-1-1 (part 1), Office Phaseouts, May-September 1975, telex from Rose Charlie, president of the Indian Homemakers' Association, to Judd Buchanan, minister of Indian Affairs, 27 June 1975 (emphasis added).

66 LAC, RG 10, box 1, file 901/1-1-1-1 (part 1), Office Phaseouts, May-September 1975, telex from Interested Mothers and Grandmothers, c/o Louise Louis to the minister of Indian Affairs, 26 June 1975.

67 LAC, RG 10, box 1, file 901/1-1-1-1 (part 1), Office Phaseouts, May-September 1975, telex from Jenny Marchand et al. to Judd Buchanan, 28 June 1975.

68 URC, minutes of the Union of BC Indian Chiefs General Assembly Held at Evergreen Hall, Chilliwack, BC, 25 April 1975.

69 Ibid.

Chapter 5: Protest

1 Ron Rose, "Indian Chiefs Warn of 'Militant May,'" *Vancouver Sun*, 23 April 1975, 44.

2 Alvin M. Josephy Jr., Joane Nagel, and Troy Johnson, eds., *Red Power: The American Indians' Fight for Freedom*, 2nd ed. (Lincoln: University of Nebraska Press, 1999), 1–2. For these scholars, Red Power is strictly a 1970s phenomenon with a limited geospatial focus. Relatedly, Daniel Cobb and Loretta Fowler acknowledged this periodization and agree that Alcatraz, the Trail of Broken Treaties March, Wounded Knee, and the Longest March traced the evolution of Red Power. While approving of the general definition of Red Power, however, Cobb and Fowler lament its overall dominance, suggesting that Red Power has come to symbolize the era and therefore overpower other forms of Indigenous activism. Cobb and Fowler, eds. *Beyond Red Power*, x–xii.

3 S. Smith, *Hippies, Indians*, 4–6.

4 "Declaration of Indian Purpose, American Indian Chicago Conference, June 13–20, 1961," in Josephy, Nagel, and Johnson, *Red Power*, 13–15.

5 Shreve, "'From Time Immemorial.'"

6 Davis, *Survival Schools;* S. Smith, *Hippies, Indians*.

7 H. Adams, *Prison of Grass*, 166–68.

8 Rutherford, "Canada's Other Red Scare," 80–81.

9 Indigenous authors Lee Maracle and Jeannette Armstrong wrote fictional accounts of political activities in British Columbia, and Maracle spoke specifically about the emergence and activities of NARP in Vancouver. Lee Maracle, *Bobbi Lee;* Jeannette Armstrong, *Slash*. For more on Red Power in Canada, see Palmer, *Canada's 1960s;* Palmer, "'Indians of All Tribes,'" 193. Rutherford suggests that Red Power arrived in Canada by the 1970s. Rutherford, "Canada's Other Red Scare," 79.

10 Bobb, "Red Power and Socialist Study."

11 Union of British Columbia Indian Chiefs Resource Centre (hereafter URC), "First Meeting of BC Chiefs Conference Planning Committee," 18 and 19 October 1969, Kamloops, BC, in Minutes of the Indian Chiefs of British Columbia Conference, 17–22 November 1969.

12 Josephy, Nagel, and Johnson, *Red Power*.

13 Davis, *Survival Schools*, 31–32.

14 URC, Minutes of the Union of BC Indian Chiefs General Assembly at Evergreen Hall in Chilliwack, BC, 24 April 1975.

15 Ibid.

16 "Indian Group Quits Occupied Hostel," *Vancouver Sun,* 29 April 1975, 10; URC, Minutes of the Union of BC Indian Chiefs General Assembly Held at Evergreen Hall, Chilliwack, BC, 21 April 1975.

17 URC, Minutes of the Union of BC Indian Chiefs General Assembly Held at Evergreen Hall, Chilliwack, BC, 21 April 1975.

18 Antoine interview, 5 June 2013.

19 Antoine interview; Joe interview, 5 June 2013; Terry interview, 30 August 2012; Eneas interview, 3 June 2012; Wayne Christian interview, 4 June 2013; Pennier interview with author, 25 July 2012.

20 S. Smith, *Hippies, Indians,* 7.

21 Palmer, *Canada's 1960s,* especially Chapters 6, 8, and 9.

22 Ron Rose, "Indians End Sit-in at Office, Start Information Picketing," *Vancouver Sun,* 12 May 1975, 1 and 2; Pennier interview with author, 25 July 2012.

23 Langston, "American Indian Women's Activism," 115.

24 Guerin interview, 16 April 2013.

25 Ibid.

26 Antoine interview.

27 Clarence, Jeanette, and Delores Jules, personal conversation with author, Tk'emlúps te Secwépemc, Kamloops, BC, 12 June 2012; Jeanette Jules, personal conversation with author, Tk'emlúps te Secwépemc, Kamloops, BC, 8 May 2016; Ignace and Ignace, *Secwépemc People, Land, and Laws.*

28 Manuel interview, 14 August 2012; Sioliya interview, 25 June 2012; Wahmeesh interview, 28 June 2012.

29 S̲k̲w̲x̲wú7mesh leader Andrew Paull was instrumental in the Allied Tribes in the early twentieth century, along with Nimpkish leader James Sewid. Sewid continued to be involved in politics, including the UBCIC, and was present at the Chilliwack meeting. In fact, at this meeting, Sewid, then an Elder, spoke out in favour of the decision to reject funding, noting how the funding issue had negatively influenced the Allied Tribes, contributing to their downfall. Sewid also lamented how funding had turned his community into a welfare village because people could not escape government bureaucracy. Antoine interview; Guerin interview, 16 April 2013; Moses interview, 11 June 2013. See also URC, Minutes of the Union of BC Indian Chiefs General Assembly Held at Evergreen Hall, Chilliwack, BC, 25 April 1975; Ron Rose, "BC Indian Chiefs Vote to Reject Government Aid," *Vancouver Sun,* 25 April 1975, 33. Nisga'a leader James Gosnell was similarly involved in provincial politics and was especially active in the Nisga'a Tribal Council.

30 URC, Minutes of the Union of BC Indian Chiefs General Assembly Held at Evergreen Hall, Chilliwack, BC, 22 April 1975.

31 URC, Minutes of the Union of BC Indian Chiefs General Assembly Held at Evergreen Hall, Chilliwack, BC, 25 April 1975.

32 "High Court Test Case Sought after 2nd Indian Fish-in," *Indian Voice* 2, no. 8 (1970): 1–2.

33 In 1973, Cowichan members also staged a week-long "Salmon for Survival" demonstration on the Quamichan reserve to agitate for their resource rights. The event was peaceful but included building illegal traditional weirs to catch salmon. The Cowichan maintained – as they had throughout the nineteenth century – that they did not recognize state-sanctioned fishing practices or regulations. Department of Fisheries records between 1893 and 1908 expose how state agencies created regulations against Indian weir fishing, particularly among the Cowichan. Cowichan members consistently resisted these, citing their traditional rights, including the right to fish using traditional weirs. These records also reveal instances where officials from the Department of Indian Affairs defended Cowichan fishermen against

Fisheries Department regulations and declared that the department was encroaching on Indian rights. Library and Archives Canada (hereafter LAC), RG 23, Department of Fisheries, vol. 583 (part 1), Fishing Regulations, Barricades; vol. 678 (part 1); vol. 1467 (part 1), Sturgeon Fishing – Complaints by Indians, 1894–1895; vol. 1467 (part 1), Fishery Regulations – Judgment re: trespass on federal property.

34 The Deep Creek fish-in ended with seven chiefs facing charges. Among these were Chief Noll Derrickson of Westbank First Nation, Chief Murray Alexis of the Vernon Band, and Chief James Stelkia of Osoyoos. These leaders would continue to play key roles in direct action across the province.

35 Dummitt, *The Manly Modern*, 9–10.

36 Clément, *Canada's Rights Revolution*. For more on Indigenous peoples and wage work, see Rolf Knight, *Indians at Work: An Informal History of Native Labour in British Columbia, 1848–1930*, 2nd ed. (Vancouver: New Star Books, 1996); Lutz, *Makúk*; Raibmon, *Authentic Indians;* Parnaby, "'The Best Men.'"

37 D. Harris, *Landing Native Fisheries*. See also C. Harris, *Making Native Space;* Newell, *Tangled Webs of History.*

38 Josephy, Nagel, and Johnson, "The Twenty-Point Proposal of Native Americans on the Trail of Broken Treaties, Washington, DC, October 1972," in *Red Power,* 44–47.

39 URC, summarized minutes, 1974 Sixth General Assembly of the Union of BC Indian Chiefs, Elks Hall, Williams Lake, BC (emphasis added).

40 Ibid.

41 "Real Issues Veiled Says Bonaparte Leader," *Nesika: The Voice of BC Indians* 3, no. 8 (1974): 5.

42 Ticoll and Persky, "Welcome to Ottawa," 16; URC, minutes of the Union of BC Indian Chiefs General Assembly Held at Evergreen Hall, Chilliwack, BC, 21–25 April 1975.

43 "BC Indians Resume Highway Road Block," *Kainai News* 7, no. 10 (1974): 1. AIM members infamously responded to Lakota Elders' calls for support on the Pine Ridge Reservation in South Dakota, which precipitated the Wounded Knee standoff in 1973. Elders explained that local resistance to Tribal Chairman Richard "Dick" Wilson and his goon squad, which had been terrorizing locals, was ineffective, and a militant response from AIM was needed. AIM was also involved in several high-profile trials against non-Indigenous men accused of murdering Indigenous men and women, and arrived to lend support to local communities throughout the trials.

44 The UBCIC's media reported this criticism and the CCNM's reaction: "Real Issues Veiled Says Bonaparte Leader," 5.

45 Cited in ibid., 5.

46 Ibid.

47 G. McKevitt, "Caravan Wants Gov. Action," *Nesika: The Voice of BC Indians* 3, no. 9 (1974): 5.

48 The subsequent arrest of CCNM member Clarence Dennis, however, led Basil to collaborate with the Kenora occupation leader Louis Cameron to arrange for a Native Peoples' Caravan to Ottawa. The caravan also importantly illustrated the deep connections forged across communities throughout the 1970s, as organizers designed the action to publicize the issues Indigenous peoples faced in Canada in terms of securing adequate housing, education, and economic development, and to arrange for the settlement of land claims and the enforcement of treaties. Ticoll and Persky, "Welcome to Ottawa," 16. The 6 September 1974 report from *Kainai News* revealed that Basil's decision to end the blockade was only temporary and that the roadblock was resumed a few days later. "BC Indians Resume Highway Road Block," *Kainai News* 7, no. 10 (1974): 1. See also Kulchyski, "40 Years in Indian Country."

49 Members of the Action Committee included Chief Adam Eneas (Penticton), Chief Victor Adrian (Seton Lake), George Harris (Chemainus), Chief Philip Joe (Squamish), Chief Jim Stelkia (Osoyoos), Jacob Kruger (Penticton), Chief Joe Mathias (Squamish), Howard Wale

(Hazelton), and George Watts (Ts'ishaa7ath). URC, "Report of the Action Committee on McKenna-McBride Cut-Off Lands," in Union of BC Indian Chiefs, Special General Assembly Information Kit, 2–4 April 1975.

50 Ibid.

51 Ibid.

52 URC, Minutes of the Union of BC Indian Chiefs General Assembly at the Evergreen Hall, Chilliwack, BC, 23 April 1975.

53 Ibid.; Eneas interview.

54 URC, Minutes of the Union of BC Indian Chiefs General Assembly at the Evergreen Hall, Chilliwack, BC, 23 April 1975.

55 Ibid.; Saddleman interview.

56 Rose, "Indian Chiefs Warn of 'Militant May,'" 44; URC, Minutes of the Union of BC Indian Chiefs General Assembly Held at Evergreen Hall, Chilliwack, BC, 21–25 April 1975.

57 Ron Rose, "Indians Begin to Beat Their War Drums," *Vancouver Sun*, 24 April 1975, 39.

58 LAC, RG 10, box 1, file 901/1-1-1-1 (part 1), Office Phaseouts, May-September 1975, letter from L.E. Wight, regional director British Columbia Region, to chiefs and councillors of the South Island District, 17 July 1975; letter from Judd Buchanan to Chief Patrick Charleyboy, Caribou Tribal Council, 17 July 1975; letter from Chief Patrick Charleyboy to Prime Minister Pierre Trudeau, 13 May 1975.

59 "Indians Start Sit-in at Interior Offices," *Vancouver Sun*, 1 May 1975, 1–2; Gerard Peters, "From 1969 to 1975: The Movement Is Born," *Nesika: The Voice of BC Indians* 3, no. 13 (1975): 2.

60 Ron Rose, "Alliance Will Honor Indian Picket Lines," *Vancouver Sun*, 26 May 1975, 1–2; P.C. Smith and Warrior, *Like a Hurricane,* 149–68.

61 LAC, RG 10, box 1, file 901/1-1-1-1 (part 1), Office Phaseouts, May-September 1975, telex from Judd Buchanan to Rose Charlie, 10 July 1975; telex from Norm Levi to Judd Buchanan, 8 July 1975; "Indians Start Sit-in at Interior Offices."

62 "Indians Maintain Blockade," *Vancouver Sun*, 5 May 1975, 34; LAC, RG 10, box 1, vol. 2, file 901/24-2-12 (part 2), Union of British Columbia Indian Chiefs, 1975–1977, Union of BC Indian Chiefs news release, Bulletin #5, 20 May 1975; box 1, File 901/1-1-1-1 (part 1), Office Phaseouts, May-September 1975, telex from L.E. Wight to P.B. Lesaux, assistant deputy minister, 5 June 1975; Eneas interview. Band members were also sometimes employed at the district offices. URC, Minutes of the Union of BC Indian Chiefs General Assembly Held at Evergreen Hall, Chilliwack, BC, 25 April 1975.

63 LAC, RG 10, box 1, file 901/1-1-1-1 (part 1), Office Phaseouts, May-September 1975, letter from Larry Wight, regional director, British Columbia Region to P.B. Lesaux, assistant deputy minister, Indian and Eskimo Affairs, 23 June 1975.

64 Rose, "Alliance Will Honor Indian Picket Lines."

65 Peters, "From 1969 to 1975"; "Province Wide Militancy Continues," *Nesika: The Voice of BC Indians* (July 1975): 7; "You've Backed Us Up as Far as We're Going to Go, We're Not Going to Go Back Any Further," *Nesika: The Voice of BC Indians* (July 1975): 4; "RCMP Storm Blockade at Gold River: 'We Saw Real Unity amongst Our People,'" *Nesika: The Voice of BC Indians* (July 1975): 2. The Westbank First Nation is a Syilx (Okanagan) nation situated in West Kelowna. The Gwawaenuk First Nation is a Kwakwaka'wakw nation situated around Port McNeill. The Tl'azt'en Nation is a Dakelh (Carrier) community situated in north-central BC.

66 LAC, RG 10, vol. 2, box 1, file 901/24-2-12 (part 2), V1990-91/045, Union of BC Indian Chiefs news release, Bulletin #6, 11 June 1975.

67 Joe interview, 5 June 2013; LAC, RG 10, vol. 2, box 1, file 901/24-2-12 (part 2), Union of British Columbia Indian Chiefs, 1975–77, news release, Bulletin #5, 20 May 1975; "We're Number 1!" *Nesika: The Voice of BC Indians* (August 1975): 3.

68 Antoine interview; Eneas interview; Joe interview; Moses interview, 11 June 2012; Pennier interview with author, 25 July 2012.

69 LAC, RG 10, box 1, file 901/1-1-1-1 (part 1), Office Phaseouts, May-September 1975, telex from Chief Tony Meyers, Stone Band, and Chief Frank Boucher, Quesnel Band, to Judd Buchanan, 19 June 1975.

70 LAC, RG 10, box 1, file 901/1-1-1-1 (part 1), Office Phaseouts, May-September 1975, telex from Chief Andy Chelsea, Alkali Lake Band, Chief Cathy Patrick, Nazko Band, and Chief Stanley Boyd, Kluskus Indian Band, to Judd Buchanan, 16 June 1975.

71 "Indians Start Sit-in at Interior Offices"; LAC, RG 10, vol. 2, box 1, file 901/24-2-12 (part 2), Union of British Columbia Indian Chiefs, 1975–1977, news release, Bulletin #5, 20 May 1975.

72 LAC, RG 10, box 1, file 901/1-1-1-1 (part 1), Office Phaseouts, May-September 1975, telex from Judd Buchanan to West Coast District chiefs, 16 June 1975.

73 LAC, RG 10, box 1, file 901/1-1-1-1 (part 1), Office Phaseouts, May-September 1975, letter from L.E. Wight, regional director British Columbia Region, to chiefs and councillors of the South Island District, 17 July 1975; letter from Judd Buchanan to Chief Patrick Charleyboy, Caribou Tribal Council, 17 July 1975; letter from Chief Patrick Charleyboy to Prime Minister Pierre Trudeau, 13 May 1975.

74 LAC, RG 10, box 1, file 901/1-1-1-1 (part 1), Office Phaseouts, May-September 1975, band council resolution, Cowichan Band Council, 8 July 1975.

75 LAC, RG 10, box 1, file 901/1-1-1-1 (part 1), Office Phaseouts, May-September 1975, telex from Chief A. Recalma, Qualicum Band, to Judd Buchanan, 4 June 1975.

76 LAC, RG 10, box 1, file 901/1-1-1-1 (part 1), Office Phaseouts, May-September 1975, telex from Judd Buchanan to Rose Charlie, 10 July 1975. See also letter from Judd Buchanan to Councillor Francis Amos, Hesquiat Band, 22 July 1975.

77 LAC, RG 10, box 1, file 901/1-1-1-1 (part 1), Office Phaseouts, May-September 1975, letter from A.M. Cunningham, regional planner, to L.E. Wight, regional director, 26 June 1975.

78 Joe interview; Eneas interview; Wayne Christian interview; LAC, RG 10, box 1, file 901/1-1-1-1 (part 1), Office Phaseouts, May-September 1975, letter from W.E. Millin to all band councils in the Thompson River and Kootenay-Okanagan Districts, 29 September 1975; letter from R.C. Pankhurst, regional superintendent of finance and administration to district supervisor, Kootenay-Okanagan District, 21 August 1975; letter from L.E. Wight to John G. McGilp, 20 August 1975.

79 Mandell interview, 12 March 2012; Rose, "Indians End Sit-in at Office"; Peters, "From 1969 to 1975." This was not the first occupation of the Vancouver office. Protesters occupied this space in 1973 as well. Tennant, *Aboriginal Peoples and Politics,* 174.

80 "Indians Continue Occupation of Downtown Gov't Offices," *Vancouver Sun,* May 10, 1975, 1 and 11. In this article, the *Sun* reporter also used the racialized term "whooping" to describe the protesters' entrance into the building. This term evoked stereotypical and polarized images of buckskin-clad warriors running through the ultra-modern glass office tower, and somewhat overpowered the notion of orderly and valid protest. This and other racially charged terminology demonstrated the stranglehold stereotypes about Indigenous peoples and politics had on British Columbians at that time. These descriptions, which concurrently emphasized images of savagery, orderliness, war, and peace focused on the protesters and method of protest while ignoring the underlying political issues. This placed Indigenous peoples outside the realm of respectable politics.

81 G. McKevitt, "Band Wants to Operate Fishing Co-op," *Nesika: The Voice of BC Indians* 2, no. 9 (1973): 2.

82 "We're Number 1!," 3.

83 Ibid.

84 "We're Number 1!"
85 Rose, "Indians End Sit-in at Office"; Peters, "From 1969 to 1975."
86 P.C. Smith and Warrior, *Like a Hurricane,* 138.
87 Rose, "Alliance Will Honor Indian Picket Lines"; Eneas interview.
88 URC, Minutes of the Union of BC Indian Chiefs General Assembly Held at Evergreen Hall, Chilliwack, BC, 23 April 1975.
89 The porous nature of organizational and geopolitical borders was also visible in Ontario during the Anicinabe Park occupation. In 1974, at Kenora, Ontario, the Ojibway Warrior Society (OWS) used a forty-day armed standoff to unite North American Indigenous peoples in opposition to colonialism. Answering calls for unity, Dennis Banks, one of the founding members of AIM, arrived with other AIM members at a conference organized by the OWS. Banks and the other AIM members were there to lend support to the occupation and the OWS. Rutherford, "Canada's Other Red Scare."
90 LAC, RG 10, vol. 2, box 1, file 901/24-2-12 (part 2), Union of British Columbia Indian Chiefs, 1975–77, news release, Bulletin #5, 20 May 1975.
91 Ibid.
92 "Indians Continue Occupation of Downtown Gov't Offices"; Rose, "Indians End Sit-in at Office."
93 Rose, "Alliance Will Honor Indian Picket Lines."
94 Photo caption, *Nesika: The Voice of BC Indians* 3, no. 13 (1975): 1; Antoine interview; Eneas interview; Joe interview; Sioliya interview; Saddleman interview, 7 February 2015.
95 Rose, "Indians End Sit-in at Office."
96 Ibid.
97 Josephy, Nagel, and Johnson, *Red Power.*
98 Ibid.
99 According to the caption, the image captured "a Native militant at the Bonaparte Reserve near Cache Creek [taking] aim at Vancouver Sun photographer Glenn Baglo, warning him to put down his camera." *Vancouver Sun,* 14 August 1974.
100 McKevitt, "Band Wants to Operate Fishing Co-op."
101 UBCIC records include specific references to four female members of AIM, and video recordings of the meeting indicate that there were more. URC, Minutes of the Union of BC Indian Chiefs General Assembly Held at Evergreen Hall, Chilliwack, BC, 23 April 1975.
102 Ibid., 22 April 1975.
103 Ibid.; Eneas interview.
104 Christopher Dummitt, Tina Loo, and Mary-Ellen Kelm likewise explored this notion of rational risk-taking as a significant component of modern masculinities. Dummitt argues that mountaineering and driving provided modern men with opportunities to engage in leisure activities that required specific knowledge and control to manage risk. Kelm demonstrates that Indigenous rodeo cowboys similarly engaged in these negotiations of risk and expertise when participating in the rugged and dangerous life on the rodeo circuit. Dummitt, *The Manly Modern;* Kelm, *A Wilder West;* Loo, "Of Moose and Men."
105 These elite masculinities were used to grant authority and direction to the grassroots political movement, while concurrently compromising it by alienating community members.
106 Canadian Broadcast Corporation, *Our Native Land;* URC, Minutes of the Union of BC Indian Chiefs General Assembly Held at Evergreen Hall, Chilliwack, BC, 23 April 1975.
107 Guerin interview, 16 April 2013; Eneas interview.
108 Eneas interview.
109 Ibid.
110 Rutherford, "Canada's Other Red Scare," 84.

111 Scott L. Morgensen, "Cutting to the Roots of Colonial Masculinity," in *Indigenous Men and Masculinities: Legacies, Identities, Regeneration,* ed. Robert Innes and Kim Anderson (Winnipeg: University of Manitoba Press, 2015), 38–61; Sam McKegney, "Warriors, Healers, Lovers and Leaders: Colonial Impositions of Indigenous Male Roles and Responsibilities," in *Canadian Perspectives on Men and Masculinities: An Interdisciplinary Reader,* ed. Jason A. Laker (Toronto: Oxford University Press, 2011); Kelm, *A Wilder West,* 66–75. Also see Keith Smith, *Liberalism, Surveillance and Resistance: Indigenous Communities in Western Canada, 1877–1927* (Edmonton: Athabasca University Press, 2009).

112 Kelm, *A Wilder West,* 66–75.

113 Lutz, *Makúk,* 9, 23–24, 46–47. See also Raibmon, *Authentic Indians,* especially Chapter 3.

114 K. Anderson, Swift, and Innes, "'To Arrive Speaking,'" 286.

115 Zirnhelt, "The Caribou Tribal Council," 19. The terms *tribal* and *tribal group* came into currency in the 1970s to reference linguistic and cultural communities and enhanced local political autonomy. Today, scholars and activists have largely replaced the concept of tribalism with those of *nation* and *nationhood,* and I have chosen to use this updated language.

116 Tennant, "Native Indian Political Activity," 121.

117 Zirnhelt, "The Caribou Tribal Council," 2, 27–28.

118 "UBCIC Courtenay 1976: 'A Bold Experiment Has Ended,'" *Nesika: A Journal Devoted to the Land Claims Movement* (May 1976): 6; URC, Minutes of the Union of BC Indian Chiefs General Assembly, 1976; anonymous interview, 25 July 2013.

119 *Nesika* reported that 118 voting delegates were present at the meeting, but the attendance list in the minutes only lists 110. "UBCIC Courtenay 1976,'" 6; URC, Minutes of the Union of BC Indian Chiefs General Assembly, 1976; URC, Union of BC Indian Chiefs Constitution.

120 LAC, RG 10, box 1, file 901/1-1-1-1 (part 1), Office Phaseouts, May-September 1975, letter from Dave Somerville, Caribou Tribal Council administrator to Judd Buchanan, minister of Indian Affairs, 22 June 1975. See also the following band council resolutions, in Office Phaseouts, May-September 1975: Kluskus Band, 21 May 1975; Nazko Band, 21 May 1975; Toosey Band, 6 June 1975; Stone Band, 22 May 1975; Alexis Creek Band, 27 May 1975; Quesnel Band, 18 June 1975.

121 URC, Minutes of the Union of BC Indian Chiefs General Assemblies, 1973–1975; "UBCIC Leaders Not Prepared to Lead," *Indian Voice* 7, no. 6 (1975): 5; Tennant, *Aboriginal Peoples and Politics,* 174.

Chapter 6: Sovereignty

1 "Canim Lake Elders Talk," *Indian World* 2, no. 9 (1980): 18.

2 This chapter will address multiple definitions and applications of terms such as *Indigenous rights, self-government, Indian government, self-determination, sovereignty,* and *nationhood.* Recognizing the multiple understandings of these terms and the tendency, at times, for them to be used interchangeably, I will clarify meanings when possible but will generally use the terms individuals chose for themselves. When it is not possible to be specific, or when I am speaking of the general movement towards sovereignty and nationhood, I will speak in terms of the *sovereignty discourse* or *sovereignty movement* for consistency and clarity. It is important to note, however, that I am not attempting to essentialize Indigenous political experience through this use of language, though I am trying to demonstrate moments of continuity within political change.

3 Self-government, self-determination, and Indigenous rights and title exist within and stem from Indigenous sovereignty. Activists used these interrelated concepts variously and sometimes interchangeably.

4 For interdisciplinary discussions on Indigenous sovereignty, see Alfred, *Wasáse;* Kiera Ladner, "Take 35: Reconciling Constitutional Orders," in *First Nations, First Thoughts: The Impact of Indigenous Thought in Canada,* ed. Annis May Timpson (Vancouver: UBC Press, 2010), 279–300; Posluns, *Speaking with Authority,* 1–3.

5 Saddleman interview, 7 February 2015; Ronald Ignace (Stsmél'ecqen), "Our Oral Histories Are Our Iron Posts: Secwépemc Stories and Historical Consciousness (PhD diss., Simon Fraser University, 2008).

6 Marianne Ignace and Ronald Ignace, *Secwépemc People, Land, and Laws,* 300–1.

7 Ibid.

8 James A. Teit, *The Salishan Tribes of the Western Plateaus,* ed. Franz Boas (Washington, DC: US Government Printing Office, 1930), 266, quoted in Carstens, *The Queen's People,* 19–20. See also Ronald Ignace, "Our Oral Histories." Coyote also plays a pivotal role among Indigenous groups across the Plateau, Great Basin, and the Plains. Robinson, *Write It on Your Heart,* 21.

9 Albert (Sonny) McHalsie, David M. Schaepe, and Keith Thor Carlson, "Making the World Right through Transformations," in Carlson, *A Stó:lō–Coast Salish Historical Atlas,* 3, 6–7; Naxaxalhts'i, "We Have to Take Care of Everything."

10 Carlson, *A Stó:lō–Coast Salish Historical Atlas,* 170–75; Carlson, "Familial Cohesion," 22–23; Drake-Terry, *The Same as Yesterday;* C. Harris, *Making Native Space;* Manuel and Posluns, *The Fourth World;* McFarlane, *Brotherhood to Nationhood;* Tennant, *Aboriginal Peoples and Politics.*

11 Wayne Christian, personal communication with author, Vancouver, BC, 10 September 2014.

12 Saddleman interview.

13 Christian, personal communication.

14 Ibid.

15 Section 91(24) of the act confers "special status," as referenced in Woodward and George, "The Canadian Indian Lobby of Westminster," 121. See also Venne, "Understanding Treaty 6"; Miller, *Compact, Contract, Covenant;* J.R. Miller, *Bounty and Benevolence: A History of Saskatchewan Treaties* (Montreal and Kingston: McGill-Queen's University Press, 2000); Union of British Columbia Indian Chiefs Resource Centre (hereafter URC), Summarized Minutes of the Union of BC Indian Chiefs 12th Annual General Assembly, 14–18 October 1980.

16 Woodward and George, "The Canadian Indian Lobby of Westminster," 121.

17 URC, Summarized Minutes of the Union of B.C. Indian Chiefs 11th Annual General Assembly, 15–18 October 1979.

18 Ibid., 14–18 October 1980.

19 URC, Union of BC Indian Chiefs, *Aboriginal Rights Position Paper,* 1980 (emphasis added).

20 Ibid.

21 URC, UBCIC Bulletins: Constitution Express, 29 October 1980.

22 URC, Summarized Minutes of the Union of BC Indian Chiefs 12th Annual General Assembly, 14–18 October 1980 (emphasis added).

23 Ibid.

24 Union of BC Indian Chiefs, *Aboriginal Rights Position Paper,* 1980.

25 The Splatsín te Secwépemc are known as the Spallumcheen in the archival materials.

26 For more on the Splatsín te Secwépemc Indian Child Caravan and child welfare bylaw, see Nickel, "'I Am Not a Women's Libber."

27 URC, Summarized Minutes of the Union of BC Indian Chiefs 12th Annual General Assembly, 14–18 October 1980.

28 Simpson, *Mohawk Interruptus,* 187.

29 For this debate, see Beth Cuthand, "Editorial," *Indian World* 3, no. 1 (1980): 2; "First Nations Constitutional Conference," *Indian World* 3, no. 1 (1980): 5; "Indian Government," *Indian World* 3, no. 3 (1980); "Knowing How Is the Key," *Indian World* 2, no. 9 (1980): 24–25; Tom Sampson, "Indian Government the Alternative to L.S.A.: In the South Island Traditional Leadership Shows the Way," *Indian World* 2, no. 9 (1980): 31–32; Saul Terry, "Indian Government the Alternative to L.S.A.: In the Central Interior DIA Is Seen as Merely a Clearing House," *Indian World* 2, no. 9 (1980): 30; "Constitutional Changes: March to Demand Full Participation," *Indian World* 3, no. 1 (1980): 4; and Marie Wilson, "Gitksan-Carrier Tribal Council Land Claims Office," *Indian World* 2, no. 9 (1980): 14–15.

30 Union of BC Indian Chiefs, *Aboriginal Rights Position Paper*, 1980.

31 "Haida/Nuu-chah-nulth Land and Sea Claim," *Indian World* 3, no. 9 (1981): 12.

32 Union of BC Indian Chiefs, *Aboriginal Rights Position Paper*, 1980; Guerin interview, 31 May 2013.

33 Coulthard, "Subjects of Empire," 438–39.

34 In 1978, the BCNWS hosted UBCIC president George Manuel and National Indian Brotherhood president Noel Starblanket at their annual assembly, where both leaders spoke about women's equality and the Indian Act. Library and Archives Canada (hereafter LAC), RG10-C-IV-7, box 1, file 901/24-2-5 (part 3), 1994–95/563 GAD, Indian Homemakers' Association of BC, 1977–1978.

35 "Membership Is a Band Affair," *Nesika: The Voice of BC Indians* 1, no. 5 (1973): 2.

36 Barker, "Gender, Sovereignty, Rights."

37 Fiske, "The Womb Is to the Nation."

38 Ibid.

39 Val Dudoward, "Editorial," *Indian World* 3, no. 5 (1980): 2.

40 LAC, RG 10, box 2, file 901/2-2-5 (part 2), Indian Homemakers' Association of British Columbia, 1976–1977, opening remarks by Rose Charlie, president of the Indian Homemakers' Association at the 13th Annual Conference, 15 September 1976.

41 "Innocent Caught in Cross Fire," *Indian Voice* 7, no. 6 (1975): 1–2; "Rose Charlie against UBCIC Decision," *Indian Voice* 7, no. 6 (1975): 1–2; "Homemaker President Urges Union of All Chiefs," *Indian Voice* 9, no. 6 (1977): 2–3; Karen Fish, "Native Women Fight Unique Battle," *Indian Voice* 9, no. 8 (1977): 17 and 19.

42 "Native Women Suffer Triple Discrimination," *Indian Voice* 9, no. 8 (1977): 8.

43 Val Dudoward, "Editorial," *Indian World* 3, no. 5 (1980): 2. For more on this trend, see Fiske, "The Womb Is to the Nation."

44 URC, UBCIC meeting minutes, 1971–1977; A. Smith, "Native American Feminism," 121.

45 Springer, "Black Feminists Respond."

46 Ramirez, "Race, Tribal Nation, and Gender," 31.

47 Barker, "Gender, Sovereignty, and the Discourse of Rights," 136.

48 Val Dudoward, "Editorial," *Indian World* 3, no. 5 (1980): 2; "Native Women Suffer Triple Discrimination," 8.

49 LAC, RG6-F-4, box 96, file 10, Canadian Organizations – National Steering Committee of Native Women, 1971.

50 LAC, RG 10, box 1, file 987/24-5, Homemakers' Club – Gen, 1973–1981, Indian Homemakers' Association Progress Report, 1 November 1973.

51 Ibid.

52 "Indian Women Are 'Citizens Minus,'" *Indian Voice* 10, no. 4 (1978): 18.

53 Fish, "Native Women Fight Unique Battle," 17 and 19; "Native Women Suffer Triple Discrimination." Mary Jane Logan McCallum's examination of Indigenous women and work in the twentieth century also addresses the uneasy relationship between Indigenous women's politics and mainstream second-wave feminism, specifically within the Registered Nurses

of Canadian Indian Ancestry, a professional organization for Indigenous nurses. McCallum, *Indigenous Women, Work, and History,* 167–224.

54 LAC, RG 10, box 1, file 987/24-5, Homemakers' Club – Gen, Indian Homemakers' Association Progress Report, 31 December 1972–1 November 1973; RG 10, vol. 2, box 2, file 901/24-2-5 (part 2), Indian Homemakers' Association of BC, 1976–1977, opening remarks by Rose Charlie, president of the Indian Homemakers' Association at the 13th Annual Conference, Richmond, BC, 15 September 1976; RG 10, vol. 1, box 16, File E6417-2254, Indian Home-makers' Association of BC, 1980–1981, Indian Homemakers' Association of BC Constitutional Position on Native Indian Children, 1981, 1 May 1981; LAC, RG 10, box 16, E-6417-2255 (part 1), B.C. Native Women's Society, 1980/08–1981/02, B.C. Native Women's Societies Policy Paper as Adopted at Their Special Meeting on 13 May 1978.

55 "Indian Leaders Warned to Halt Discrimination against Women," *Indian Voice* 2, no. 7 (1977): 9, reprinted from the *Globe and Mail,* 26 May 1977.

56 Ibid.

57 This moratorium applied to future marriages only, and did not include reinstating membership that had already been lost. Ibid.; Kathleen Bell-Younger, "Moratorium on Section 12(1)(b) Declared by Munro," *Indian Voice* 12, no. 8 (1980): 2.

58 Bell-Younger, "Moratorium on Section 12(1)(b) Declared by Munro."

59 Kathleen Bell-Younger, "Section 12(1) B in Effect Because of Lack of Band Action," *Indian Voice* 12, no. 10 (1980): 2.

60 LAC, RG 10, vol. 1, box 16, file E6417-2254, Indian Homemakers' Association of BC, 1983, notes for a speech by Hon. John Munro to the Indian Homemakers' Association of BC, 30 April 1981.

61 "Indian Leaders Warned to Halt Discrimination"; Bell-Younger, "Moratorium on Section 12(1)(b) Declared by Munro."

62 Kitty Sparrow, "Discrimination of Indian Women Taken to UN," *Indian Voice* 12, no. 6 (1980): 1; Barker, "Gender, Sovereignty, and the Discourse of Rights," 137–42; Canadian Broadcasting Corporation, "Native Women Fight for Equal Rights."

63 Sanders, "The Indian Lobby," 311.

64 "Constitutional Changes: March to Demand Full Participation," *Indian World* 3, no. 1 (1980): 3; "First Nations Constitutional Conference," *Indian World* 3, no. 1 (1980): 4.

65 "Prime Minister Offers No More than Observer Status at Constitutional Talks," *Indian World* 3, no. 1 (1980): 6 (emphasis added).

66 URC, UBCIC Bulletins: Constitution Express (November 1980): 1; URC, "Constitution Express: Newsclippings, Trip to Ottawa November 1980," in summarized minutes of 6th Special General Assembly, Union of British Columbia Indian Chiefs, 14–15 May 1981.

67 George Manuel arrived in Ottawa before the Constitution Express but fell ill and ended up in an Ottawa hospital, where he watched the event unfold. Manuel's son Robert (Bobby) took charge of the delegation. Art Manuel, telephone conversation with author, 24 July 2012; Arthur Manuel and Grand Chief Ronald M. Derrickson, *Unsettling Canada: A National Wake-Up Call* (Toronto: Between the Lines, 2015), 67–68.

68 Manuel interview, 14 August 2012; Manuel and Derrickson, *Unsettling Canada,* 67–68.

69 Manuel and Derrickson, *Unsettling Canada,* 69.

70 "A Journey to Nationhood," *Indian World* 3, no. 8 (1980): 4–6.

71 URC, UBCIC Bulletins, Constitutional Bulletin, 17 December 1980. Indigenous organizations across Canada did not fully support the UBCIC's position against entrenchment. The Assembly of First Nations, the Inuit Tapirisat, and the Native Council of Canada accepted the government's demands for entrenching Indigenous rights, while the Indian Association of Alberta, the Four Nations Confederacy, and others opposed this stance. See Archie Pootlass, "Dilemma at NIB," *Indian World* 3, no. 10 (1981): 8.

72 "Constitution Express Re-awakened Our Nations," *Indian World* 3, no. 9 (1981): 6–7.

73 "Russell Tribunal Finds Canada Guilty," *Indian World* 3, no. 8 (1980): 10; "Petition and Bill of Particulars on the Standing of Indigenous Tribes and Bands under the Protection of the British Government in the Face of Impending Canadian Independence," http://constitution.ubcic.bc.ca/node/128.

74 George Manuel, "President's Message," *Indian World* 3, no. 10 (1981): 7; Carlson, *Stó:lō–Coast Salish Historical Atlas;* Tennant, *Aboriginal Peoples and Politics.*

75 "Council of Chiefs Deliberate," *Indian World* 3, no. 9 (1981): 12; "If We're a Nation We Have to Act Like One," *Indian World* 3, no. 9 (1981): 30.

76 Harder and Patten, "Looking Back on Patriation and Its Consequences," in *Patriation and Its Consequences: Constitution Making in Canada,* ed. Lois Harder and Steve Patten (Vancouver: UBC Press, 2015), 13.

77 Sanders, "The Indian Lobby," 318–21.

78 "Another Termination Attack: Indian Government Bill," *Indian World* 3, no. 10 (1981): 22. See also "Prime Minister Offers No More than Observer Status."

79 *Constitution Act, 1982,* s35, being Schedule B to the Canada Act 1982 (UK), 1982.

80 Trudeau's Liberal government initially seemed favourable to Penner's recommendations, but 1983 and 1984 witnessed the elections of John Turner and then Brian Mulroney. The latter resulted in subsequent changes to personnel in the Department of Indian Affairs, which helped to solidify the new government's oppositional stance.

Reflections

1 Union of British Columbia Indian Chiefs Resource Centre (hereafter URC), Minutes of the Union of BC Indian Chiefs 9th Annual General Assembly, Prince George, 26–28 April 1977.

2 Ibid.

3 Woolford, *Between Justice and Certainty.*

4 Blomley, "'Shut the Province Down.'"

5 Ibid., 9–10.

6 Don Bain, personal communication with author, Union of BC Indian Chiefs Offices, Vancouver, BC, 5 April 2012.

7 Blankinship, "Alternatives to the British Columbia Treaty Process."

8 The "cede, release, and surrender" clause is present in most of the treaties negotiated between the Crown and Indigenous peoples and, according to Crown interpretations, stipulates that, in exchange for the treaty, Indigenous peoples will give up interest in the lands not covered in the treaty. Indigenous peoples, on the other hand, have always interpreted treaties as land-sharing rather than land-cession agreements. Morris, *The Treaties of Canada;* Sharon Venne, "Understanding Treaty 6."

9 Joe interview, 5 June 2013.

10 Blankinship, "Alternatives to the British Columbia Treaty Process."

11 Moses interview, 11 June 2013.

12 Pennier interview with author, 25 July 2012; Sioliya interview, 25 June 2012; Terry interview, 30 August 2012; Wayne Christian interview, 4 June 2013; Guerin interview, 31 May 2013.

13 Bain, personal communication.

14 Ibid.

15 Coulthard, *Red Skins, White Masks,* 24.

16 Pennier interview with author.

17 Terry interview.

Bibliography

Archival Collections

Library and Archives Canada (LAC)
"Interviews with Native Indian Leaders Relating to Our Chiefs and Elders Portfolio and
Exhibition." Sound recording [ca. 1980–1991], series R5729-1-8-E
RG 6, Department of the Secretary of State
RG 10, Department of Indian Affairs
RG 148, Canadian Human Rights Commission

Union of British Columbia Indian Chiefs Resource Centre (URC)
Minutes of the Indian Chiefs of British Columbia Conferences and General Assemblies

Interviews

Anonymous. Interview with author, 25 June 2013.
Antoine, Janice. Interview with author. Merritt, BC, 5 June 2013.
Charles, Archie. Interview with Melissa McDowell. Seabird Island First Nation, Agassiz,
BC, 2 June 2002. SRRMC, Oral History Collection, Sardis, BC.
Charlie, Rose. Interview with Koni Benson. Sts'ailes (Chehalis) First Nation, Agassiz, BC,
3 June 1998. SRRMC, Oral History Collection, Sardis, BC.
Christian, Wayne. Interview with author. Splatsín te Secwépemc First Nation, Enderby, BC,
4 June 2013.
Eneas, Adam. Interview with author. Penticton First Nation, Penticton, BC, 3 June 2012.
Guerin, Delbert. Interview with author. Xʷməθkʷəy̓əm (Musqueam) First Nation, Vancouver,
BC, 16 April and 31 May 2013.
Joe, Percy. Interview with author. Merritt, BC, 5 June 2013.
Jules, Clarence. Interview with author. Tk'emlúps te Secwépemc, Kamloops, BC, 12 June 2012.
Kelly, Marge. Interview with author. Soowahlie First Nation, Cultus Lake, BC, 3 May 2012.
Malloway, Ken. Interview with author and Katya MacDonald. Coqualeetza Longhouse,
Sardis, BC, 22 June 2007. SRRMC, Oral History Collection, Sardis, BC.
Mandell, Louise. Interview with author. Vancouver, BC, 12 March 2012.
Manuel, Arthur. Interview with author. UBCIC Offices, Vancouver, BC, 14 August 2012.
Moses, Don. Interview with author. Merritt, BC, 11 June 2013.
Naxaxalhts'i (Albert "Sonny" McHalsie). Interview with author. Stó:lō Research and Resource
Management Centre, Sardis, BC, 20 April 2012.
Pennier, Clarence (Kat). Interview with author. Stó:lō Tribal Council Offices, Agassiz, BC,
25 July 2012.

–. Interview with Martin Hoffman, 17 May 2011. SRRMC, Oral History Collection, Sardis, BC.

–. Interview with Melissa McDowell. Stó:lō Nation Office, Chilliwack, BC, 31 May 2002. SRRMC, Oral History Collection, Sardis, BC.

Point, Steven. Interview with Mandy Fehr and Andree Boisselle. Stó:lō Nation Offices, Sardis, BC, 29 June 2007. SRRMC, Oral History Collection, Sardis, BC.

Saddleman, George. Interview with author. Vancouver, BC, 7 February 2015.

Sioliya (June Quipp). Interview with author. Cheam First Nation, Rosedale, BC, 25 June 2012.

Terry, Saul. Interview with author. Vancouver, BC, 30 August 2012.

Wahmeesh (Ken Watts). Interview with author. Ts'ishaa7ath (Tseshaht) First Nation, Port Alberni, BC, 28 June 2012.

Ware, Reuben. Interview with author. Vancouver, BC, 20 August 2012.

Primary Sources

An Act for the Gradual Enfranchisement of Indians, the Better Management of Indian Affairs, and to Extend the Provisions of the Act, SC 1869, c 42.

An Act to Amend and Consolidate the Laws Respecting Indians, SC 1876, c 18.

"British Columbia Bands and Agencies." Collections Canada. http://www.collections canada.gc.ca/bands-agencies/005008-3000-e.html.

Canadian Broadcasting Corporation. "American Indian Movement Shakes Up Canada." *Our Native Land.* https://www.cbc.ca/player/play/1851655876. Accessed 18 November 2017.

–. "Native Women Fight for Equal Rights," *Our Native Land.* 2 March 1985. http://www. cbc.ca/archives/entry/our-native-land-native-women-fight-for-equal-rights.

–. "War Chief: George Manuel." *Ideas.* 3 May 1994, ID 9427.

"Celebrating Women's Achievements." Library and Archives Canada. http://www.collections canada.gc.ca/women/030001-1108-e.html.

Charlie, Rose. "Grand Chief Rose Charlie – The Birth of the UBCIC." Video from UBCIC Annual General Assembly, 2009. https://www.youtube.com/watch?v=SS5LpSedQ1c& feature=relmfu.

Constitution Act, 1982, s 35, being Schedule B to the *Canada Act* 1982 (UK), 1982.

Department of Indian Affairs. *Annual Report.* [1973–76.] Ottawa: Information Canada, 1973–76.

Hawthorn, Harry Bertram. *A Survey of the Contemporary Indians of Canada: A Report on Economic, Political, Educational Needs and Policies.* Ottawa: Indian Affairs Branch, 1966.

Indian News. Published by the Department of Indian Affairs, 1955–75.

Indian Voice. Published by the British Columbia Indian Homemakers' Association, 1969–81.

Indian World. Published by the Union of BC Indian Chiefs, 1980–83.

Lex'yem. Published by the Kamloops Indian Band, 1979.

Native Voice. Published by the Native Brotherhood of BC, 1966–68.

Nesika: A Journal Devoted to the Land Claims Movement. Published by the Union of BC Indian Chiefs, 1976.

Nesika: The Voice of BC Indians. Published by the Union of BC Indian Chiefs, 1972–77.

"Petition and Bill of Particulars on the Standing of Indigenous Tribes and Bands under the Protection of the British Government in the Face of Impending Canadian Independence." http://constitution.ubcic.bc.ca/node/128.

Report of the Royal Commission on Indian Affairs for the Province of British Columbia. Volume 2. Victoria: Acme Press, 1916. https://www.ubcic.bc.ca/mckenna_mcbride_royal_ commission.

UBCIC. *A Declaration of Indian Rights: The BC Indian Position Paper*. 17 November 1970. http://d3n8a8pro7vhmx.cloudfront.net/ubcic/pages/1440/attachments/.

–. Union of BC Indian Chiefs General Assembly, 21–25 April 1975. Video. https://www.ubcic.bc.ca/Resources/Digital/7thAGAMIC.htm. Accessed 5 February 2012.

Unity: Bulletin of the Union of British Columbia Indian Chiefs, 1970–71.

Secondary Sources

Adams, Howard. *Prison of Grass: Canada from a Native Point of View*. Rev. ed. Saskatoon: Fifth House, 1989.

Adams, Ian. "The Indians: An Abandoned and Dispossessed People." *Weekend Magazine*, 31 July 1965, 2–6.

Alfred, Taiaiake. *Wasase: Indigenous Pathways of Action and Freedom*. Toronto: University of Toronto Press, 2005.

Anderson, Kim, and Bonita Lawrence, eds. *Strong Women Stories: Native Vision and Community Survival*. 3rd ed. Toronto: Sumach Press, 2006.

Anderson, Kim, John Swift, and Robert Alexander Innes. "'To Arrive Speaking': Voices from the Bidwewidam Indigenous Masculinities Project." In *Indigenous Men and Masculinities: Legacies, Identities, Regeneration*. Edited by Alexander Innes and Kim Anderson, 283–307. Winnipeg: University of Manitoba Press, 2015.

Anderson, Mark, and Carmen Robertson. "The 'Bended Elbow' News, Kenora, 1974: How a Small-Town Newspaper Promoted Colonization." *American Indian Quarterly* 31, no. 3 (2007): 410–40. https://doi.org/10.1353/aiq.2007.0027.

Armstrong, Jeannette C. *Slash*. 6th ed. Penticton, BC: Theytus Books, 1996.

Arndt, Grant. "Indigenous Agendas and Activist Genders: Chicago's American Indian Center, Social Welfare, and Native American Women's Urban Leadership." In Krouse and Howard, *Keeping the Campfires Going*, 34–55.

Barkaskas, Patricia. "The Indian Voice: Centering Women in the Gendered Politics of Indigenous Nationalism in BC, 1969–1984." Master's thesis, University of British Columbia, 2009.

Barker, Joanne. "Gender, Sovereignty, and the Discourse of Rights in Native Women's Activism." *Meridians: Feminism, Race, and Transnationalism* 7, no. 1 (2006): 127–61. https://doi.org/10.2979/MER.2006.7.1.127.

–. "Gender, Sovereignty, Rights: Native Women's Activism against Social Inequality and Violence in Canada." *American Quarterly* 60, no. 2 (2008): 259–66. https://doi.org/10.1353/aq.0.0002.

Berger, Dan, ed. *The Hidden 1970s: Histories of Radicalism*. New Brunswick, NJ: Rutgers University Press, 2010.

Blankinship, Jennie L. (Nahumpchin). "Alternatives to the British Columbia Treaty Process: Community Perspectives on Aboriginal Title and Rights." Master's thesis, University of Victoria, 2006.

Blomley, Nicholas. "'Shut the Province Down': First Nations Blockades in British Columbia, 1984–1995." *BC Studies* 111 (Autumn 1996): 5–35.

Bobb, Ray. "Red Power and Socialist Study in Vancouver, 1967–1975." In *Onkwehon:we Rising: An Indigenous Perspective on Third Worldism and Revolution*. https://revolutionary-initiative.com/2012/04/26/overview-of-red-power-movement-in-vancouver-1967-1975/

Boldt, Menno. *Surviving as Indians: The Challenge of Self-Government*. Toronto: University of Toronto Press, 1993.

Campbell, Lara, Dominique Clément, and Gregory S. Kealey, eds. *Debating Dissent: Canada and the Sixties*. Toronto: University of Toronto Press, 2012.

Cardinal, Harold. *The Unjust Society*. Vancouver: Douglas and McIntyre, 1999.

Carlson, Keith Thor. "Familial Cohesion and Colonial Atomization: Governance and Authority in a Coast Salish Community." *Native Studies Review* 19, no. 2 (2010): 2–41.

–. *The Power of Place, the Problem of Time: Aboriginal Identity and Historical Consciousness in the Cauldron of Colonialism*. Toronto: University of Toronto Press, 2010.

–. "Rethinking Dialogue and History: The King's Promise and the 1906 Aboriginal Delegation to London." *Native Studies Review* 16, no. 2 (2005): 1–38.

–, ed. *A Stó:lō–Coast Salish Historical Atlas*. Vancouver/Seattle/Chilliwack: Douglas and McIntyre/University of Washington Press/Stó:lō Heritage Trust, 2001.

–. *You Are Asked to Witness: The Stó:lō in Canada's Pacific Coast History*. Chilliwack, BC: Stó:lō Heritage Trust, 1997.

Carstens, Peter. *The Queen's People: A Study of Hegemony, Coercion, and Accommodation among the Okanagan of Canada*. Toronto: University of Toronto Press, 1991.

Clément, Dominique. *Canada's Rights Revolution: Social Movements and Social Change, 1937–82*. Vancouver: UBC Press, 2008.

Cobb, Daniel M. *Native Activism in Cold War America: The Struggle for Sovereignty*. Lawrence: University of Kansas Press, 2008.

Cobb, Daniel M., and Loretta Fowler. *Beyond Red Power: American Indian Politics and Activism since 1900*. Santa Fe, NM: School for Advanced Research, 2007.

Collier-Thomas, Bettye, and V.P. Franklin, eds. *Sisters in the Struggle: African American Women in the Civil Rights–Black Power Movement*. New York: New York University Press, 2001.

Collins, Patricia Hill. "Shifting the Center: Race, Class, and Feminist Theorizing about Motherhood." In *Mothering: Ideology, Experience, and Agency*. Edited by Evelyn Nakano Glenn, Grace Change, and Linda Rennie Forcey, 45–65. New York: Routledge, 1994.

Coulthard, Glen Sean. *Red Skin, White Masks: Rejecting the Colonial Politics of Recognition*. Minneapolis: University of Minnesota Press, 2014.

–. "Subjects of Empire: Indigenous Peoples and the 'Politics of Recognition' in Canada." *Contemporary Political Theory* 6, no. 4 (2007): 437–60. https://doi.org/10.1057/palgrave.cpt.9300307.

Culhane, Dara. "Their Spirits Live within Us: Aboriginal Women in Downtown Eastside Vancouver Emerging into Visibility." In Krouse and Howard, *Keeping the Campfires Going*, 76–87.

Davis, Julie L. *Survival Schools: The American Indian Movement and Community Education in the Twin Cities*. Minneapolis: University of Minnesota Press, 2013.

Drake-Terry, Joanne. *The Same as Yesterday: The Lillooet Tribal People Chronicle the Takeover of Their Territory*. Lillooet, BC: Lillooet Tribal Council, 1989.

Drees, Laurie Meijer. *The Indian Association of Alberta: A History of Political Action*. Vancouver: UBC Press, 2002.

Dummitt, Christopher. *The Manly Modern: Masculinity in Postwar Canada*. Vancouver: UBC Press, 2007.

Fiske, Jo-Anne. "Carrier Women and the Politics of Mothering." In *British Columbia Reconsidered: Essays on Women*. Edited by Gillian Creese and Veronica Strong-Boag, 198–216. Vancouver: Press Gang, 1992.

–. "Colonization and the Decline of Women's Status: The Tsimshian Case." *Feminist Studies* 17, no. 3 (1991): 509–35. https://doi.org/10.2307/3178288.

–. "The Womb Is to the Nation as the Heart Is to the Body: Ethnopolitical Discourses of the Canadian Indigenous Women's Movement." *Studies in Political Economy* 51, no. 1 (1996): 65–95. https://doi.org/10.1080/19187033.1996.11675329.

Fixico, Donald. "Witness to Change: Fifty Years of Indian Activism and Tribal Politics." In Cobb and Fowler, *Beyond Red Power*, 2–15.

Foster, Hamar. "A Romance of the Lost: The Role of Tom MacInnes in the History of the British Columbia Indian Land Question." In *Essays in the History of Canadian Law: In Honour of R.C.B. Risk*. Vol. 8. Edited G. Blaine Baker and Jim Phillips, 171–212. Toronto: University of Toronto Press, 1999.

–. "'We Want a Strong Promise': The Opposition to Indian Treaties in British Columbia, 1850–1900." *Native Studies Review* 18, no. 1 (2009): 113–37.

Galois, R.M. "The Indian Rights Association, Native Protest Activity and the 'Land Question' in British Columbia, 1903–1916." *Native Studies Review* 8, no. 2 (1992): 1–34.

Hall, Tony. "Blockades and Bannock: Aboriginal Protests and Politics in Northern Ontario, 1980–1990." *Wicazo Sa Review* 7, no. 2 (1991): 58–77. https://doi.org/10.2307/1409066.

Harmon, Alexandra. *Rich Indians: Native People and the Problem of Wealth in American History*. Chapel Hill: University of North Carolina Press, 2010.

Harris, Douglas. *Landing Native Fisheries: Indian Reserves and Fishing Rights in British Columbia, 1849–1925*. Vancouver: UBC Press, 2008.

Harris, R. Cole. *Making Native Space: Colonialism, Resistance, and Reserves in British Columbia*. Vancouver: UBC Press, 2002.

Hodgins, Bruce W., David McNab, and Ute Lischke, eds., *Blockades and Resistance: Studies in Actions of Peace and the Temagami Blockades of 1988–89*. Waterloo, ON: Wilfrid Laurier University Press, 2003.

Hughes, Celia. "Negotiating Ungovernable Spaces between the Personal and the Political: Oral History and the Left in Post-War Britain." *Memory Studies* 6, no. 1 (2013): 70–90. https://doi.org/10.1177/1750698012463895.

Ignace, Marianne, and Ronald Ignace. *Secwépemc People, Land, and Laws: Yeri7 re Stsqeyskucw*. Montreal and Kingston: McGill-Queen's University Press, 2017.

Indian Association of Alberta. *Citizens Plus*. Edmonton: Indian Association of Alberta, 1970.

Jamieson, Kathleen. *Indian Women and the Law in Canada: Citizens Minus*. Ottawa: Advisory Council on the Status of Women, 1978.

–. "Sex Discrimination and the Indian Act." In Pointing, *Arduous Journey*, 112–36.

Janovicek, Nancy. "'Assisting Our Own': Urban Migration, Self-Governance, and Native Women's Organizing in Thunder Bay, Ontario, 1972–1989." In Krouse and Howard, *Keeping the Campfires Going*, 56–75.

Kelm, Mary-Ellen. *A Wilder West: Rodeo in Western Canada*. Vancouver: UBC Press, 2011.

Knickerbocker, Madeline, and Sarah Nickel. "Negotiating Sovereignty: Indigenous Perspectives on the Patriation of a Settler Colonial Constitution." *BC Studies* 190 (Summer 2016): 66–87.

Krouse, Susan Applegate, and Heather A. Howard, eds. *Keeping the Campfires Going: Native Women's Activism in Urban Communities*. Lincoln: University of Nebraska Press, 2009.

Kulchyski, Peter. "40 Years in Indian Country." *Canadian Dimension* 37, no. 6 (2003): 33–36.

Ladd-Taylor, Molly. *Mother-Work: Women, Child Welfare, and the State*. Urbana: University of Illinois Press, 1994.

Lambertus, Sandra. *Wartime Images, Peacetime Wounds: The Media and the Gustafsen Lake Standoff*. Toronto: University of Toronto Press, 2004.

Langston, Donna Hightower. "American Indian Women's Activism in the 1960s and 1970s." *Hypatia* 18, no. 2 (2003): 114–32.

Leger-Anderson, Ann. "Women's Organizations in Saskatchewan: Report for Culture, Youth, and Recreation." 31 March 2005, 1–63. www.publications.gov.sk.ca/documents/96/98075-Women'sOrgs.pdf.

Loo, Tina. "Of Moose and Men: Hunting for Masculinities in British Columbia, 1880–1939." *Western Historical Quarterly* 32, no. 3 (2001): 296–319. https://doi.org/10.2307/3650737.

Lowe, Lana. "A Strategic Analysis of the Union of British Columbia Indian Chiefs." Master's thesis, University of Victoria, 2004.

Lutz, John S. *Makúk: A New History of Aboriginal-White Relations*. Vancouver: UBC Press, 2008.

Lyons, Scott. *X-Marks: Native Signatures of Assent*. Minneapolis: University of Minnesota Press, 2010.

Manuel, George, and Michael Posluns. *The Fourth World: An Indian Reality*. Don Mills, ON: Collier-Macmillan, 1974.

Maracle, Lee. *Bobbi Lee: Indian Rebel*. Toronto: Women's Press, 1990.

–. *I Am Woman: A Native Perspective on Sociology and Feminism*. 2nd ed. Vancouver: Press Gang, 1988.

McCallum, Mary Jane Logan. *Indigenous Women, Work, and History, 1940–1980*. Winnipeg: University of Manitoba Press, 2014.

McFarlane, Peter. *Brotherhood to Nationhood: George Manuel and the Making of the Modern Indian Movement*. Toronto: Between the Lines, 1993.

Miller, J.R. *Compact, Contract, Covenant: Aboriginal Treaty-Making in Canada*. Toronto: University of Toronto Press, 2009.

–. *Skyscrapers Hide the Heavens: A History of Indian-White Relations in Canada*. Toronto: University of Toronto Press, 1989.

Million, Dian. *Therapeutic Nations: Healing in an Age of Indigenous Human Rights*. Tucson: University of Arizona Press, 2013.

Milne, Jennifer. "Cultivating Domesticity: The Homemakers' Clubs of Saskatchewan, 1911 to the Post-War Era." Master's thesis, University of Saskatchewan, 2004.

Mills, Sean. *The Empire Within: Postcolonial Thought and Political Activism in Sixties Montreal*. Kingston and Montreal: McGill-Queen's University Press, 2010.

Mitchell, Darcy Anne. "The Allied Tribes of British Columbia: A Study in Pressure Group Behaviour." Master's thesis, University of British Columbia, 1977.

Moran, Bridget. *Stoney Creek Woman, Sai'k'uz Ts'eke: The Story of Mary John*. Vancouver: Arsenal Pulp Press, 1999.

Morris, Alexander. *The Treaties of Canada with the Indians of Manitoba and the North-West Territories*. 1880. Reprint, Calgary: Fifth House, 1991.

Naxaxalhts'i (Albert McHalsie). "We Have to Take Care of Everything That Belongs to Us." In *Be of Good Mind: Essays on the Coast Salish*. Edited by Bruce Granville Miller, 82–130. Vancouver: UBC Press, 2007.

Nickel, Sarah. "'I Am Not a Women's Libber, Although Sometimes I Sound Like One': Indigenous Feminism and Politicized Motherhood in British Columbia." *American Indian Quarterly* 41, no. 4 (2017): 299–335. https://doi.org/10.5250/amerindiquar.41.4.0299.

–. "'You'll Probably Tell Me That Your Grandmother Was an Indian Princess': Identity, Community, and Politics in the Oral History of the Union of British Columbia Indian Chiefs, 1969–1980." *Oral History/Forum d'histoire orale* 34 (2014): 1–19.

Ouellette, Grace J.M.W. *The Fourth World: An Indigenous Perspective on Feminism and Aboriginal Women's Activism*. Halifax: Fernwood, 2002.

Palmer, Bryan D. *Canada's 1960s: The Ironies of Identity in a Rebellious Time*. Toronto: University of Toronto Press, 2009.

–. "'Indians of All Tribes': The Birth of Red Power." In Campbell, Clément, and Kealey, *Debating Dissent*, 193–210.

Parker, Peter. "'We Are Not Beggars': Political Genesis of the Native Brotherhood, 1931–51." Master's thesis, Simon Fraser University, 1992.

Parnaby, Andrew. "'The Best Men That Ever Worked the Lumber': Aboriginal Longshoremen on Burrard Inlet, BC, 1863–1939." *Canadian Historical Review* 87, no. 1 (2006): 53–78.

Perks, Robert, and Alistair Thomson, eds. *The Oral History Reader*. London: Routledge, 1998.

Posluns, Michael W. *Speaking with Authority: The Emergence of the Vocabulary of First Nations' Self-Government*. New York: Routledge, 2007.

Raibmon, Paige Sylvia. *Authentic Indians: Episodes of Encounter from the Late Nineteenth-Century Northwest Coast*. Durham, NC: Duke University Press, 2005. https://doi.org/10.1215/9780822386773.

Ramirez, Renya K. "Race, Tribal Nation, and Gender: A Native Feminist Approach to Belonging." *Meridians* (Middletown, CT) 7, no. 2 (2007): 22–40. https://doi.org/10.2979/MER.2007.7.2.22.

Ramos, Howard. "Aboriginal Protest." In *Social Movements*. Edited by Suzanne Staggenborg, 71–80. Don Mills, ON: Oxford University Press, 2012.

Raunet, Daniel. *Without Surrender, without Consent: A History of Nishga Land Claims*. Vancouver: Douglas and McIntyre, 1984.

Robertson, Leslie, and Kwaguʼł Gixs̱am Clan. *Standing Up with Gaʼaxstaʼlas: Jane Constance Cook and the Politics of Memory, Church, and Custom*. Vancouver: UBC Press, 2012.

Robinson, Harry. *Write It on Your Heart: The Epic World of an Okanagan Storyteller*. Edited by Wendy Wickwire. Vancouver: Talon Books, 1989.

Rouse, Jacqueline A. "'We Seek to Know ... In Order to Speak the Truth': Nurturing the Seeds of Discontent – Septima P. Clark and Participatory Leadership." In Collier-Thomas and Franklin, *Sisters in the Struggle*, 95–120.

Rutherford, Scott. "Canada's Other Red Scare: The Anicinabe Park Occupation." In Berger, *The Hidden 1970s*, 77–94.

Sanders, Douglas. "The Indian Lobby." In *And No One Cheered: Federalism, Democracy, and the Constitution Act*. Edited by Keith Banting and Richard Simeon, 301–32. Toronto: Methuen, 1983.

Shreve, Bradley G. "'From Time Immemorial': The Fish-in Movement and the Rise of Intertribal Activism." *Pacific Historical Review* 78, no. 3 (2009): 403–34. https://doi.org/10.1525/phr.2009.78.3.403.

Simpson, Audra. *Mohawk Interruptus: Political Life across the Borders of Settler States*. Durham, NC: Duke University Press, 2014.

Smith, Andrea. "Native American Feminism, Sovereignty, and Social Change." *Feminist Studies* 31, no. 1 (2005): 116–32. https://doi.org/10.2307/20459010.

Smith, Linda Tuhiwai. *Decolonizing Methodologies: Research and Indigenous Peoples*. New York: Zed Books, 1999.

Smith, Paul Chaat, and Robert Allen Warrior. *Like a Hurricane: The Indian Movement from Alcatraz to Wounded Knee*. New York: New Press, 1996.

Smith, Sherry. *Hippies, Indians, and the Fight for Red Power*. New York: Oxford University Press, 2012.

Springer, Kimberly. "Black Feminists Respond to Black Power Masculinism." In *The Black Power Movement: Re-thinking the Civil Rights–Black Power Era*. Edited by Joseph Peniel, 105–18. New York: Routledge, 2006.

Sterritt, Angela. *Racialization of Poverty: Indigenous Women, the Indian Act and Systemic Oppression: Reasons for Resistance*. Vancouver: Vancouver Status of Women, 2007.

Straus, Anne Terry, and Debra Valentino. "Gender and Community Organization Leadership in the Chicago Indian Community." In Krouse and Howard, *Keeping the Campfires Going*, 22–33.

Teit, James A. *The Salishan Tribes of the Western Plateaus: Forty-Fifth Annual Report of the Bureau of American Ethnology (1927–1928)*. Edited by Franz Boas. Washington, DC: US Government Printing Office, 1930.

Tennant, Paul. *Aboriginal Peoples and Politics: The Indian Land Question in British Columbia, 1849–1989*. Vancouver: UBC Press, 1990.

–. "Native Indian Political Activity in British Columbia, 1969–1983." *BC Studies* 57 (Spring 1983): 112–35.

–. "Native Indian Political Organization in British Columbia, 1900–1969." *BC Studies* 55 (Autumn 1982): 3–49.

Ticoll, David, and Stan Persky. "Welcome to Ottawa: The Native Peoples' Caravan." *Canadian Dimension* 10, no. 6 (1975): 14–31.

Titley, Brian. *A Narrow Vision: Duncan Campbell Scott and the Administration of Indian Affairs in Canada*. Vancouver: UBC Press, 1986.

Turner, Dale A. *This Is Not a Peace Pipe: Towards a Critical Indigenous Philosophy*. Toronto: University of Toronto Press, 2006.

Venne, Sharon. "Understanding Treaty 6: An Indigenous Perspective." In *Aboriginal and Treaty Rights in Canada: Essays on Law, Equity, and Respect for Difference*. Edited by Michael Asch, 173–207. Vancouver: UBC Press, 1997.

Voyageur, Cora J. "Female First Nations Chiefs and the Colonial Legacy." *American Indian Culture and Research Journal* 35, no. 3 (2011): 59–78. https://doi.org/10.17953/aicr.35.3.tx7pth12527049p7.

–. "Out in the Open: Elected Female Leadership in Canada's First Nations Community." *Canadian Review of Sociology/Revue canadienne de sociologie* 48, no. 1 (2011): 67–85. https://doi.org/10.1111/j.1755-618X.2011.01250.x.

Weaver, Sally M. *Making Canadian Indian Policy: The Hidden Agenda, 1968–70*. Toronto: University of Toronto Press, 1981.

Wolfe, Patrick. "Settler Colonialism and the Elimination of the Native." *Journal of Genocide Research* 8, no. 4 (2006): 387–409. https://doi.org/10.1080/14623520601056240.

Woodward, Michael, and Bruce George. "The Canadian Indian Lobby of Westminster, 1979–1982." *Journal of Canadian Studies/Revue d'études canadiennes* 18, no. 3 (1983): 119–43. https://doi.org/10.3138/jcs.18.3.119.

Woolford, Andrew John. *Between Justice and Certainty*. Vancouver: UBC Press, 2005.

Zirnhelt, David. "The Caribou Tribal Council." Master's thesis, University of British Columbia, 1976.

Index

vs participation in settler systems, 153; sovereignty before, 148–51; terminology for rights, 164–65; trilateral federalism proposal, 151–52, 166; UBCIC's roles, 151–53, 161–67. *See also* UBCIC, sovereignty and constitutional patriation

Cook, Jane, 178*n*22

Coqualeetza Cultural Centre, 98–99

Coulthard, Glen, 7, 153, 172–73

Courtenay, UBCIC meeting (1976), 143–44, 198*n*119

Cowichan, 37, 133, 135, 193*n*33

Dakelh (Carrier), 11, 21(f), 27

David, Chief Basil, 37, 122

A Declaration of Indian Rights (Brown Paper, UBCIC), 53–54, 76

Deep Creek fish-in, 124–25, 194*n*34

Demerais, Lou, 75

Dept. of Fisheries. *See* Fisheries and Oceans, Dept. of; fishing protests

Dept. of Indian Affairs. *See* DIA (Dept. of Indian Affairs); DIA, resistance to

Dept. of Secretary of State. *See* DSS (Dept. of Secretary of State)

DIA (Dept. of Indian Affairs): about, 35; devolution of services, 71, 73–76; districts, 22, 23(f), 45, 174(t)–175(t); funding for organizations, 74, 77, 92–93, 95(t); goal of provincial jurisdiction, 76; homemakers' clubs (IHC), 11, 25–26, 28–30, 44; Indian Act consultations, 159; media, 28; moratorium on women's exclusion for marrying out, 160–61, 201*n*57; off-reserve services, 78; recognition of Indigenous organizations, 45, 46, 169; response to funding rejection, 101; UBCIC funding, 95(t); UBCIC leaders as liaisons, 86; White Paper on abolishment of, 50. *See also* Indian Act; settler colonialism

DIA, resistance to: about, 130–34; AIM security force, 134–35, 140; alliances, 131–32; band lobbying of, 127; fears of DIA influence on UBCIC, 58; goal of local control of services, 76, 130, 133–34, 137; lobbying by women, 30–31, 67, 103, 105–7, 159; occupations of offices, 9, 114, 129–38, 196*n*79; protests as radical masculinity, 138–42; UBCIC cut-off lands

committee, 128–29, 134–38; UBCIC lobbying of, 71, 127; UBCIC's dilemma of refusal vs participation in settler systems, 58. *See also* land claims; UBCIC, finances and refusal of funding (1975–76); UBCIC, resistance

Dick, Agnes, 103, 107, 109

Douglas, Chief Albert and Edna, 82, 121

Douglas Lake, 5, 21

Douglas treaties, 33–34, 181*n*62

Drees, Laurie Meijer, 9

DSS (Dept. of Secretary of State): funding for organizations, 29, 73–75, 94, 95(t)

Dudoward, Val, 154–55, 157

Duncan, William, 36

Eneas, Angeline, 139

Eneas, Chief Adam, 15, 68, 84, 86, 122, 129, 137, 139–41, 194*n*49

England. *See* Britain

Fairclough, Ellen, 43–44

Fairweather, Gordon, 159

feminisms, new Indigenous: about, 11–12, 63, 68, 156–58; citizenship and sovereignty, 152–58; heteronormative sexualities, 67–68; individual vs collective rights, 157; intersectionalism, 11–12, 156–57; *Lavell* case on marrying out, 63–65, 66–67, 158, 161; NIB's opposition to, 64, 157; non-Indigenous alliances, 157–58; responses to 1975 funding refusal, 104, 111–12; terminology, 12; transnational networks, 63; variation in identification with, 111–12. *See also* Indigenous women and politics

Ferguson, Hattie, 59

First Citizens' Fund, 73–74, 95(t)

First Nations: bands in districts, 174(t)–175(t); maps of DIA districts and bands, 21(f), 23(f); statistics on, 4, 6. *See also entries beginning with* Indigenous peoples

First Nations Summit, 171

Fish, Karen, 156, 158

Fish Lake Accord, 5, 21–22

Fisheries and Oceans, Dept. of: regional protests, 99–100, 124–25, 129–30; UBCIC opposition, 78, 129–30; weir regulations, 135, 193*n*33

Fisheries Association of BC (FABC), 43

of many influences, 54; patriarchy, 142; "pre-contact" sovereignty, 148–50; recognition of Indigenous concerns, 45, 50–51; standards for Indigenous homemakers, 26–27; as unfinished, 10. *See also* constitutional patriation; DIA (Dept. of Indian Affairs); DSS (Dept. of Secretary of State); Indian Act; treaties, settler-Indigenous; White Paper (1969)

Sewid, James, 121, 122, 193*n*29

Sewish, Chief Adam, 107

sexuality and heteronormativity, 24–25, 67–68. *See also* gender

Seymour, Larry, 79–80, 85

Simpson, Audra, 7, 152

Sinclair, James, 43, 46

Sioliya (June Quipp), 82, 121

Smith, Paul Chaat, 136

Smith, Sherry, 116, 120

social class, 70, 79–80, 87, 158–59

Social Credit government, 125

South Island District (later Nanaimo District), 23(f), 106–7, 130, 133, 175(t)

sovereignty: about, 14, 146–53, 165–67; *Aboriginal Rights Position Paper* (UBCIC), 150–52; constitutional patriation, 146–47, 165–67; defined, 147; embedded sovereignties, 152–53; as flexible concept, 167; inherent pre-colonial sovereignty, 146–50, 153; Laurier Memorial (1910), 38–39, 149; multiple sovereignties, 152–53; and oral traditions, 148–50; petitions and lobbying, 38–39, 149–50; power inequities, 153; refusal vs participation in settler systems, 153; settler recognition by Indigenous peoples, 125, 151–53; sexism in rights movements, 156–57; terminology, 198*nn*2–3; tribal councils, 142–44; trilateral federalism proposal, 151–52; UBCIC's role in political recognition, 147, 150–53; women's citizenship, 153–61. *See also* constitutional patriation; Indigenous peoples and governance; UBCIC, sovereignty and constitutional patriation

Splatsín, 152

Springer, Kimberly, 28

Squamish, 21(f), 37, 40–41

Stamp, Mary, 101

Starblanket, Noel, 200*n*34

Status of Women Council of BC, 157–58

Stelkia, Chief James, 102, 124–26, 194*n*34, 194*n*49

Stó:lō, 21(f), 31, 98–99, 118

Stoney Creek, 104

Strauss, Anne Terry, 28

Student Union for Peace Action (SUPA), 47–48, 120

students. *See* Indigenous youth

St'uxwtews: international lobbying, 37; UBCIC support, 127. *See also* Cache Creek blockade

Supreme Court of Canada: *Lavell* case on marrying out, 63–65, 66–67, 158, 161

A Survey of the Contemporary Indians of Canada (Hawthorn), 53

SVITF (Southern Vancouver Island Tribal Federation), 6, 17–18, 20, 44, 46

Swift, John, 142

Syilx, 5, 21–22, 37, 38–39, 118, 124–25, 149

Tate, Charles M., 37

Teit, James, 36, 38, 42, 148

Tennant, Paul, 9, 35, 36, 44, 74, 181*n*62

terminology and Indigenous peoples, 7–8, 176*nn*1–2, 198*n*115, 198*nn*2–3

Terry, Chief Saul, 77, 173

Tetlenitsa, Chief John, 38, 122

Thomas, Sophie, 104

Thompson, Chief Charlie, 93–94

Thompson-Nicola District (later Central District), 5, 21–22, 23(f), 131, 134, 175(t)

Titley, Brian, 35

Tizya, Rosalee, 86

Tk'emlúps. *See* Kamloops (Tk'emlúps)

Tl'azt'en Nation, 132, 189*n*7

Toosey Band, 144

Trail of Broken Treaties March (1972), 114, 125–26, 162, 192*n*2

transnational networks: about, 7, 9–10, 48–49, 116–18, 126–27; AIM networks, 136–37, 197*n*89; CEDAW convention (UN), 161; decolonization, 48–49, 116; gendered political issues, 28; militant May activism, 114–16; networks, 9–10, 126–27; 1960s movements, 47–49, 120; 1970s movements, 114–16, 126–27; nonviolent strategies, 48–49, 117–18; sexism, 156–57; women's networks, 63; youth